SAM HOUSTON'S WIFE

A Biography of Margaret Lea Houston

Sam Houston's Wife

A Biography of Margaret Lea Houston

BY

WILLIAM SEALE

UNIVERSITY OF OKLAHOMA PRESS : NORMAN

By William Seale

Texas Riverman: The Life and Times of Captain Andrew Smyth (Austin, 1966)

Sam Houston's Wife: A Biography of Margaret Lea Houston (Norman, 1970)

International Standard Book Number: 0–8061–0926–2

Library of Congress Catalog Card Number: 77–123341

 Composed and printed at Norman, Oklahoma, U.S.A., by the University of Oklahoma Press. First edition.

For Eugenia Broocks Seale

Preface

On Sunday, May 22, 1836, the sun appeared, ending a rainy season that had curtained New Orleans for six weeks. In the streets, candy and fruit hawkers competed with the cathedral's bells for the attention of the moving people, who, had it not been for the sudden coming of dry weather, would not have been so numerous in the open air.

That morning on the New Orleans wharves an estimated five thousand people awaited the arrival of the ship bearing Sam Houston, military leader of Texas' popular rebellion against Mexico. He had been wounded a month before in the decisive Battle of San Jacinto. The Gulf voyage necessary for his return had raised doubts whether or not Houston would live long enough to reach the New Orleans surgeons.

The noisy crowd included a tourist party of Alabama schoolgirls, chaperoned by the Reverend Mr. and Mrs. McLean, master and matron of the Pleasant Valley Academy, near Marion, Alabama. When the Scotsman McLean urged his flock nearer to the Mississippi's edge, one of the pupils, seventeen-year-old Margaret Lea, gained an advantageous position from which to view the arrival of the hero of the Battle of San Jacinto.

At noon the schooner *Flora* appeared downriver in tow behind a steamboat. As she came closer she proved to be an ugly vessel, her sails and rigging sagging, her scaling wooden bow slapping against the current. Though it was finally verified that Houston was aboard, he could not be recognized among the passengers on the deck. An enthusiastic fringe of onlookers crossed the plank as it was lowered; so many people followed them aboard that the *Flora* rolled in the water and the captain cried out that his ship was going to sink. By the time order was restored, Sam Houston had been assisted from his cot to the gunwale, where he faced the throng and the sun-bathed rooftops of New Orleans. Weak, pale, and covered with blood from his shattered ankle, Houston addressed the people. A Baptist preacher years afterward tried to recall Houston's words to the populace: "My kind physicians say I must not speak," Houston began, "yet I must thank you for your sympathy for Texas. . . . But, fellow citizens, remember while Texas has conquered Santa Anna and his bloody soldiers . . . she has another grander victory to gain before she is really free and great; she must conquer herself, her passions, and her sins. And in this second greater battle we need large recruits of pious women and ministers of the gospel." The audience began to cheer while a band played rousing airs. Sam Houston collapsed when he attempted to leave the *Flora*. He was carried unconscious to the coach of his friend William Christy.

Margaret Lea, who was enthralled by the idea of heroes, saw her first real hero with tearful emotion. She later described having a premonition that she would some day meet Sam Houston. But she told that story many years later, after she had become his wife and the single most important influence upon his life, after the schoolgirl's destiny had taken its strange turns. She and her husband, in their rare moments of privacy, verbally sewed this and other histories into a tapestry of romance whose threads have endured since their deaths more than one hundred years ago.

This book attempts to waken Margaret Lea's life from a historical sleep even deeper than the obscurity in which she enveloped herself as the wife of Sam Houston. I think Margaret Lea's biography casts a fresh, penetrating, and heretofore unknown light on Sam Houston, both personally and politically. My story is based principally upon the vast number of Houston letters. With only the published letters of Sam Houston, a biography of Margaret Lea could not have been written. Houston descendants have given me unrestricted use of two superb family collections of manuscripts. Neither collection has been previously seen by scholars, though recently a part of one of the collections was photographed for the University of Texas Library. In addition, I have consulted the works of the legion of Houston historians before me. Contemporary diaries and newspapers, together with carefully researched word restorations of sites the Houstons knew in Texas, Alabama, and Tennessee have provided the setting for my work.

The assembled information has assumed mighty proportions; however, no single item within the mass provides even a vague outline which might serve as a guide. I am fortunate in that the material is sufficiently abundant to allow me to shun the obvious course of seeing Margaret Houston entirely from the perspective of her husband. Some of the parts which ultimately composed this portrait persisted in eluding interpretation, kindling my curiosity, and maintaining my interest throughout the four years devoted to the project.

William Seale

Beaumont, Texas
September 1, 1970

Acknowledgments

Mrs. Jennie Morrow Decker, Colonel and Mrs. Edward A. Everitt, Mr. and Mrs. Sam Houston Hearne, Mr. and Mrs. James A. Darby, and Mrs. F. Starr Baldwin, all Houston descendants residing in Houston, Texas, gave invaluable assistance in locating hundreds of manuscripts and relating family traditions. Mrs. John L. Little, Sr., of Beaumont, Texas, provided material on her Lea ancestors. Professor Robert H. Woody of Duke University, Durham, North Carolina, directed the original version of this manuscript as a doctoral dissertation and was a careful critic. The late Mrs. W. E. Sampson of Houston gave me encouragement when the project might otherwise have been abandoned.

Professor James B. Renberg of Waukesha, Wisconsin, has been a faithful reader of countless revisions. Mr. Neal D. Cannon, Jr., of Houston was my host during much of the Texas research. Dr. William J. Murtagh of Alexandria, Virginia, made available many sources of research in Virginia and Washington, D.C. Professor Gary S. Horowitz of New York City aided in my research there. Mr. and Mrs. James W. Moody, formerly of Nashville, Tennessee, and now residing in Richmond, Virginia, introduced me to Middle Tennessee and its vast historical resources. Mrs. Joan M. Hartwell of Mobile and Miss Annie Lee Nichols of Marion greatly increased my knowledge of Alabama.

I wish to thank also Mr. and Mrs. Jack B. Osborne, Mrs. Curtis Franklin Scott, Miss Llerena B. Friend, Mr. R. Henderson

Shuffler, Miss Mattie Russell, Mrs. Carroll E. Ward, the late Mrs. Dan O'Madigan, the late Mr. and Mrs. Roland Jones, Mrs. Charles S. Pipkin, Sr., Mr. and Mrs. Robert Sims, Miss Julia Plummer, Miss Mickey Johnston, Professors R. Beeler Satterfield and Preston B. Williams, Mrs. O. B. Sawyer, Dr. F. Peel Allison, Mrs. Carmen Whatley, Miss Helen Bailey, Mrs. Major Bell, the late Professor Earl W. Fornell, Miss Ruth Hartmann, Mr. James E. Holland, Mr. and Mrs. Bryan Butts, Mrs. John D. Clark, Mrs. Cade Downs, Professor Allan Going, Mrs. Ben E. Pickett, Mr. and Mrs. Charles Fisher, Miss Lucinda L. Smith, Mr. and Mrs. Allan Vance Briceland, Mrs. George Markley, Mr. and Mrs. Joe H. Tonahill, Mrs. Lon Cartwright, Mrs. Jerome Head, Mrs. Ralph Ellis Gunn, Mrs. Ben Calhoun, Mrs. Dorothy Knepper, Mrs. Dwight Lee, Miss Ima Hogg, Mr. David Warren, Miss Ruth Crawford, Miss Mattie Lee Seymour, Mrs. Fisher Osborne, Mr. Dorman Winfrey, Mr. James M. Day, Miss Mary Beth Fleischer, Mrs. Willie Belle Coker, Mr. Chester V. Kielman, Mr. Paul Adams, Mr. L. Tuffly Ellis, Mr. Philip Fry, Miss Angele Gingras, Mrs. Barbara Whitehead, Mr. William Whittliff, Mrs. Grace Longino, Mr. Ogden Robertson, Mr. Blaine Hickey, and Miss Sue Flanagan.

William Seale

Contents

	Preface	*page* vii
	Acknowledgments	xi
1.	The Major's Toast	3
2.	Love Letters	34
3.	The Four-poster	72
4.	History's Hallways	83
5.	Raven's Roost	107
6.	Sweet Rocky	131
7.	A Lady Waiting	172
8.	The Grand Finals	190
9.	Fierce Winds at Cedar Point	210
10.	Steamboat House	222
11.	The Receding Lantern	234
	On the Sources	259
	Selected Bibliography	264
	Index	275

Illustrations

Margaret at the time of her marriage *following page* 112
The Engagement Cameo
Senator Sam Houston of Texas, 1846
Henry Lea, Serena, and Varilla
Galveston as Margaret knew it
Margaret at thirty
Ashbel Smith
Antoinette Lea Bledsoe
Loggia of the Huntsville house
Nancy Lea
Maggie, Mary William, and Nannie Houston
Sam Houston wearing his linen duster
George W. Samson
Independence
Margaret at forty
Sam Houston as governor of Texas, 1860
Margaret Houston in 1860
Austin in the 1860's
Sam Houston after the departure from Austin
Nannie at fifteen
Nettie and Mary William
Posthumous portrait of Margaret

Sam Houston's Wife

A Biography of Margaret Lea Houston

1.

The Major's Toast

In central Alabama the old town of Marion rises from level land which is stripped of its native forests. The countryside's only emotional quality is in its sky. A pedestrian in Perry County who wanders away from the rampant vegetation of the creek banks and the protective trees along the neglected fences exposes himself to the temperament of the sky, which, most of the year, is amiably blue. The thunderheads that collect in the brief, chilly winter give way to summer's balmy dome, and fierce sunlight beams on the cottonfields and filters through the branches of the oak trees, cedars, sycamores, and willows that shade the houses and dusty streets of the town.

During the early years of the nineteenth century Marion was a cluster of log shanties. Those were the hard years in the fields; courthouse records reveal the despair of the pioneers who wearied and left, and the vitality of the settlers who remained and, with luck, prospered. By the 1830's a sawmill had opened, providing the deacons of Siloam Baptist Church with finished lumber for the steeple of the new building. The steeple was even painted. It was later that a permanent courthouse was built, giving a certain feeling of unity to the disjointed town. However, there were good stores around the square, and the citizens proudly pointed out the Lafayette Hotel. Judson Female Institute, in addition to several lesser academies, lent a cultured air to Marion.[1]

Better houses replaced some of the cabins. Sweet olive, rose bushes, and blooming quince tangled behind the whitewashed palings of gardens where sewing and embroidery were the relished pastimes of women whose detached kitchens had become the responsibility of Negro slaves. The landowners of the region invested heavily in slaves. Overseers were seldom hired. At daybreak the planter was present to watch the first hoes in the reddish soil; some country families continued to work alongside their Negroes, though most men of means returned to their houses when the sun got hot. Marion had many citizens whose early toil had been rewarded with the leisure time in which to hunt bear or deer or to seek self-improvement at the bookcase or the pianoforte.

Two blocks west on Greensboro Street from Marion's principal square stood the tall, whitewashed house of Henry Lea. Using pine boards, pegs, and bricks, the carpenters had achieved in the Lea house a compromise between the Greek Revival vogue and common-sense construction principles. Senator Henry Lea was an important man at the state capitol in Montgomery, and his house bespoke his position.[2]

From her native Virginia, Senator Lea's young wife Serena had brought cedar seedlings and iris bulbs to beautify the yard. The predictable fence of white palings defined a front flower garden, allowing the broad façade of the residence to conceal the slave cabins, the kitchen, the chicken yard, the vegetable garden, the

[1] Annie Lee Nichols, "Early Days in Marion," unpublished lecture delivered at Judson College in 1962.

[2] Frances Youngblood, *Historic Homes of Alabama and Their Traditions*. From a photograph of Henry Lea's house taken ca. 1858.

horse lot, the privies, the smokehouse, and the well house behind.

A raised cottage is what the main house would have been called in those days, not only because the age responded to the cozy connotation of the word cottage, but also because the size of the house was disguised by architecturally emphasizing the second story, a classical pavilion of wood, with blinds hinged to its windows. This second or principal floor rested exactly atop a rusticated, elevated basement of brick, which Serena had screened with a wisteria arbor. A dining room was the main downstairs room. Most of the upstairs rooms contained beds. There was a heavy, square-columned piazza, which was connected to the ground by a pair of steep, uncovered stairs.[3]

Notwithstanding its spaciousness, the Lea house was for a time uncomfortably crowded with people. Besides Henry and Serena Lea and their two children, Henry's widowed mother Nancy Lea, under the pretense of wanting to place her two younger daughters in town schools, had come in from the country to live with Henry, her eldest son. With Nancy Lea had come Vernal, the younger of Henry's two brothers, and the youngest two of his three sisters, Antoinette and Margaret. But within three years of the advent of Nancy Lea and her children, the senator and Serena had the house to themselves again. Vernal went to read law at the University of Georgia and eloped with a demure girl whose name survives merely as Mary. Antoinette, promptly after her eighteenth birthday, married William Bledsoe, a rich Mobile merchant. Nancy Lea moved west, and in the parlor of the Greensboro Street house, on May 9, 1840, Margaret was married to Sam Houston.[4]

[3] County records, Marion, Alabama, Perry County; Willis Brewster, *Alabama: Her History, Resources, War Record, and Public Men*; Albert James Pickett, *History of Alabama.*

[4] Marriage license, Perry County, Alabama, May 9, 1840. Amelia W. Williams and Eugene C. Barker, (eds.), *The Writings of Sam Houston*, II, 350 (hereinafter referred to as *Writings*).

It was curious that of the vibrant Leas, Margaret, the least extravagant of all, made the most irrational alliance. Of the younger three children of Temple and Nancy Moffette Lea, Margaret had been the least likely to be attracted to the bizarre. She was said to have inherited the good sense of her father, Temple Lea; certainly she, like Temple Lea, was the embodiment of gentleness. The widow, though possessed of what coastal people called *éclat*, was anything but gentle. Antoinette could have married the Texan and not surprised anyone, because she was headstrong and impulsive, and after four months of marriage still seemed to her elders too tart tongued. Even Vernal's elopement had proved surprisingly sensible in that it had instilled in the youngest Lea son, at twenty-two, a sense of duty. The elder children, Henry, Martin, and Varilla, more than a full decade older than the others, had married, and in the instance of Varilla Lea Royston, had children nearly as old as Margaret. The three oldest Lea children, energetic, ambitious people, had long disapproved of the insolent laughter of Antoinette and Vernal and had been protective of the scholarly, introspective Margaret.

A month before her marriage Margaret had celebrated her twenty-first birthday. Because of her museful nature, the Leas' protectiveness toward her was understandable. Margaret was often wise, but seldom aggressive. Her thirst for ethereal beauty was whetted by books of romance. Pretty mail-order editions of *Ivanhoe*, *The Naval Foundling*, *Harry O'Reardon, or Illustrations of Irish Pride*, and *Swallow Barn* lined the shelves beside Henry's law books and his own copy of *The Vicar of Wakefield*. Over the previous two years, the dream world of Margaret Lea had been disturbed from time to time by evangelical questions which she could not answer, questions which cast her into deep depressions. Henry Lea's library provided her only escape. "I have taken my seat in the library. For several reasons it is a favourite resort. Now in the early morning it looks out upon a range of wild hills still slightly obscured by the mists of night.... How solemn the place! Sacred to holy musings and communion with the genius of ages gone by! I am in the midst of a band of heroes, ideal and real, and sages with their wisdom and philosophy are here and orators and poets with their dusty laurels. A majestic host!"[5]

The family stood by helpless to console the fifteen-year-old Margaret in her highly demonstrative grief over her father's death. Temple Lea had been a Baptist preacher and a dreamer. His wife had invested her inheritance from the Moffettes in Alabama land and developed a cotton plantation with fifty slaves, all while her husband preached over the countryside, unworried about the source of the maintenance of his family. Nancy Lea had been devoted to him. She likewise loved Margaret and believed that because she had known Temple Lea so well, she could better perceive Margaret's nature than could the rest of her family. She did not hesitate to criticize Margaret or quickly dismiss many of her daughter's depressions as "the glooms."

Margaret's conversion to religion occurred during chapel at the Pleasant Valley Academy, near the Lea farm, when she was nineteen.[6] Soon afterward she was baptized by the Reverend Peter Crawford of Siloam Baptist Church. At Judson Female Institute, in which she subsequently enrolled, she received vigorous Bible instruction. Religion gave her a sense of purpose, and her religious endeavors pleased her family.

Toward her literary interests the Leas were condescending,

[5] Margaret Lea to Sam Houston, Marion, July 17, 1839, University of Texas Archives. Unless otherwise designated, it will be understood that the collection's catalog title is under the name of the author of the particular letter to which the footnote refers.

[6] Margaret Lea Houston to Sam Houston, Huntsville, March 11, 1856, University of Texas Archives.

though seeming fully aware that Margaret's keen fascination with the idea of eternity was what led her to desire to perpetuate every moment of her life in verse.

Why have I sought thee out, loved flower?
To gaze upon thy radiant bloom?
Or doth some tranquilizing power
Breathe in thy rich perfume?

He placed thee in my hand, that friend
Who now doth distant roam
I took thee, little thinking then
How dear thou would'st become

Thou sweet memento! Gentle flower!
Say, will he cherish me,
And love me, too, in that dark hour,
As now I cherish thee?[7]

The subject of "Lines To a Withered Pink" was a flower Sam Houston had given her. Sentimental poems such as this one mirrored the days Margaret felt well. Somber rhymes reflected the bad seasons of asthma or other regular sicknesses from which she suffered.

Piousness was a family characteristic. Most of the Leas were good Baptists, reserving proper reverence for Heaven and appropriate fear for Hell. Nancy Lea herself had been immersed, praying and singing, in a Georgia creek under the hand of an evangelist.[8] She had come up strengthened to marry and bear seven children, six of whom grew to maturity. A little boy, Gabriel,

[7] Margaret M. Lea, "Lines To A Withered Pink," Camden, Alabama, June, 1839, Sam Houston Memorial Museum.

[8] Margaret Decker Everitt, "Notes On The Lea Family," Houston, 1965, author's collection.

had died of the colic in his second year. In spite of her wish to guide Margaret into adulthood, Nancy Lea more typically provided sympathy and pity. The mother became a sanctuary which was too available for Margaret's good.

Margaret was twenty and attending Judson Institute when the young Baptist preacher William Carey Crane traveled through Marion, was introduced to her, and remembered her many years later as "fascinating." He was certain that she "attracted young hearts," because "her language indicated high intelligence," among other "graces and virtues."[9] She was tall, with "beautiful dark brown hair . . . quite full of waves." Her face was an oval with arresting violet eyes.[10] A daguerreotype of disputed date shows Margaret at perhaps twenty-one or twenty-two. Her hair is parted neatly in the middle and it is shiny, its arrangement forming a long Gothic arch over soft and inquisitive eyes. The silk sleeves are tight at the shoulders, broadening to the wrists in patterns of ribbon and lace. Margaret's expression is grave and old, though the picture's general impression is one of a whimsical child.

[9] William Carey Crane, *Life and Select Literary Remains of Sam Houston of Texas*, 253; see also Crane's article in *The Houston Post*, 1884, cited in R. Henderson Shuffler, *The Houstons at Independence*, 48–49. A curious document survives in the University of Texas Archives to record an old romance of Margaret's; it is an essay entitled "To Margaret," written March 1, 1837, by a youth named Joseph. In conclusion, Joseph laments, "Just as our acquaintance begins, we are called to part. After beholding the magnificent outlines of the Temple of Truth, we must shake hands in the vestibule. Engaged awhile in picking up a few pebbles on the shore, we have to leave each other to explore separately the great ocean of truth. . . . Tho' I should return to my native state, while you remain in yours, let us remember that as the waters of the James & those of the Cahawba flow into the same great Ocean, so do the streams of our influence tend toward eternity." Margaret labeled the essay "Sympathetic and Affectionate," but she failed to record Joseph's last name.

[10] Marie Lea Hume to Miss Underwood, Houston, n.d., Margaret Lea Houston Collection, University of Texas Archives; also see daguerreotype, Sam Houston Memorial Museum.

In her diminutive gloved hand she conceals her spectacles, which she kept secured to her dress by a cord.

Margaret and Sam Houston met in May of 1839 at a garden party in Mobile.[11] It was Antoinette's party, a strawberry festival in honor of Nancy Lea, though Mrs. Lea was emphatic about having come to Mobile for the express purpose of doing business. When Judson Institute recessed for the summer, Margaret decided to accompany her mother and visit Antoinette. The sisters' reunion was the first since Antoinette's marriage the previous winter. Nancy Lea often closeted herself with William Bledsoe to discuss investments, giving Antoinette time to show Margaret the sights of Mobile. Mrs. Lea had sold her farm, the Cane Brake, with all its stock and seed, for a good price. Her visit with her son-in-law was for the purpose of ascertaining where best to invest the money from that sale. Hard times had hit Alabama.[12] The widow was tired of unpredictable cotton markets. She wanted to begin buying and selling western land, for her success in selling the Cane Brake had convinced her that she had a bright future in real estate.

Sam Houston was in Mobile publicizing a townsite company in which he was involved, offering properties at Sabine Pass on the Texas Gulf Coast near the international boundary east of Galveston Island.[13] The forty-six-year-old Houston, having lately finished his term as president of the Texas Republic, had traveled to New Orleans, then to Mobile, and planned to visit in Tennessee before returning to Texas. In Mobile a fast rapport developed

[11] Sam Houston to Margaret Lea Houston, Washington, D.C., March 7, 1849, Sam Houston Hearne Collection.

[12] Marquis James, *The Raven: A Biography of Sam Houston*, 309; see also Durant Daves to Ashbel Smith, May 10, 1839, Ashbel Smith Manuscript, University of Texas Archives.

[13] *Proprietor's Notice Concerning the City of Sabine*, May 1, 1839, *Writings*, II, 312–13.

between Houston and Margaret's brother Martin A. Lea, a well-known promoter in the city. Their association led to a friendship, and in the course of their being together, Lea introduced Houston to William Bledsoe. It occurred to Bledsoe that Nancy Lea's eagerness to invest her money might be satisfied in Texas.

Houston's appointment with Mrs. Lea happened to be on the day of Antoinette's garden party. The general accompanied Bledsoe home, where the serene atmosphere of the flower garden captured his fancy. He spoke to the guests, including Margaret, to whom he is said to have paid flattering compliments. When he had completed an interview with Nancy Lea, he returned to the party and lingered into the late afternoon talking with the ladies. At dusk, he and Margaret walked in the garden.[14]

Nancy Lea was too astute a businesswoman to oppose Margaret's initial courtesies to the general. Still, the widow Lea remembered Margaret's experience in New Orleans that May three years before. Margaret had said she would someday meet Sam Houston, and she had now done so. One of Margaret's fantasies had come true.[15]

During the days that followed Antoinette's party, Houston calculated regularly with the widow over her Texas maps. He convinced her of the Republic's wondrous future and so intrigued her, and even Bledsoe and Martin, that by the last of May, William Bledsoe set sail for the Republic of Texas to see for

[14] Margaret Lea Houston to Sam Houston, Galveston, December 7, 1840, Franklin Williams Collection.

[15] Generally speaking, the New Orleans incident must be labeled as a very probable legend. The Houston children all said that it was true and that their parents had told them. Parts of the story were being told as early as 1846 by C. Edwards Lester, Houston's first biographer. Rufus Burleson of Baylor University told the story and included Margaret Lea circa 1885 in a newspaper interview in Houston, and the interview was reprinted in J. H. H. Ellis, *Sam Houston and Related Spiritual Forces*. *The Bee* and the *Commercial Register* chronicle General Houston's arrival at New Orleans.

himself.[16] Bledsoe was ready to abandon his wholesale grocery business and dissolve his Number Four Commerce Street partnership with F. V. Cluis.

If her own anxiousness to amass profit blinded her momentarily, the plump, black-haired Nancy Lea soon realized that General Houston's great interest in the Leas was because of Margaret. A courtship had gone on before the widow's eyes. Nancy Lea was distraught. She reasoned that, hero or not, Sam Houston was an old man compared to Margaret, a girl of twenty. Houston's personal reputation was unsavory, and Nancy Lea had heard the stories about his drinking. He had separated from his wife a decade before, while he was governor of Tennessee, and people still spoke of the incident as a scandal. Mrs. Lea decided she must end the romance between Houston and her daughter, and she attempted to do so, subtly. Watching the two from afar, she made leading remarks on subjects of religion and morality. One afternoon she made an even bolder attempt. Houston complained of sickness, whose source seems to have been liquor. When he went to bed in the Bledsoe house, Nancy Lea slipped into his room armed with two servants and a Bible. A servant was stationed at Houston's head and one at his feet on the pretense that he was delirious and might do physical harm. Situating herself near the patient, Nancy Lea read aloud specific passages of the Bible she believed he should know.[17]

Early in June, Margaret's mother, utterly frustrated in her efforts to drive Houston away, announced that she and Margaret would return to Marion. In business relations, Mrs. Lea was satisfied with Sam Houston. She had made her decision to invest in Texas land, and if Bledsoe's report was good, she would move

[16] Margaret Lea to Sam Houston, Marion, July 17, 1839, University of Texas Archives.

[17] Daughters of the Republic of Texas, *Fifty Years of Achievement*, 335.

to Galveston, where she could direct her endeavors on the spot.

Before they left Mobile, Margaret told her mother that General Houston had proposed marriage. Nancy Lea's opposition was vehement. But Margaret was determined, and, without her mother's permission, she agreed to become Sam Houston's wife.

Houston had already notified Andrew Jackson and the William G. Hardings and his other old friends that he would come to Nashville. Seeking to fulfill a dream, Houston was planning to establish a Texas plantation in the healthful Gulf breeze. It was his idea to equip his plantation in the Tennessee manner, like The Hermitage or Traveler's Rest. "There are five things on earth which I love," he wrote that June to one of the Polks of Middle Tennessee, "a fine woman, a fine horse—a fine dog. . . . A Game Cock, and fine arms."[18] Houston indulged himself with the things he liked. When he hunted on his five-thousand-acre Galveston Bay property, he had a large variety of firearms from which to select. That summer he would purchase horses at Belle Meade and several other Nashville farms on credit. Galveston's best sporting houses nightly matched game cocks; and Tom Edmundson would, by autumn, deliver Houston "one dog and two bitches" on Galveston Bay.[19]

He wanted Margaret to marry him before she left Mobile. Margaret refused, because she was moved by her mother's genuine concern. So that everything would be socially correct, it would be necessary that Houston call on the Leas in Marion at Henry's house.[20] Margaret wanted her brothers to know Houston, but Houston seems to have been less than enthusiastic about meeting Henry Lea. He begged Margaret to marry him immediately.

[18] Sam Houston to L. J. Polk, Columbia, Tennessee, June 13, 1839, Polk Collection, University of North Carolina Archives.

[19] *Ibid.*

[20] Margaret Lea to Sam Houston, Marion, August 1, 1839, Franklin Williams Collection.

Undoubtedly Margaret was tempted. Houston promised a life of excitement to a girl who had seen little of the world outside Marion and who had always dreamed about being in the midst of the momentous. Her ambitions, however, did not overshadow her respect for Nancy Lea. Assuring Sam Houston that she had experienced "the beginning of a new existence," she told him that he would have to visit her home before she would discuss a wedding date.[21] He finally agreed to be there in mid-July. To symbolize their engagement, Houston presented her with a cameo portrait of himself. A happy Margaret fastened green ribbons to the sculptured profile and hung it around her neck. In the coach with a disgruntled Nancy Lea she returned to Marion, composing love poems about Sam Houston along the way.[22]

From Nashville later that summer, Houston wrote to suggest that Margaret join the Bledsoes at the Blount Springs resort, approximately halfway between Nashville and Marion, where Bledsoe had gone to recover from a fever he had developed during his brief stay in Texas.[23] Margaret replied that Blount Springs was only a "trifling journey" from Marion, so it was even more feasible for Houston to come and visit her if he planned to go to Blount Springs for a vacation. Houston's ardor was high, but he made every effort to avoid an encounter with Margaret's assembled kin. On Greensboro Street, Henry tired of waiting and went to Montgomery on business. Varilla wept bitterly over Margaret's engagement and blamed Nancy Lea for permitting the courtship.

[21] Margaret Lea Houston to Sam Houston, Galveston, December 7, 1840, Franklin Williams Collection.

[22] The cameo is in the San Jacinto Museum of History on loan and is the property of Sam Houston Hearne; "Lines To A Withered Pink" is one of Margaret's love poems, and the manuscript is in the Sam Houston Memorial Museum.

[23] Margaret Lea to Sam Houston, Marion, August 1, 1839, Franklin Williams Collection.

Sam Houston tried a last resort in psychology. He wrote and told Margaret that his country needed him, seeming to feel certain that Margaret's patriotic spirit would change her mind. Early one morning in the window of Henry's library Margaret wrote her reply. "Far be it from me to raise my voice against that of your country! No—if she requires your presence, go without delay! . . . When her cries of oppression are hushed, we will welcome you again to my Native State."[24] A wearied hero of San Jacinto went home in defeat.

In the months that followed, letters from Texas appeared at the Marion stage stop. Henry Lea's sister gathered them up and wrote replies in her dainty hand. The betrothal seems not to have excited Marion, for Margaret wrote that "politics is the engrossing theme," and added, "I prefer my books, music, and needle-work."[25] Her friends did not take her romance seriously. She comforted Houston's doubts, reminding him that he was the first "gentleman" she had ever "addressed."

Late in October the family was together on Greensboro Street. The beautiful, bright-eyed Antoinette, troubled by Bledsoe's sickly appearance, returned with her husband to Marion. The mineral baths seem to have improved Bledsoe. He "delighted" the family recounting his tour of the Texas wilderness. On the basis of his descriptions, Nancy Lea packed her trunks. Henry purchased all but two of her slaves and saw that some of her furniture was crated. In the excitement of the moment, Varilla and Robert Royston decided they would plant one more crop in Alabama and then go also to Texas; they sowed corn, because they feared cotton would delay them. Texas became a mania in the Lea house. Henry and Serena talked of going west after Henry's term of office expired.

[24] *Ibid.*
[25] *Ibid.*

At the end of the month, the punctual Bledsoe took Antoinette and Nancy Lea to a steamer at Mobile. Martin joined them at Galveston in December. Back in Marion, Margaret was left with her needlework, sometimes going in the carriage to call on friends in the country. She amused herself trying to learn Spanish and studying Texas geography.

The mails brought many letters urging Margaret to come to Texas. Houston had expected her to come with her mother. Surprised that she had not done so, he insisted that there was no possibility of his traveling to Alabama, and that, besides, he had already met most of the family. He was busy with politics, having been elected to the Congress of the Republic, sitting at Austin, which he called "the most unfortunate site upon earth for the Seat of Government."[26]

Margaret promised to think about moving to Texas, but did not encourage her fiancé. "I stated to you . . . that it was the wish of myself and relations that you should visit Marion. . . . Our opinions are unchanged. I have never yet taken sides in any affair of moment without being guided in a great measure by my relations." She would not deceive him. "In this case . . . I shall rely entirely on their discretion."[27]

They exchanged more letters in the passing weeks and months. A February wedding date was set. Sam Houston could not be there, so it was postponed to April. Then in April Margaret saw a vague hope for May. She sat in the shade of Serena's wisteria and sewed the three dresses of her trousseau, a white satin, a purple silk, and a blue muslin.[28] Her trunks were packed with linens,

[26] Sam Houston to Anna Raguet, Austin, December 10, 1839, *Writings*, II, 322.

[27] Margaret Lea to Sam Houston, Marion, August 1, 1839, Franklin Williams Collection.

[28] Margaret Lea to Nancy Lea, Marion, April 25, 1840, University of Texas Archives.

silver, and clothing; her parlor grand piano was dismantled and crated. The "young Negro woman Viannah, the Negro girls Eliza and Charlotte and the boy Jackson," whom Temple Lea had bequeathed her, would accompany their mistress.[29] Eliza, her body servant, was her constant companion.

On April 25, Margaret wrote a letter to Texas. "Dearest Mother I had hoped long before this to have been with you . . . but I might have forseen the probability of a disappointment. . . . Marion is much the same. . . . One or two marriages have varied the monotony a little." She eagerly awaited Sam Houston: "The Gen. will certainly be here this evening. If he is you may be sure I will not detain him long."[30]

It was not, however, until the seventh of May, a Thursday, that Sam Houston stepped from the stagecoach into the uncertain camp of Margaret's kin. Martin was with him, but none of his old Texas friends had come. After he registered at the Lafayette Hotel, Houston went to call on the family on Greensboro Street. To pay for the trip to Alabama, he had borrowed $250 during his brief stop in New Orleans.[31]

Margaret did not hesitate. Her promise to her family was fulfilled. Houston was in Marion, where the friends and cousins could meet him. Never once had Margaret challenged the wisdom of her mother, brothers, and sisters. For the last time in her life Margaret had allowed the opinions of others to dictate her conduct toward Sam Houston.

The marriage took place on a Saturday.[32] The windows and

[29] Will of Temple Lea, August 22, 1834, Record Book 57, Perry County, Alabama.

[30] Margaret Lea to Nancy Lea, Marion, April 25, 1840, University of Texas Archives.

[31] Sam Houston to James S. Holman, New Orleans, May 3, 1840, *Writings*, IV, 66.

[32] *Selma Free Press*, May 23, 1840.

tables of the tall, wooden parlor were festooned with flowers from Serena's garden. The Reverend Peter Crawford faced the guests, who overflowed into a bedroom and out into the hall. Martin Lea was best man, in the absence of Houston's friend Dr. Ashbel Smith of Galveston. Two little Moffette cousins, grandchildren of Nancy Lea's brother, were flower girls, and Mrs. L. J. Goree, wife of the president of Judson Institute, was matron of honor.[33] Margaret, in the white satin dress over which she and Eliza had labored during the lonely past spring, entered beside Henry Lea.[34] To the guests who were intimate with the family, the presence of the senator must have seemed a surrender on his part to that which they knew he had opposed. Henry Lea's participation probably more accurately indicated that he had reached some understanding with Margaret and Sam Houston, although it is obvious that he was close to neither of them in years to come.

Peter Crawford knew Nancy Lea, and he had known her children since he had come to Marion to assume the ministry of Siloam Baptist Church. Margaret's marriage had everything against it. She was twenty-six years younger than General Houston, to begin with, and she was a protected young lady. Peter Crawford remembered how sincerely she had testified aloud at the Pleasant Valley Academy.[35] Afterward, he himself had baptized her with a party of other young people.[36] A man Sam Houston's age, and one of his infamous temperament, was likely to grow impatient with Margaret Lea's religious depressions. The Texan

[33] Nichols, Annie Lee, "Early Days in Marion," 8–9; see also Mrs. Sam W. Jackson to Miss Emma Burleson, Madisonville, Texas, n.d., Houston Manuscripts, University of Texas Archives.

[34] *Selma Free Press*, May 23, 1840.

[35] Margaret Lea Houston to Sam Houston, Huntsville, March 11, 1856, University of Texas Archives.

[36] Julia Murfee Lovelace, *A History of the Siloam Baptist Church, Marion, Alabama*, 7–10.

seemed hardened to weaknesses in other people and remarkably indulgent of his own. The face of San Jacinto's hero looked older than middle age. He was pale and thin,[37] and his worldliness was a strange contrast to Margaret's innocence.

Sam Houston had been born to an easy life on his father's Timber Ridge farm in the back country of Virginia in the spring of 1793. When young Houston was fourteen, Major Samuel Houston died, and the widowed Elizabeth Paxton Houston, with her children and possessions, migrated to cheap lands in Tennessee before debt took Timber Ridge. Elizabeth Paxton Houston, a strong woman, was idolized by young Sam.

The boy had no use for Maryville, Tennessee. He saw his brothers working with their few Negro slaves in the thick fields of corn, but he preferred to read and swim and fish, as he had done back home at Timber Ridge. Pioneer life in Tennessee was laborious. Young Sam Houston began to run away, never far, but frequently, and with explanations given only to his mother, who tried to sympathize with him. His rambles led him among the Cherokee youths, whose forest world appealed to his imaginative pantheism. At home the community criticized him for abandoning his family, who needed him on the farm. Houston variously attended a small academy, clerked in a store, and taught school; but he was too unsettled to prevail in any one endeavor very long and returned to the Cherokees intermittently. His brothers resented him, and, when at nineteen Houston joined the United States Army, only his mother and his beloved sister Mary thought sadly of it.

Elizabeth Houston's son surprised the Maryville people. His military daring while fighting the Creek Indians in Alabama made

[37] Ashbel Smith to B. E. Bee, Galveston, May 22, 1840, University of Texas Archives; Sam Houston to Margaret Lea Houston, Austin, January 16, 1841, Franklin Williams Collection.

him a minor hero. Gravely wounded by an Indian arrow in a dramatic siege which he led, Lieutenant Houston gained General Andrew Jackson's admiration. While Houston was in Maryville recovering from the wound in his thigh, Jackson achieved renown for leading the Americans to victory against the British at New Orleans. Houston's friendship with Jackson, as time passed, led to a commission in the army, a career in law, and an introduction into Tennessee public life. Sam Houston found his calling in politics, and he advanced rapidly.

The 1820's promised great political opportunities for unknowns. Jackson's circle sought to place the general in the White House, and ambitious young men were attracted to the Jackson following. The Old Chief and his entourage gained support in every part of the disjointed United States. Jackson's relationship with his young friends was often paternalistic. The hospitality of The Hermitage was always available to them, and many of them, like Sam Houston, thought of it as a home.

The Hermitage was what Timber Ridge might have become. Attorney and minor politician Houston wandered in Jackson's stable and ate at "Aunt Rachel's" board, which was abundant and garnished with rich plate, of the sort Elizabeth Paxton Houston might have had if affairs in Virginia had taken a different turn. The tall, well-made Houston, nearing thirty, attracted attention every place, from the plantation balls to the political rallies to the Sunday horse races adored by Nashvillians. Lavish clothes, ruffled and pinned with jeweled ornaments and buttons, glamorized an already romantic figure. He had thick auburn hair and blue eyes, which, if the miniature painter was accurate, gave a certain piquant quality to the otherwise rough-drawn outdoorsman. Men liked him and he knew how to talk to them, whether on horseback on the Lebanon Pike, on the torchlit political platform, or at late-hour revelry in the Nashville Inn. His political ideas were not original.

A Jacksonian in Nashville was not different from one in Pittsburgh. The trade secret was to have those prescribed ideas expounded by an orator who was a personable, dramatic, and caustic entertainer, who seemed to be expressing what most people felt. Houston was adept and was rewarded.

When Jackson met defeat in the 1824 presidential election, the rush began toward the election of 1828. United States Congressman Sam Houston was soon walking in the mud streets of Washington. He was General Jackson's friend and therefore the enemy of President John Quincy Adams. Back home, the political organization developed other plans for its prodigy. Following a stump tour, Sam Houston was elected governor of Tennessee.

In 1828, Andrew Jackson won the presidential race, and the Jacksonians began packing their bandboxes and trunks. Governor Houston rode out to Gallatin and proposed to a pretty blonde named Eliza Allen. Her father, John Allen, was an old friend of General Jackson and the late Mrs. Jackson. The arrangement was ideal; at eighteen Eliza would be the first lady of Tennessee. All the best people of Middle Tennessee attended the wedding in January, 1829. The governor moved his bride into rooms in the Nashville Inn.

Abruptly, on an early morning three months later, Eliza packed her belongings and went home to her parents. As news of the separation spread over Nashville, the people looked to Sam Houston for an explanation. Houston's powers of persuasion were great, but this time no statement was forthcoming from the governor of Tennessee. People gathered in the street and watched the upper windows of the inn. Gossips strained their abilities to suggest grotesque reasons why Eliza Allen Houston had left. Houston's affection for nudity, acquired from the Indians, had frightened the timid girl, according to one story. His unhealed wound, received during the Creek War, supposedly repulsed her. In another report, Eliza was said to have been apprehended kneeling on the hearth burning love letters another man had sent her. The truth is that neither Eliza nor Sam Houston ever revealed why they separated. Houston's life was one of mysteries and puzzles, but that secret was the best kept of all.

Street mobs jeered in that pleasant spring night beneath the light of torch flames that illuminated the locked shutters of the Houston apartment. Terrified Jacksonian Democrats slipped in the back entrances of the inn and demanded that the governor issue a statement. When Houston refused, they raced to Gallatin, but Eliza's family met them at the door and sent them away.

Sam Houston penned an eloquent, noncommittal resignation from the governorship. Wearing the clothing of the plain frontiersman, he carried his baggage through the crowded street to the steamboat wharf. That walk was one of the more theatrical acts of his career, and it would be well remembered in Nashville long after Sam Houston's political opponents had swarmed like scavengers in his wake, and long after his wandering had taken him elsewhere.

Bitter and alone, Houston evaluated the extent of his losses. He was hurt by the coldness of the people. Eliza, too, had seemed cold. Alone on the deck on the steamboat, Sam Houston contemplated suicide. He was not the type. Contemplate, perhaps, but there was no chance of his trading what he knew with some certainty for an unknown hereafter. Summer found him deep in the Cherokee country with the friends of his boyhood. As a youthful runaway he had been taken into the tribe as a brother. His connection was recognized, and the Raven or the Rover, as he was variously called, became a citizen of the Cherokee Nation and an intimate of its ruling families.

The country was a timbered frontier. Farms and ranches had been established in the short time since the Cherokees had blazed their pioneer trails into the Arkansas lands. Some of the richer families owned Negro slaves. Sam Houston bought an interest in a trading post, and by Cherokee law he took an Indian wife, a blacksmith's widow named Diana Rogers Gentry, who was part Cherokee and whose family Houston had known as a boy. At their Wigwam Neosho, she and Houston operated an apparently successful business and maintained small herds as well. Diana Rogers Gentry is a baffling character in Houston's life. Some years his senior she seems to have offered him temporary peace in which he tried to regain his emotional strength.[38]

At length, Houston wearied of Wigwam Neosho, and boredom took him to the United States military installation, Cantonment Gibson, where he joined the officers in their off-duty pastime of drinking. The Raven had been a pleasure drinker of some repute back in Nashville. On the Indian frontier, whisky made him forget his tragedy. The old Creek War wound hurt him. His worries drew him deeper into the bottle, and he went home to Diana more and more in a state of drunkenness. The Indians, seeing him in this state, nicknamed him Big Drunk.

In spite of his hard drinking, Houston was not without a certain discipline over himself. The love of political involvement was merely dormant in him. By 1832 the unfair practices of white encroachers into the Cherokee Nation had aroused his indignation sufficiently to induce him to accept the ambassadorship from the Cherokees to the United States. Clad in full Cherokee regalia, feathered and turbaned, he journeyed to Washington, D.C., to plead for justice.

Never afterward did he return to Diana or the Cherokees for a significant period of time. His old friends received him warmly, and the familiar savor of the capital kindled in him an anxiousness

[38] For a scholarly account of Diana (or Tiana) Rogers Gentry, see Rennard Strickland and Jack Gregory, *Sam Houston With the Cherokees.*

to reconstruct his career. A reunion with Andrew Jackson convinced him that he must emerge from obscurity. He visited The Hermitage on his way back to the Cherokee Nation. In Nashville, in a gesture typical of him, he draped himself in a toga and had his portrait painted as Marius among the ruins of Carthage. Marius, he later wrote, "was one of the proudest Romans!"[39]

He restlessly paced the puncheon floors of Wigwam Neosho. On his trip he had frantically made business contacts in what seemed to be an effort to obligate himself to return to civilization. He attended Indian meetings, however, and became involved in the Cherokees' constant threats of going to war with other tribes. A message came from Andrew Jackson, offering Houston the opportunity to travel through Texas as United States emissary to the Comanches, with the explicit purpose of collecting information relative to the country and to the feasibility of the government's sponsoring a great council which might meet to discuss Indian affairs peacefully.

In December of 1832, Houston crossed the Red River into Texas, the northernmost territory of the Mexican republic. That part of Mexico had been in his mind for years, considering its potential for land speculation. Its boundaries were not defined; its eastern woodlands were a continuation of those of the United States, with equal agricultural promise. And where the woodlands ended, a vast plain swept westward to the Pacific Ocean, and southward into the old Spanish viceroyalty of New Spain, which was now the independent, but unstable, Republic of Mexico. Idly, perhaps, Houston pondered an empire for himself in Texas, policed by Cherokee armies. The dream was not an original one, though in his case, and considering his influence with the Cherokees, it was perhaps more plausible.

[39] Sam Houston to Sam Houston, Jr., Austin, April 7, 1860, *Writings*, VIII, 457–58.

In any event, he attended to his business and settled in Texas, after short stays in Louisiana and Arkansas, where he referred to himself as "special agent." Sam Houston was usually optimistic about his future in Texas. He was a celebrity among the Anglo-American farmers and floaters scattered over the land's wilderness and crude towns. Hard toil's first profits were being realized by some of the settlers. Mexico was bleeding from governmental turmoil of a quasi-criminal flavor, and she paid little attention to her frontiers.

Toward the predominantly Anglo-American population, which was required to swear allegiance to Mexico and join the Roman Catholic church, the Mexican government was dangerously undependable in its policies, particularly regarding the security of the Texas land titles. Years before, in Nashville, Houston had worked with the Nashville Company in trying to clear up confusing titles in Texas. As a resident of Texas, Houston showed no reluctance to fan fires of unrest. An acute resentment on the part of the Anglo-American community already in control did not stop him. He rose in the eyes of the settlers, partially on the basis of his personal fame and his political connections back in the United States. Few people seem to have been aware of Houston's dealings with New York land speculators. In fact, for several years past and all his years to come, he was able to conceal his consistent association with buying and selling land. Political success on the frontier required the gift of anticipating an audience's feelings in advance and the ability to be before that audience at the right time in spite of the difficulty of traveling in that undeveloped land. Sam Houston was a master at both. He had the advantage of being from the same political environment as most of the Texas settlers—the Jacksonian South. His ideas were echoes from home, brightening the spirits of the discontented pioneers, who were at best uncomfortable under Mexican domination.

When revolution broke out in the autumn of 1835, Sam Houston was made commander-in-chief of the Texans' inadequate little army. Immediately after the fall of the Alamo in the spring of 1836, General Antonio López de Santa Anna elaborately divided his formidable force and sent armies to capture strategic parts of Texas. Santa Anna then personally headed the pursuit of the Texas governmental officials, and the Texans began a mass flight toward the United States border at the Sabine River. Sam Houston's army, increased daily by the arrival of United States volunteers, threaded a haphazard system of ferries across rivers, bayous, and creeks, all of them swollen by the incessant spring rains. Slow trains of terrified civilians clattered ahead of Houston's army, agreeing with the soldiers that Houston was a coward for not facing the enemy. The Texans' main hope lay in General Edmund Pendleton Gaines, who, with a large force of United States troops, had moved from Fort Jesup, in the interior of Louisiana, to the banks of the Sabine. Yet on the afternoon of April 21, 1836, at a crossing on the San Jacinto River, some one hundred twisting, bogged miles west of the Sabine, the Texans achieved a military victory which ended the war.

Santa Anna had chased the government officials to Galveston Bay, where they escaped by fleeing to Galveston Island. Instead of pursuing them to the island, Santa Anna, continuing an already long march, rounded the edge of the bay to the mouth of the San Jacinto River, whose closest crossing was Lynch's Ferry, some distance upriver. At the ferry he ordered his exhausted troops to camp and await the arrival of supplies and a rendezvous with other parts of his dispersed army. By deciding to camp in the marshy land, Santa Anna placed his force in a vulnerable position. Perhaps because of the great size and superiority of the equipment of his army, the Mexican president seems not to have worried about danger.

Houston, meanwhile, in an apparent effort to thwart overpowering insubordination among his soldiers, had turned from the path of the civilians onto another, less crowded Louisiana road, which led to the Opelousas Trail but necessitated crossing Lynch's Ferry. It is not known whether Houston was impatient to bypass the slow civilians, or whether he was bound for the Neches River, which Andrew Jackson had considered the international boundary, or whether he was riding for the more distant Sabine. He reached Lynch's Ferry in the night of April 20, but, seeming to realize the futility of making a crossing in such a short time, he camped to await the enemy. Learning of Santa Anna's planned rendezvous with other parts of the invading force, Houston knew the only course was to attack the Mexicans before the reinforcements, some of which arrived that night, created impossible odds. Vince's Bridge on Sims Bayou, which would have served the reinforcements, was burned, thus complicating Santa Anna's rendezvous. In midafternoon of April 21, 1836, the Texan army staged a surprise attack while most of Santa Anna's camp was still resting from the forced marches of the previous days. The Battle of San Jacinto lasted eighteen minutes, during which the Texan force suffered nine casualties. Among the 730 Mexican prisoners taken was Santa Anna, and 630 Mexican soldiers lay slain in the tall, watery grasslands that had been the battlefield. Houston was one of a small number of Texans who were wounded. His ankle was shattered, and in May he sailed to New Orleans to seek proper medical attention.

If some of the army persisted in considering Sam Houston a coward, the Texas settlers called him their hero. In the controversy over the proper epithet, the praise stood predominant, and Houston knew how to take advantage of it. The Texans, most of whom had fled to safety in Louisiana, knew few of the details of the San Jacinto victory. They had heard about the great battle after it was over, and they were satisfied to learn that the well-known Sam Houston had commanded an army that had won. Those civilians elected Houston first president of the Republic of Texas. Houston relished his glories. It pleased him that the capital city was named for him; Independence Day was discreetly set on March 2, Sam Houston's birthday, rather than on the anniversary of the signing of the Texas declaration of independence, which had actually taken place on another day. As president, Houston did his job well. In the midst of the Republic's extravagant ambitions, he sought out and followed the realistic path. Though he was cautious and quite aware of the political danger in making mistakes, Houston's private schemes for Texas were imaginative. As the Republic grew older, he became more optimistic about her future. In the quiet of his quarters he penciled fantasies of a nation that stretched to the Pacific Ocean and even southward into Mexico.

Necessarily the president was always on the move. In the capital he shared a shanty with bachelor friends. A guest in other cities, he visited in the houses of families whose home life appealed to him. He fell in love with Anna Raguet of Nacogdoches, and for a short while he sincerely believed that if he married her she would give him a stable life. At San Jacinto he had made her a wreath of oak leaves, calling his creation the Laurels of San Jacinto.

A constant siege of rain muddied the streets of Houston City and chilled the humid air. Sam Houston's old wound—and the crippling new one from San Jacinto—began to ache. Five lesser wounds on the front of his body dealt him misery in particularly humid times. He turned to whisky, the only painkiller he knew. And he found that it soothed the pain of loneliness as well. His drinking became more prodigious than ever. Ashbel Smith, Houston's doctor, wrote that liquor did not seem to affect Houston's competence in office but lamented that it was ruining his health.

The general lost weight quickly. His susceptibility to sickness increased, and he refused to care for himself. Backroom jokes about his drunkenness circulated beyond the Sabine. Houston's retort was not abstinence but a retreat to his quarters, where he drank alone, heavily, and frequently. Though he sought seclusion at times, privacy was seldom his privilege.[40]

Letters from the Redlands ended his correspondence with Anna Raguet. Her family discovered that Houston was not divorced from Eliza Allen; his attentions to Anna Raguet were improper. Immediately, in an act of questionable legality, though one practiced very often in Texas, Houston sent a divorce petition through the court at San Augustine, apparently using every influence to keep the news from his political opponents and to please the Raguets. He was unsuccessful at both attempts. The public criticism of his actions was small, but quite evident, and in the midst of the embarrassment, Anna Raguet eloped with Dr. Robert Irion, one of Houston's roommates in the bachelor house in Houston City.

His term of office ended. By the dictates of the constitution, he could not succeed himself as president. Houston in retirement seems to have curbed his drinking slightly, perhaps because of his health. Drinking, however, was still one of his consuming pastimes, and once he started drinking, he was incapable of moderation. He was lonely and bored. Texas was too unbounded. Brothels, saloons, and cock-pits amused the predominantly male populations of Houston City and Galveston. Wrapped in a leopard skin or an Indian blanket, the former president sloshed through the streets, drank on credit at the bars, then walked home to drink more. His scars, windburn, and thin, sun-reddened hair made him look older than he was. The lonely and temporary characteristics

40 Ashbel Smith, description of Sam Houston, n.d., University of Texas Archives.

of his life were of his own making. Fame's mystique had always appealed more to Houston than the threat of imprisonment among cornstalks, rail fences, and plows. When he had been a younger man he had sought the domestic existence only occasionally, when he wanted a place in which to regain his spirits. As a man nearing fifty he missed the solidarity of a home.[41]

Houston's affection for Margaret Lea was genuine. She represented the kind of decency and gentility that Elizabeth Paxton Houston had given him in his boyhood, and which he had seldom known since. He found comfort in Margaret's seriousness, just as her girlishness amused him. From Marion, Margaret had written to him: "My heart . . . is like a caged bird whose weary pinions have been fold[ed] for weeks and months—at length it wakes from its stupor, spreads its wings and longs to escape. . . . Last night I gazed long upon our beauteous emblem, the *Star of my Destiny*, and my thoughts took the form of verse, but I will not inscribe them here, for then you might call me a romantic, star-struck young lady."[42] Houston was charmed. To a Texan he wrote that Margaret was a "clever gal," and, "I hope to show her to my friends as such."[43] But Margaret warned that if he did not hurry to Marion as prescribed, then "you will not see your Esperanza for *ages* (months I mean) to come."[44]

The morning of the wedding many of the Leas remained un-

[41] For biographies of Sam Houston, see William Carey Crane, *Life and Select Literary Remains of Sam Houston of Texas*; Llerena B. Friend, *Sam Houston: The Great Designer*; Marquis James, *The Raven: A Biography of Sam Houston*; C. Edwards Lester, *The Life of Sam Houston, Hunter, Patriot, and Statesman of Texas*; see also *Writings*, I–VIII.

[42] Margaret Lea to Sam Houston, Marion, July 17, 1839, University of Texas Archives.

[43] Sam Houston to Robert Irion, Austin, Texas, January 27, 1840, Collection of J. R. Irion II.

[44] Margaret Lea to Sam Houston, Marion, July 17, 1839, University of Texas Archives.

convinced of the wisdom of Margaret's marriage. They could perhaps envision Margaret as a minister's wife, but not as the wife of Sam Houston. Houston praised religion merely to conceal his contempt for churches. For all Houston's politeness, his past was unsavory. His robust manner masked the telling thinness of his body and pallor of his face.[45] His excessive use of alcohol was a serious problem.[46] But Margaret was convinced she could reform him.[47] Although everything was against the marriage and heartbreak inevitable for Margaret, Peter Crawford and the Leas could do no more than pray that God protect her. Sam Houston would doubtless take care of himself.

The minister completed his ceremony, which Houston commemorated with a small gold band.[48] Margaret preferred plain jewelry "of good quality."[49] Following the marriage there was a luncheon, after which General Houston and Margaret went to Houston's hotel, where they lived for a week, until Margaret's

[45] *Alabama State Review*, Montgomery, September 17, 1845.

[46] Though Houston's drinking is usually discussed in a humorous way, liquor had gotten such a hold on Houston that his habit seems to have been anything but humorous. Ashbel Smith, whose intimate friendship with Houston gives credence to his many notes on the general, plainly states that Houston's drinking had made him a public spectacle, but that at the time of his marriage to Margaret, Houston had begun drinking alone in his quarters. Poor health in Houston was attributed by Smith to liquor and the wounds. In a temperance speech in the east Texas Redlands in the summer of 1853, Houston said, "I believe that total abstinence is the only way by which some intemperate drinkers can be saved. I know it from my own personal experience. When a person's appetite for stimulating beverages becomes uncontrollable, he should 'touch not handle not.' If I cannot indulge in the use of the same in moderation, it is my misfortune." See *Writings*, VI, 21–26. Smith's notes on Houston are in the University of Texas Archives. Margaret's later letters to Houston clearly indicate the seriousness of Houston's drinking problem.

[47] Crane, *Life and Select Literary Remains*, 253–57.

[48] Author in conversation with Mrs. Jennie M. Decker, Houston, January 10, 1965.

[49] *Ibid.*

crates and trunks were hauled to Mobile and Margaret had recovered from a mild fever she developed after the wedding. It was decided best that Eliza accompany Margaret to Texas, while Margaret's three other slaves would travel with Martin.

General Houston addressed the citizens of Marion at the Lafayette Hotel one evening during the week.[50] Another function was a dinner party in his honor, during which a group of girls stood up and sang an "Original Ode," to the tune of "The Bucket."

There dwells in the patriot's bosom, a feeling
Of pride for his country he never can quell,
Whether joy for her triumph—or sorrow be stealing
For wrongs she has suffered, 'tis idle to tell.

O! They who have flung out the banner of battle,
And nailed it undaunted to Liberty's tree,
May be sure, tho' the hard storms of conflict now rattle,
Will yet proudly wave o'er the land of the free.

Our Washington's name has been hallowed in story,
As founder of freedom's retreat in the west,
Another has risen to share in his glory—
The TEXIAN PATRIOT—our own honored guest![51]

The most provocative tribute of the week was offered by one Major Towns at a subscription barbecue held in honor of the Houstons in the oak grove adjoining the graveyard of Siloam Baptist Church. As "President of the Day" it was Major Towns's office to propose a toast. When he rose he addressed not Sam Houston, as everyone else had done, but Margaret, the daughter

[50] *Marion Herald*, May 16, 1840; see also an undated typescript, presumably by Martin Lea Royston, Barker Texas History Center, University of Texas Library.

[51] *Telegraph and Texas Register*, Houston, July 1, 1840.

of his old friend Temple Lea. The toast named her the "Conqueress of the Conqueror."[52] And all the people present, even Margaret herself, could well have wondered if there was truth to it.

[52] *Marion Herald*, May 16, 1840.

2.

Love Letters

The steamer *New York* turned her green and white hulk northward full steam toward Galveston Island. Her passengers marveled at the clouds of seagulls that climbed skyward and floated down in the sunlight. The water changed from a deep blue-green to brown and became choppy as the boat neared the land. A salt-laden wind blew, seemingly without direction. Without exception the passengers collected at the wooden rail to watch the barren shores of the Texas Republic.

General and Mrs. Houston spent the last four days of their wedding trip among the passengers of the *New York*. The possibility of Houston's weakening to the temptations of Mobile and New Orleans had worried Margaret. The family had told Margaret not to be surprised if her husband left the narrow path he had followed in Marion. There was a bar aboard the *New York*, but, comforting Margaret's fears with more than promises, Houston had begun drinking mild bitters in an effort to break the liquor habit gradually. Margaret was proud of him and turned her thoughts to the new life around her.[1]

[1] Margaret freely told of her project to reform Houston, and the story, with

On Galveston Bay, but not in view of the Gulf shore, was Houston's farm, Cedar Point, which could be reached by sailing over the bay and a short distance up Cedar Bayou. A log residence had been begun there in a cornfield whose green sprouts probably screened the house from the bayou that June. Margaret anticipated going to Cedar Point soon, to relax in the peace of the country. The general had spoken highly of the salt air's healing powers, and Margaret saw the air as her ally in restoring Sam Houston's health.

The city of Galveston presented itself as a cluster of boxlike wooden buildings on the bay side of the island. In an otherwise unchanging landscape of sea, sky, and sand, its appearance was startling. The *New York* edged to the wharves. Dilapidated schooners, keelboats, and rafts docked in great numbers among the better ships. French, German, and Spanish could be heard mingled with the more typical English dialects. Since the Revolution, four years before, Galveston had grown from an island camp into a significant trade center, with ships from the United States, Europe, and the West Indies.

Nancy Lea had rented a house in Galveston after her arrival there in the previous autumn. She had lived with the Bledsoes before they moved to the Brazos River, then to a permanent location on the Trinity River. Rural Texas was too arduous for Nancy Lea, so she continued to reside on the island in spite of the yellow fever epidemic which was only beginning to subside. Margaret's meeting with her mother ended eight months of separation, the longest period they had ever been apart. From Marion, Mar-

variations, persists in the Houston family. The letters of Margaret and General Houston leave no doubt that a definite arrangement was made in an effort to ease Margaret's worries. The bitters are referred to on several occasions, for example, Sam Houston to Tom Bagby, Houston, December 18, 1842, *Writings*, III, 236.

garet had written: "Dearest Mother, I will not now attempt to reconcile my feelings during your voyage, nor the sweet thankfulness to Heaven that has enlivened my heart ever since I heard of your safe arrival. No, my pen would grow lame."[2]

During her residence in Texas, Nancy Lea had even conceived a certain fondness for Sam Houston. Being mother-in-law of Texas' most celebrated citizen might have warmed her more had she not been so domineering. She did not soften toward Houston until she had triumphed over him. In the previous November, when she had arrived at Galveston, she had seen Houston standing on the dock awaiting her ship. Obviously he had not received the letter in which Margaret told him she would not accompany her mother to Texas. Mrs. Lea scowled disapproval at the pageantry with which Houston called attention to his presence. The general inquired about Margaret. "General Houston," began Nancy Lea, "my daughter is in Alabama. She goes forth in the world to marry no man. The one who receives her hand will receive it in my home and not elsewhere."[3] Mrs. Lea had not bowed to the Texan, and afterward a genuine respect and affection developed between them. But neither of them ever yielded in their contest over Margaret.

General and Mrs. Houston established temporary residence at Nancy Lea's, choosing to ignore the fever and Margaret's terror of epidemics like the one that had taken her father's life six years before. The callers were few. Houston's friends had fled the city, except for Ashbel Smith, the only physician who had remained in town to help the fever victims.[4] At Houston's insistence, Smith had paid considerable attention to Margaret's mother. He was thirty-

[2] Margaret Lea to Nancy Lea, Marion, April 25, 1840, University of Texas Archives.

[3] James, *The Raven*, 313.

[4] Smith's experiences in the epidemic are documented in his MS collection, University of Texas Archives.

two, pale and light haired, with a boyish beard around his chin. Like Vernal, he was very meticulous, and made an avocation of trying to appear urbane. Born in Connecticut, Smith had pursued medical studies in Scotland and France, where he had met as many of the great and powerful as he could. It had been his pleasure in Paris to dine with General Lafayette, thus gaining a curio for his gentlemanly diary. He was a scholar and seemed frankly out of place in Texas. When Houston asked him to serve as best man in the wedding, he regretted that the "unsentimental obstacle" preventing his attendance was money.[5] The bachelor had seen more noble service at home in the yellow fever epidemic. Not once had he entertained romantic fantasies about Houston's decision to marry. He was probably even yet gravely concerned over the union of the general and "Miss Lee." To Bernard Bee he had written, "General Sam Houston left Galveston for Alabama . . . in truth to take the irrevocable step. . . . His health is very feeble and he disregards it in a manner that cannot be approved. I need not say what I think of the part he is about to enact." Colonel Bee had been adamant in his disapproval of the marriage. Smith wrote, "No difference of opinion exists between us."[6]

Margaret was anxious to see Antoinette, who, besides being her sister, was her closest friend. The rest of the family was worried about the Bledsoes. William Bledsoe's Trinity River property was being partially cleared for sugar planting in a thick forest twenty miles upstream from the town of Liberty, near the inland village of Grand Cane. The sickness that had troubled Bledsoe in Alabama was growing worse. His financial situation sank as he awaited return from real estate investments overly bold. There were seven

[5] Ashbel Smith to Radcliffe, Galveston, June 1, 1840, University of Texas Archives.

[6] Ashbel Smith to Bernard Bee, Galveston, May 22, 1840, University of Texas Archives.

slaves at the Bledsoe farm to keep the vegetable garden and make attempts at land clearing. Until his speculations paid off, however, the sugar plantation was merely a goal. With her supply of United States money, Nancy Lea had paid the Galveston bills left by the Bledsoes.[7]

Late in June, Houston left Margaret in Galveston with her mother, and he and Smith took a boat to Houston City, where the former president delivered an oration from the old capitol of the Republic. Margaret's happiness at his return was dampened by his plans for the coming weeks. He had accepted other engagements, and Margaret resigned herself to a long stay at Nancy Lea's. Houston was gone for most of the summer. In Galveston, Nancy Lea joined the Baptist church and applied herself to setting up a firm foundation for Margaret. The best of the Christian populace took notice of the devout Leas. Nancy Lea saw good in this, for Galveston presented a more genteel environment than rowdy Houston City or Austin, which faced threats by Indians. The longer Houston's absences lasted, the more eagerly Mrs. Lea sought to encourage social ambitions in Margaret.

Margaret's interest was not in society. Cedar Point was a two-hour boat ride away and seldom accessible by land. Sailboats for hire occasionally appeared at the docks; it was a matter of going there and bargaining, a service one of Houston's Negroes, Ben Blue or Esaw, performed for Margaret. The ships were leaky wrecks dredged from peninsula sand at Bolivar and tarred so that they would float again and taxi customers to points on the bay.

At Cedar Point, a flat, virtually treeless expanse of land greeted Margaret. There was a small house of logs standing unfinished in the clearing, which provided a distant view of the bay. It was a

[7] Sam Houston to Margaret Lea Houston, San Augustine, September 4, 1840, Franklin Williams Collection; see also public records, Galveston County, Texas. Mrs. Lea did a large amount of business in land.

two-room house, reminiscent of old ones Margaret must have remembered seeing in Perry County. Down the center the usual hallway was left open at each end, to attract the Gulf winds. The bride was delighted, except for the name, which she thought inadequate for her first home. She remembered the name Ben Lomond from one of Scott's romances. And Ben Lomond the cabin became.

Houston loved the "cabbin of unhewn logs."[8] The few rangy cedars that grew near the house shaded a plainer manor than he probably had foreseen. His Negroes were kept busy with farm work, however, and he thought little of houses. At Margaret's suggestion he had the slaves plant a grove of oak trees in the clearing; the trees extended orchardlike to the bayou and grew well.[9]

During the summer of 1840, Margaret made regular excursions from her mother's house out to Ben Lomond. The servants, with the exception of Eliza, were moved there and probably occupied the loft room and one of the downstairs rooms until a slave quarter was built. Furniture was slowly moved to Ben Lomond and a small flower garden was planted, with a catalpa tree in it. Margaret could not have gone so freely to the country had not Ashbel Smith or another friend, George Hockley, been usually willing to go along. Both men had farms near Cedar Point. Smith built a substantial house on his land, and when he was through he proudly nailed a sign to the gate: HEADQUARTERS. Soon a sign appeared on Hockley's unpretentious portal: HINDQUARTERS.[10]

For a man in his thirties, Pennsylvanian George Washington

[8] Sam Houston to Washington D. Miller, Cedar Point, May 31, 1841, collection of Mrs. F. S. Baldwin.

[9] Author in conversation with Mrs. Jennie Morrow Decker, May 1, 1965, Houston.

[10] Undated paper, Ashbel Smith manuscripts, University of Texas Archives.

Hockley had lived a full life. He had known Sam Houston before Houston had been elected governor of Tennessee. He had become one of the heroes of San Jacinto because of his command of the Twin Sisters, gift cannon from the United States. Like most of the Republic's citizens, Hockley was out to make his fortune as soon as possible. His interest was in sugar-cane planting.

Margaret enjoyed the bachelors. They were usually within calling distance, and she was often lonely. They liked books, as she did, and they seem to have taken her away from the hard stares of Nancy Lea.

The political situation was becoming difficult, attracting Houston into its midst. The public was disclaiming as extravagant and quixotic the policies of his successor Mirabeau B. Lamar. Houston was the most vocal opponent of the theatrical nationalism with which Lamar sought to draw the Republic toward self-sufficiency. Margaret found political involvements incompatible with Houston's promises to retire from public life. She tried selfishly to get Houston to concentrate upon her.

It was tiresome to be banished with her mother and Eliza. Eliza, a small, wiry girl, had a quick sense about necessity, and often directed the other house servants with whom Margaret was sometimes ill-tempered. Charlotte, a mulatto, resided also at Cedar Point. Margaret traded the coachman Jackson to Nancy Lea for a field hand named Frankey. Mrs. Houston's own efforts to perform housework were token, for she loathed mundane tasks. Eliza and Nancy Lea took care of most household business. Otherwise, details could simply take care of themselves. There were greater, more heroic endeavors for the wife of Sam Houston.

When General Houston told Margaret late in August that he would ride north to the Redlands country to attend to his law practice there, she insisted upon going, and Houston was pleased. The Redlands, whose principal town was San Augustine, covered a forty-mile sprawl of farms and forest running from the Sabine west. Sam Houston's name was in the race for congressman from that district. It was San Augustine and the neighboring Nacogdoches where many of Houston's friends lived. His law office which had been closed for a year since the death of his partner, was in San Augustine also.

Houston prepared for the journey, which would exceed 150 miles by the bridgeless ruts the Republic called roads. He borrowed a coach and rented four mules. "They will be needful," he once said of the road, "and all the caution possible, to save the Ladies & the carriage."[11] Eliza would go along to attend to Margaret. August was in its last week when they ferried from Galveston to the mainland.

Two days later the coach rolled through the Trinity River bottomlands to Grand Cane. The Bledsoe house, which was about three miles from town, was an unassuming log place of several rooms and a porch, beyond which, through a small green valley, lay the Trinity River, a muddy body that steamed in the hot August sun.[12] Heat and rich black land spell sugar country. Antoinette and William Bledsoe were but two among hundreds who set their aims on sugar gold in the wilds of Texas. Louisiana had set the formula, and thus far it had applied successfully to the new land.

It was the Houstons' plan to rest only overnight at the Bledsoes. The waterways part of the journey to San Augustine was over. From now on, monotonous upcountry forests, bogs, and Indian dangers would surround them. The young slave Joshua carried a

[11] Sam Houston to Margaret Lea Houston, San Augustine, September 4, 1840, Franklin Williams Collection.

[12] Author in conversation with Mrs. Jennie Morrow Decker, January 12, 1964, Houston; see also Ellis, *Sam Houston and Related Spiritual Forces*; cisterns and portions of the garden of the Bledsoe home remain in the Martinez Survey, Liberty County, Texas.

rifle, and Sam Houston kept another one in his saddle scabbard, besides the brace of pistols that were his trademark.

Perhaps it was Margaret's uneasiness over Houston's candidacy, coupled with the harrowing ferry crossings and poor roads, that made her ill. Shortly after entering Antoinette's house, she was carried to bed. Antoinette could probably have calmed Houston's anxieties, for she knew Margaret's frequent illnesses and Margaret's mental susceptibility to any disease that she heard about. Doubtless the unhappy diagnosis that Captain Bledsoe's sickness was consumption had inspired Margaret. But Antoinette was like Nancy Lea in believing Houston too inconsiderate of her sister. With problems of her own, Mrs. Bledsoe had no intention of comforting Sam Houston.

Joshua was given the general's horse and a message for Ashbel Smith. Days passed. Smith was on a holiday in Houston City and was fast asleep when the rider arrived. He rose at once and made the thirty-five-mile ride "in the interior." General Houston rushed him to Margaret's side.[13] Smith diagnosed Margaret as exhausted and said that she could not travel. Anxiety and the prospect of camping on the roadside would overtax her. The reprobate Texas climate required an adjustment Margaret had not made. General Houston did not want to leave her. So tender were his attentions to the bedridden Margaret that Ashbel Smith, back in Galveston, wrote to a friend, "Gen. Houston was a model of domestic propriety and kindness."[14]

However, Sam Houston rode away through the sweetgums and pinoaks, leaving Margaret at Grand Cane with the Bledsoes. Early September was hot and still, and Margaret opened her first letter from the traveling politician. He had been indisposed—"bled

[13] Ashbel Smith to Kincaid, Galveston, August 30, 1840, University of Texas Archives.

[14] *Ibid.*

myself last evening. . . . Sickness has been universal in Texas. I am more lonely each day. . . . To see you engrasps my greatest desires. But for a while I must be reconciled and pray for your health, safety, and happiness."[15]

With seemingly endless time in which to think, Margaret became worried over Sam Houston. Gossips spoke idly of her marriage, though she seems to have heard only fragments of what they said in Grand Cane. Houston had been called a bigamist because of his questioned divorce.[16] A greater problem, however, was liquor. Margaret had no way of knowing how well he practiced the abstinence he had promised when they married. The mere fact of the promise, and recent good behavior, had not changed the popular image of Houston as a drunkard. Margaret feared the possibility of truth in the stories, for she knew better than anyone else the depth of Houston's involvement with liquor. She believed she was God's instrument to aid him in his reformation. But her efforts seemed frustrated because she could not keep him within her reach.[17]

His letters were frequent. "Everybody is anxious to see you in the Redlands. I would be right 'appie' to see you myself." She must come at once. Bring "Captain Bledsoe and Sis" and journey by the lower, better-known route, for "persons are *killed* on the upper road—by the Indians! !"[18]

Margaret and Eliza crossed the gangplank to Galveston Island. In desperation, Margaret wrote a long letter spilling out her fears.

[15] Sam Houston to Margaret Lea Houston, Crockett, Texas, August 22, 1840, Franklin Williams Collection.

[16] Gen. T. J. Green to Col. B. E. Bee, Velasco, July 19, 1840, University of North Carolina Archives. Green also accused Houston of "beastly and infamous" conduct "since his marriage."

[17] William C. Crane, *Life and Select Literary Remains*, 253.

[18] Sam Houston to Margaret Lea Houston, San Augustine, September 4, 1840, Franklin Williams Collection.

Houston replied, "Today is drizzling and damp, and I am depressed and melancholy! I cannot be happy but where you are!" And as for her worries, "My love I do sincerely hope that you will hear no more slanders of me. It is the malice of the world to abuse me, and really were it not that they reach my beloved Margaret, I would not care one picayune—but that you should be distressed is inexpressible wretchedness to me!"[19]

Margaret liked to sit and analyze her marriage. Now and then household problems arose and interrupted her. Either because of dislike of Margaret or fear of Nancy Lea, who had assumed management at Cedar Point, discontent brewed in the slave quarter. To eliminate the friction and to provide income, Houston hired some of the men out to other people. During the process of exchange, Tom and Esaw disappeared and were not apprehended. They had fled to Mexico. A disgruntled Houston borrowed one hundred dollars Texas money in San Augustine to repay Nancy Lea for Margaret's expenses. "I regret," wrote Houston, "that I cannot send you a million in gold."[20]

He was at home in mid-November, having been elected to the Texas Congress. Ignoring Margaret's wish to move to Ben Lomond, he decided to establish residence in a rent house he owned in Houston City. He arranged to ship the furniture to Houston City, where the rosewood piano is said to have attracted a crowd when it arrived, still crated, aboard a boat on the bayou.

Margaret found that Houston City's notorious reputation masked an agreeable society. Legend confidently states that she established a pleasant home for Sam Houston in the city that bears his name, though little is known of their private lives there. Char-

[19] Sam Houston to Margaret Lea Houston, Austin, January 16, 1841, Franklin Williams Collection.

[20] Sam Houston to Margaret Lea Houston, San Augustine, September 4, 1840, Franklin Williams Collection.

lotte was brought from Cedar Point to assist Eliza, with whom she constantly bickered. Trunks were opened, yielding lace curtains and tablecloths. Brass candlesticks and the mellow glow of Alabama store-bought mahogany stood against common unceiled walls.

Margaret wearied quickly of Houston City. Life there was too active. Constant parties interrupted her reading, callers broke into her thoughts, and it was necessary to keep the house in order. Houston City was a muddy, populous place not safe to explore alone. Too, there was the theater, and the usual saloons with the noisy brothels above. The city was never quiet. Balls were held in the big, peach-colored building that had housed the capitol and its records before the removal to Austin. Margaret missed the sand streets and orange trees of Galveston. When Houston left in December and rode westward 150 miles to Austin for the opening of the Congress, not a day longer did Margaret remain in Houston City. She sailed to Galveston to join Nancy Lea.

At her mother's home she went into seclusion to pursue the rest and reading which were her only joys in Houston's absences. "This is the holy sabbath and Momma is gone to church and has left me to commune with my heart and to think of you. Oh how delightful is solitude when absent from the idol of your soul!" She anticipated his letters eagerly, reconciled to not seeing him until the Congress had adjourned. "I am here alone—alone and my mind steals back to the scenes of other days. Ah many a bright vision of joy and gladness rises up from the bosom of the past to greet me."[21]

Solitude brought both pain and pleasure to Margaret. Since her baptism she had avoided remembering the religious doubts that had frightened her once before. Mr. McLean, Professor Goree, or the Reverend Peter Crawford had never been far away, and

[21] Margaret Lea Houston to Sam Houston, Galveston, December 7, 1840, Franklin Williams Collection.

they were strong. Margaret's public testimony had not been wholly satisfying, and she had allowed Peter Crawford to baptize her when perhaps she should have waited until she better understood what she was doing. To her way of thinking, each step she made in religion was vital.

Lonely times brought up old questions which somehow could no longer be answered by youth's optimism. It only increased her anxiety to know that Houston mocked the religious matters she took so seriously. "Oh my beloved," she wrote, "why has our heavenly father made us so happy unless he intended that we should be grateful and useful in his cause!"[22] Sam Houston refused to attend church. "Our God whom *you* serve," he had reminded her.[23] He respected Margaret's devoutness, but respect was no compensation for Margaret. She shuddered to think of his laxness. There were considerations beyond this life—"death! The world hath pleasures which the foolish employ to screen their vision from the horrid object, but it avails him nothing, for it is ever before the eye, distinct as the handwriting upon the wall!" It was foolish to ignore the truth, she insisted. One could "forget awhile the . . . danger . . . yet everyone has his hours of solitude, and then comes the dreadful reaction!"

She exhorted Houston to force himself to think of these important things. "Let us not abuse a blessing so rarely bestowed on human beings, nor be too secure in our present state. . . . The heart is very deceitful and may possibly grow selfish under the influence of prosperity, and bye and bye we would become . . . presumptious, and imagine that the blessings which surround us were nothing more than our rights." She closed her letter with, "I would tell you that my health is very good now if I did not fear that you

[22] *Ibid.*

[23] Sam Houston to Margaret Lea Houston, San Augustine, September 4, 1840, Franklin Williams Collection.

would take encouragement to remain from me longer than you might otherwise do."[24] He was not at home for New Year's vacation during 1841. Mrs. Houston sailed to Cedar Point frequently during the mild January to see the great progress Nancy Lea had made toward its completion.

During January, Vernal and his wife Mary arrived at Galveston, seeking a new life in which they might forget the death of their infant son. The weak, chronically ill Mary needed a new climate, and Vernal asked Sam Houston's advice about finding a livelihood. If family connections could help Vernal comfortably situate himself, he was willing to take the opportunity. There was apparently little left of his inheritance. He had lived well as a student at the University of Georgia. When his money was depleted, Henry supplied him with an allowance. Vernal was more mature for his experience. He and Margaret left Mary with Nancy Lea and visited Houston City together. They enjoyed being together, a fact Margaret mentioned in a letter to General Houston, who replied with the jealous-sounding remark that Margaret would not have a real protector until Sam Houston was at home. Vernal missed "Nettie," as he called Antoinette. So early in February he and Mary boarded a boat up the Trinity to the Bledsoes', where they offered their services while the captain was ill.

General Houston was overdue at home. National affairs were his obsession: "All the evils of which Texas has now to complain were brought upon her by ignorance and corruption. . . . We have none to rule but in misrule, and the President is so mean, and base." Houston's capacity for writing letters was prodigious. In small ways he alluded to the next president—to be elected in 1841—who he would be, and what would be his problems: after

[24] Margaret Lea Houston to Sam Houston, Galveston, December 7, 1840, Franklin Williams Collection.

the disillusion of liberal optimism, the "next administration" would be "so involved . . . that it cannot extricate the nation."[25]

Margaret would have liked to join the general in Austin, even though the family, and her husband, discouraged her from doing so. Houston had complained that there was not a single house between the capital of Texas and Santa Fe. Open to Indian attacks, Austin's citizens were already hardened to reports of hunters being found scalped and white women being carried away to the plains. Margaret was afraid of Indians and did not want to hear the stories of the frequent massacres in remote outposts. The city of Austin seemed safe, but the safeness was merely an illusion created by prosperity. Mexican troops moved freely through the lands between the Nueces and the Río Grande. They had come close to San Antonio, which was only sixty miles from Austin. Houston insisted that Margaret remain on the coast, near the regular stopping places of the steamers. If necessary, she could be safely back in Alabama within ten days to two weeks, depending upon the weather at sea.

The capital city excitement which Houston described was far removed from the tellurian existence that characterized most of the Republic. In Austin, political popularity was the measure of success. "When I cease to speak the ladies leave and the galleries are empty!"[26] Sam Houston relished flattery, but Margaret could see nothing but the chance that the capital's glitter might take him away from her.[27] Rumors traveled down the Austin road. "You my love will smile," Houston comforted, "at the nonsense malignity inspires."[28] The tales of his drunkenness were not necessarily

[25] Sam Houston to Gen. William G. Harding, Cedar Point, July 17, 1841, Harding manuscripts, University of North Carolina Archives.

[26] Sam Houston to Margaret Lea Houston, Austin, January 16, 1841, Franklin Williams Collection.

[27] Friend, *The Great Designer*, 98.

unkind. Houston was accustomed to the often-good-naturedly ribald stories in which people liked to feature him. He made jokes about the bitters he drank now instead of whisky at the insistence of his pious wife. A measure of Houston's human appeal was in his self-deprecation, yet his admirers were mistaken if they believed he loved them more than himself. He had little use for people. He had no doubt of his superiority, and he had an uncanny talent of convincing audiences to believe in it as well. That the people sometimes made him the subject of vicious talk did not alarm Houston.[29]

In the interest of his young wife, however, Houston became irritated at gossips. As a public official he was admittedly public property, but Margaret deserved her seclusion. She knew nothing of politics; she was gentle and tenaciously loyal to people she loved. He denounced the "malicious slanders, calculated to create hatred." Margaret must learn to turn her head.

> Were I, as I am represented to be, my enemies would be satisfied, and silent. It would be gratification to see me a drunken sot. But my dear *they* see that my constitution is daily returning and my complexion becoming pure and clear! These are painful symptoms to my adversaries . . . Do not be distressed. I cannot forget my love, and admiration for Margaret! I would not inflict one pang to your dear heart for Empires![30]

Margaret believed him and molded her fear of the public tongue into a peculiar feeling of contempt. Newspapers lay un-

28 Sam Houston to Margaret Lea Houston, Austin, January 16, 1841, Franklin Williams Collection.

29 Ashbel Smith, "Reminiscences of the Texas Republic," University of Texas Archives.

30 Sam Houston to Margaret Lea Houston, Austin, January 16, 1841, Franklin Williams Collection.

opened on her table. Her attitude sometimes amused Houston, who could not resist an opportunity to tease her. After a wedding reception he wrote—"I drank one cup of coffee! but not even one glass of *wine!*"[31]

If he seemed to be making fun of Margaret, he was misinterpreted. "I find that total abstinence will make me all that I ever was in point of health and constitution." The effects were already felt. "But there is more than this to be considered! The feelings of my dearly beloved Maggy—whose only dread is that I may abandon myself at some time to *intemperance*!!!!" He asked her not to worry. Be patient, for "*when we meet you will be satisfied!*"[32]

The Houstons' talk of his retirement and the plans for building a permanent house at Cedar Point seemed curiosities from the past. They had not yet spent time at Ben Lomond; they had not even seen each other in months. And Margaret missed him. "My mind . . . fixes itself on the bright hour in which we first *met* and *loved*. Ah how sweetly the lone evening star shone upon our village home! I trembled to think that there was one dearer to me than all the hallowed ties of kindred . . . yet there was a strange joy in my heart. . . . I felt that the majestic being who sought my hand combined all the ideas of human greatness and excellence that had haunted the visions of my youth. I thought not of disappointment except to know and feel that I would rather suffer misfortune with *him* than enjoy prosperity with another."[33]

Margaret was depressed, and as lonely as she had been as a recluse in her brother's library back in Marion. Her family still uselessly pitied her. "The world," she wrote, "would call this the

[31] *Ibid.*

[32] *Ibid.*

[33] Margaret Lea Houston to Sam Houston, Galveston, December 7, 1840, Franklin Williams Collection.

language of girlish romance. Be it so—it is a romance that elevates the thoughts from the groveling things of earth."[34] She kept to her bed long hours because of asthma and coughs. Nancy Lea and Eliza nursed her and insisted that she not exert herself, and apparently she did not.

Now political rumors began to worry her. Sam Houston was said to have announced his candidacy for president. Hearing that, Margaret's vision of Ben Lomond vanished. She wrote a letter, to which Houston replied:[35]

Austin 3rd Feby 1841

By the enclosed News Paper, my *Beloved* will see, that I have *not consented to become a Candidate for the Presidency!* The affections and happiness of my endeared Margaret are more to me than all the Gewgaws of ambition; or the pageantry of Royalty.

Should she desire me to do so, I will consent but not otherwise! My *Love* must decide! And let her regard *her own* happiness.

Mine will consist in *her felicity*. The determination of my Love I will abide by.

Thy People shall be my People; and thy God shall be my God! On tomorrow I suppose we shall adjourn.

Thy devoted
Husband
HOUSTON

To Lady Margaret.

Late in February they sailed to Ben Lomond, where they remained five weeks. General Houston left by sailboat several times for short speaking engagements, but most of his political business

[34] *Ibid.*

[35] Sam Houston to Margaret Lea Houston, Austin, February 3, 1841, Franklin Williams Collection.

was conducted at home. In Austin he had been the main spokesman decrying the failures, and minimizing the successes, of President Lamar's romantic nationalism. His ideas were as Jacksonian as his manner of disclaiming Lamar. Margaret must have known her husband would run for president, regardless of her wishes to the contrary. Shortly before the first of April, Houston took Margaret back to Nancy Lea's in Galveston and hastened alone to the Redlands, which was always the place of beginning for him in politics.

When Nancy Lea went to the Bledsoes', Margaret hesitated to follow, lest she miss the general on his return to Galveston. After mid-April, Nancy Lea hired a wagon and had Jackson drive her to Antoinette's with a load of household furniture. It was the first of several trips she would make for the purpose of moving her possessions from the Galveston house. Captain Bledsoe's condition was so uncertain that the widow was needed on the Trinity to help Antoinette manage the farm.

Alone in Galveston, Margaret mused over a picture Sam Houston had given her. It was a likeness of himself.

Dear gentle shade of him I love,
I've gazed upon thee till thine eye,
In liquid light doth seem to move
And look on me in sympathy!

An image starts within my mind,
As in a shadow from the past,
On some sweet dream of olden time,
Has suddenly my heart o'er cast.

Yes—yes, it must be so! the same
Proud form of majesty, the one
That o'er my girlish vision came,
And that my heart hath loved alone.[36]

The poem was longer, for Margaret liked to write very long poems. She coined a title, "To My Husband's Picture," and folded the poem into her next letter as a surprise for Sam Houston.

Oblivious to the newspapers' ridicule of her husband, Margaret directed Eliza to pack for a trip to Grand Cane. Coastal economic interests usually motivated Galveston, and Congressman Houston, seeking to appeal to an ever widening public, had made indiscreet remarks which had alienated his supporters among the land speculators in the Redlands. Although the coastal interests usually opposed him, the general found that factions in Houston City appreciated what he had been saying. With their prosperity in decline since the government's removal to Austin, Houston City capitalists were alarmed. Alliances were made, and a Houston City group nominated Sam Houston for president of the Republic of Texas.

Margaret, meanwhile, in disappointment, was with Eliza somewhere on the road to Grand Cane. The gloomy forests around Antoinette's house were a humid shade beneath the hot, unmoving sun. Margaret knew she would see little of the general now that he was a candidate for president. Already the bitter electioneering had begun. Politicians annoyed Margaret with their cruelty, and the old stories about the general's drunkenness were circulating in the campaign propaganda of David G. Burnet, Houston's opponent.[37]

William Bledsoe's poor health restricted his business activities, and some of his property was sold at public sale in Galveston. Nancy Lea and Antoinette, sometimes morose anyway, were nurturing their unhappiness, and Margaret felt imprisoned in the

[36] Margaret Lea Houston, "To My Husband's Picture," Galveston, April 15, 1841, University of Texas Archives.

[37] Sam Houston to Margaret Lea Houston, Austin, January 16, 1841, Franklin Williams Collection.

country. Abruptly one morning Margaret and Eliza sailed to Galveston, where Margaret spent her twenty-second birthday alone. Away from her piano and her books she looked for a means of occupying herself. She grew fond of walking on the beach in the afternoon. Customarily she wore a shawl, in the Mexican manner, and a mantilla to protect her pale complexion from the sun.[38] Beach walking was a popular pastime among the islanders. When they saw the solitary woman and her maid, they doubtless knew nothing about her. Sam Houston's wife lived in anonymity.

Galveston newspapers endorsed the idea that the epidemic that was burning over the city had come from a foreign sailor on a ship in the port. Some feared it was a return of the black vomit, the common name of yellow fever. The argument raged, and some of the papers found their way up the Trinity to the quiet house in the hackberry and myrtle trees. It was Captain Bledsoe's custom to go to the edge of the Gulf and flag the riverboats in order to buy available newspapers. The papers were still printing reports on the sickness when Nancy Lea arrived in Galveston to fetch Margaret and return her to the safety of the country. Margaret emphatically refused to go, and the widow sent her coachman Jackson riding to the Redlands with a message.

By mid-May Margaret was strumming her guitar for General Houston in the peace of Ben Lomond. Her real talent was the Spanish guitar, though she preferred the pianoforte. When he wearied of music, Margaret amused him with poems she had written.

And oh that smile! I know it well,
It minds me of the eve in May,
When soft the rising starlight fell
Upon the flowers at close of day.

[38] Author in conversation with Mrs. Jennie Morrow Decker, January 12, 1964; also see clippings ca. 1899, collection of Mrs. F. S. Baldwin.

And first my trembling lips did own
Thy love returned, that holy hour
Sure nature smiled in unison,
Through every tree and vine and flower.[39]

It was a happy summer. Houston wrote epistolary campaign articles under the title *Truth* for publication in Texas newspapers. On the bay shore, Margaret gathered wildflowers. "My dear wife is trying to keep house," wrote Houston to a friend, "and I make a fair hand in the field! True my dear fellow!"[40] Political friends rowed up the bayou to enjoy the Houstons' hospitality at Cedar Point. The dining table was set in the hall, and for the guests' amusement, there were good saddle horses, a sailboat, and several shelves of books. Margaret's interest in domestic details was fleeting. The house was the special charge of Eliza, who was in the kitchen all day preparing food. A half-century afterward, Eliza, who could neither read nor write her name, told how an Indianola sugar planter had offered two thousand dollars cash for her and how Margaret had refused.[41]

Margaret was not well advised if, as Eliza said, her attitude about money was otherwise flippant. One reason the Houstons were in the country is probably because they could live there at virtually no expense. Besides the costs of the campaign, which were covered by contributions and personal loans, Houston was in such need that some of his slaves remained hired out and the Houston City house was up for sale. Houston bought and sold land occasionally, but as for a dependable income, he had none. Impecu-

39 Margaret Lea Houston, "To My Husband's Picture," Galveston, April 15, 1841, University of Texas Archives.

40 Sam Houston to Washington Miller, Cedar Point, May 31, 1841, collection of Mrs. F. S. Baldwin.

41 Author in conversation with Mrs. Ruth Sanders Johns, April 20, 1961, Georgetown, Texas.

niosity was a marked characteristic of the Houstons' friends. Ashbel Smith and George Hockley had moved to their farms on the bay, where Smith was writing a scholarly treatise on yellow fever and the Texas epidemic which had just ended.[42]

General and Mrs. Houston passed the summer at Ben Lomond, out of hearing of the political enemies who were making a major issue of Sam Houston's moral weaknesses. Houston could not escape the mystery of his past. It is not known how much of the truth of that past Margaret ever knew. Eliza Allen was still living in Tennessee; Diana Rogers Gentry had remarried two weeks prior to San Jacinto.[43] Margaret's children later maintained that Houston revealed the secret of his first marriage to her, but one wonders if Margaret was curious to know. She and the general seldom dwelled upon the past in their letters. Although she was jealous of anything that took him away from her, she never doubted his love for her, and more than anything else she was engrossed in her present life with him.

Houston's newspaper articles condemning President Lamar and Judge Burnet were as sharp as those written against him by his opponents. In the beginning Margaret scanned the articles; however, she stopped doing so and even ceased reading many of her husband's speeches, which were usually printed in entirety.[44] She had not been exposed to the tactics of public men on the frontier, nor had she campaigned with Henry Lea in Alabama. Houston respected her wish for privacy and conducted his campaign at home and quietly.

[42] Ashbel Smith, "On Yellow Fever," University of Texas Archives. This paper was presented before the Royal Society in London when Smith was there in conjunction with service in the Texas diplomatic corps.

[43] Ernest C. Shearer, "The Mercurial Sam Houston," *The East Tennessee Historical Society's Publication*, Vol. XXXV, 9.

[44] Sam Houston to Margaret Lea Houston, Washington, D.C., January 6, 1855, Franklin Williams Collection.

But in the passing weeks Houston became restless. He worried over his recent unpopularity in the Redlands. Hockley and Smith came regularly to the Houston house in the newly planted oak grove. Sam Houston's nervousness was more easily understood by them than by Margaret, who was content in the country. Ashbel Smith wrote that Houston followed dreams through life, and that money and the making of money bored him when his dreams intervened: political power was the only self-gratification the general wanted. Indians and Mexicans threatened the well-being of the Republic. Houston assumed he could solve the problem if he were again president of the nation. "Were I its *ruler*," he once said of the United States, "I could rule it well. . . . To govern well is a great science."[45]

Although the summer of 1841 could probably have lasted forever and Margaret would not have complained, Houston decided in July that he must go to the Redlands. He wanted Margaret to accompany him, apparently as a stimulant to the angry voters who might be appeased seeing the child bride of the man who had exposed his misery to them in other days. Margaret protested that she was ill, and Houston turned to writing more articles. When on the eve of departure her illness worsened, the trip was postponed again.

August came, and Margaret sat up in bed with her lap-desk. "Ben Lomond," she wrote, "Cedar Point, 1841."

> *Yes dearest, we are happy here*
> *In this sweet solitude*
> *Of ours, no heartless ones come near*
> *Or tiresome scenes intrude.*

[45] Sam Houston to Margaret Lea Houston, Washington, D.C., April 22, 1858, *Writings*, VII, 99–100.

The Mock-bird on our green yard tree
Sings through the live-long night,
And greets the moon, his heart less free
Than ours, his hopes less bright!

At eve beside our cottage door
We watch the sky's last hue
And listening to the ocean's roar
Our thoughts the day review.

Would that we thus might ever be,
Far from the world's dark snares!
Mid nature's wildwood purity,
Untrammeled by earth's cares![46]

August progressed, and the election was set for mid-September. Houston wrote, "Things move on . . . coolly and very dryly—*Dryly* because we have had no rain for the last nine weeks, *drily* because we have no liquor." Of liquor he must leave no doubt. "I do not taste one drop of it, nor will I do it!"[47] He had his friends save orange peel for him to use with bitters on occasions.

Ashbel Smith came to Cedar Point visibly worried about talk he had heard on a visit to Houston City. The vindictive newspaper articles the general had written might be turning into a disadvantage in the election because they were clearly directed at Mirabeau B. Lamar, more than at his opponent Burnet, and Lamar had many friends in Texas. Undecided voters in the Redlands and the Gulf Coast might be swayed against Houston in reaction to the attacks of *Truth.* Smith had in his hand a letter suggesting that the doctor go to Cedar Point and effect an amiable

[46] Margaret Lea Houston, "Cedar Point—Ben Lomond," June 1, 1841, University of Texas Archives.

[47] Sam Houston to Samuel Williams, Cedar Point, July 28, 1841, *Writings*, II, 369–70.

truce between Houston and the outgoing president. Admittedly Smith liked Lamar as a person, calling him a "Princely Trubador." Margaret took the letter and read the proposal. She expressed herself in favor of it. Those newspaper wars would stop; the contest would be reduced to an exchange of ideas between Houston and the real opponent, Burnet. Ashbel Smith agreed with Margaret. Soon Houston became impatient with their presumption to guide his career. "Mr. Smith, the interests of history and of *Truth* are of far more importance than General Lamar's support of Sam Houston can ever be."[48]

Another date was set for the Redlands trip, and Margaret came down with a second ailment. Dr. Smith had returned to Galveston, to which place Frankey carried a note: "If you can, come over. Mrs. H—— is affected, she thinks, with 'bronchitis'—she is ill anyhow!"[49]

On the last day of August, Houston told Margaret he would have to go alone, since the election was two weeks away. He packed his saddlebags. Margaret rallied when she saw she could not change his mind; if he must go, then she would go too, rather than to stay at home and be lonely. Though he knew she would arouse interest in the Redlands, Houston was opposed to her making the journey. But he acquiesced and engaged in Houston City "an eminent physician," Dr. Fosgate, to travel with them in case Margaret should develop ill effects from camping out.[50]

That month of September, Margaret was exposed to many raw aspects of Texas life. The springless coach bumped along the roads, which, weed grown, trickled through walls of pine and oak. At

[48] Diary of Ashbel Smith, entry for October 13, 1841, University of Texas Archives.

[49] Sam Houston to Ashbel Smith, Cedar Point, August 25, 1841, *Writings*, II, 374.

[50] Harriet Smither (ed.), "The Diary of Adolphus Sterne," *Southwestern Historical Quarterly*, Vol. XXXII, 178.

night Joshua unhitched the mules, set up the tent, and gathered a bed of leaves for the general and Margaret. A big fire was built between the tent and the coach. For six days they traveled. Camp meetings, weddings, balls, and barbecues were welcome grounds for political campaigning. They had been in Nacogdoches only a while when it was announced that Houston had won the presidency.

Hardly was there a moment for congratulations. Margaret was back in the coach and off one hundred miles southwest to Washington, where a barbecue was being held in Houston's honor. A great feast was served with, according to one guest, "barbecued hogs and two thundering big beeves well roasted with lots of honey, *taters*, chickens, and goodies in general." The same guest remarked that it was "cold water *doins*." Sam Houston did not drink the "smallest drop of the ardent during his stay."[51]

Dr. Fosgate could not endure the schedule. At Washington he took the public coach back to Houston City. Tuesday night, September 28, 1841, in a drizzling mist, Joshua drove the coach again through the Redlands eastward to San Augustine. The president of the Republic of Texas rode the Tennessee mare he had bought the summer he met Margaret. Even in the night, Margaret, inside the coach, could doubtless sense the unique quality of these Redlands. The source of the name was obvious. No land was more scarlet; its hills rose and fell in an easy terrain of creeks and forests and hillside cotton fields reminiscent of parts of the eastern United States. From the top of a gradual slope the road meandered down into the outskirts of San Augustine, which, unless, as now, the populace was expecting the president-elect, had few lighted windows. Neat whitewashed cottages slumbered behind picket-fenced yards that bordered red dirt streets. Different

[51] Henry Gillett to Ashbel Smith, September 17, 1841; Edward Winfield to Ashbel Smith, September 22, 1841, cited in Friend, *The Great Designer*, 101.

from the other Texas towns Margaret had seen, San Augustine greeted her with ornamental trees instead of the bareness that usually accompanied Anglo-American civilization into the wilderness.

The Houstons were the guests of the rich merchant Iredell D. Thomas. His tall, galleried house stood on a corner of the courthouse square, which tilted down from the abrupt peak of a hill. Late that night Margaret was shown to one of Penelope Thomas's prized rosewood beds, the kind of furniture San Augustine, in strange contrast to the rest of the Republic, seemed to have in abundance.[52]

Blue skies and sunshine the next morning brought many callers to meet the president-elect and his lady. Sam Houston was particularly fond of San Augustine, and there is a story that he built a house in a meadow east of town and hoped to make it his permanent home. He and Margaret often expressed an interest in living in the Redlands, though they never did move there. Small outbreaks of violence had erupted between land speculators and the poor farmers in the Redlands, dimming future prospects for the whole countryside. Yet, as surely as some people complained of a "state of decline," the *Red-Lander*, San Augustine's newspaper, boasted, "The beauty and fashion of this city and vicinity, can vie with any portion of the United States."[53]

Margaret proved herself an "accomplished and amiable Lady," according to the *Red-Lander*. Her "course through the country has won a popularity, by her kind and Ladylike manner, greater if possible than that which clings to her patriotic husband."[54] Having already spent a brief visit in the country with the Philip Subletts, the Houstons decided to return there and finish their visit. Five

[52] Collection of Mrs. Roland Jones, a descendant of Penelope Thomas, contains a portion of the contents of the house in which the Houstons were guests; see also in the Jones collection, photograph of the Thomas house, ca. 1900.

[53] The *Red-Lander*, October 14, 1841.

[54] The *Red-Lander*, October 28, 1841.

miles out from town the Sublett place stood refreshingly quiet in its cedar grove. Mrs. Sublett was much older than Margaret, and they seem to have had very little in common. Houston, however, was very fond of Phil Sublett, saying he was the only San Jacinto veteran of his acquaintance still in Texas. It was in the Sublett house that Houston had recuperated from the San Jacinto wound; in other times the Subletts had given him shelter in periods of drunkenness.

That night Houston and Sublett rode back to San Augustine to attend *Pizarro*, which was being presented by the all-male San Augustine Thespian Society in the Greek Revival opera house atop Berry's Saloon.[55] Houston, it is told, had once played Othello at Berry's opposite Will Ochiltree, who played the part of Desdemona.

Because of weakness from travel Margaret was unable to leave as soon as Houston had planned. San Augustine took the opportunity of the delay and held a "Complimentary Ball" in early October. Guests were attracted from the next county, and what the Houstons failed to record about the event, the effervescent *Red-Lander* more than adequately reported: "It was numerously attended by the gay and fashionable Ladies and Gentlemen of this city and county. . . . We can safely assert that San Augustine never produced a more lovely and interesting company of Ladies; joy beamed on the faces of all. Never in any assembly have we witnessed or heard more hillarity and sociability of feeling; all were easy and competent in their manners, for it seemed that it gave each one pleasure to render others happy."[56]

In mid-October, Houston took advantage of an invitation sent to him and Margaret by the Adolphus Sternes of Nacogdoches. Eva Sterne had been Houston's godmother in his token conversion

[55] Harriet Smither, "The Diary of Adolphus Sterne," 179.

[56] The *Red-Lander*, October 14, 1841.

to Catholicism, effected soon after his arrival in Texas. Like Houston, Adolphus Sterne, a German Jew, had obeyed the Mexican law concerning the state church. A man of erratic political convictions, Sterne had been one of those Redlanders who opposed Houston and voted against him in the election of the previous month. If Sterne still had misgivings about Houston, he had nothing but compliments for Margaret, writing in his private diary that she was, if not beautiful, a good wife for Sam Houston.

Nacogdoches' stylish society seemed inconsistent with the appearance of the old city, which was only touched by whitewash here and there, crowded in clumps of pine, and had red dirt streets leading to corrals. It was a drab contrast to San Augustine. A mass of citizens came forward to congratulate the president-elect at a public barbecue.[57] In the course of the affair a country man stepped up to Margaret and asked in a loud voice if she had ever been in Shelby County. Margaret replied that she had not, and he said that she should go, for the general had a number of children over there—children, that is, who were named for him. The crowd, and Sam Houston, were greatly amused. An embarrassed Margaret moved closer to her husband, who admonished the jokester to try to keep his statements in better order thereafter.[58] Margaret had to expect a certain rowdiness among the throngs that went to the public functions and stood in the torchlight to hear Houston's speeches. Private fêtes were more to her taste. At Charles Chevallier's party, Margaret met Dr. and Mrs. Robert Irion. Anna Raguet Irion was pregnant and appearing in public, which would have been unthinkable in Marion. But people waltzed in Texas too and were not so bold back home.

The last night of the visit in Nacogdoches, Anne Simmons held a dinner party, and Margaret bravely emerged from Houston's

[57] *Ibid.*

[58] John Salmon Ford, "Memoir," 216–17, University of Texas Archives.

side and let herself be known. Adolphus Sterne went home and wrote the opinion that his violet-eyed guest was a "first rate musician, on the piano-forte & guitar—on which latter instrument she excells."[59]

Early the next morning the Houstons prepared to leave Nacogdoches. Houston deeded his town lot in Nacogdoches to the Sternes' new baby Eugenia as a birthday present. At one time he had planned to build a house on the property and settle in that town. When he lost Anna Raguet, he abandoned the idea of living in Nacogdoches.

A half-day later the coach stopped on the Angelina River before the log farmhouse of the Irions, and for about three days the Houstons and the Irions were together. Anna was a beautiful blonde, the master of several languages, and a student of theology. She was a woman of wide capabilities, very unlike the pampered, introverted Margaret. The general impression is left that the Houstons and the Irions were not compatible. Still they remained friends, for some years later Margaret embroidered a baby blanket for Anna Raguet's first son, Sam Houston Irion.[60]

Back on the road in early November, Margaret tensed against the chilly wind that blew in the coach. Creek crossings required a stop and endless delays. The ferries were dangerous and not dependable. Exhausted, Margaret went to bed when she reached Houston City.

On November 9, cannons boomed. Margaret participated in the presidential parade which began at nine in the morning. The notoriously unco-ordinated Houston Dragoons, the Fanin Artillery, and the Milam Guards marched ahead of Margaret's carriage as an honor guard. At ten o'clock the parade stopped before

[59] Harriet Smither, "Diary of Adolphus Sterne," 182.

[60] Susan Miles, "A Famous Romance," *West Texas Historical Association Yearbook*, Vol. XXXVIII, 137.

the Main Street Presbyterian Church. The wives of the other dignitaries were already seated in the church, awaiting the president-elect and his entourage. Noisy street crowds always frightened Margaret, so she probably showed her joy at being in the protection of the church. Sam Houston addressed the full room "with his accustomed gallantry," beginning by bowing toward the ladies' section.[61]

Revelry continued all afternoon and night in the streets. The rival militia companies contributed to the noise by firing twenty-two gun salutes in competition. After dark, candles glowed from the windows of Houston City. The fashionable people attended a ball at the City Hotel. Some of the most elegant ladies of the Republic were present, adorned after the style of the day, in leg-of-mutton sleeves and high-piled curls festooned with cut flowers and Spanish silver combs. What a man might wear to such an occasion was anybody's guess. Sam Houston loved red and wore the color freely with vests of antelope or leopard and sweeping evening cloaks lined in satin. The dress Margaret wore was probably old unless she had with forethought borrowed one of Antoinette's fine gowns from Mobile days. The Houstons had little cash to spend on clothing. Houston had closed his San Augustine office, realizing a small profit in land but not in money.

On December 1, Sam Houston bade Margaret goodbye and joined his friends on the road to Austin for the inaugural ceremony. Margaret did not go because the trip was difficult, as well as expensive, and she would delay the other travelers in the party. The Redlands tour had shown Margaret's incapacity for long journeys. It would take rest and Eliza's herb medicines to restore her health.

The reports of the presidential inauguration arrived in Houston City shortly after New Year's Day. General Houston had made

[61] Houston *Morning Star*, November 9, 1841.

his speech and had taken his oath in buckskin, explaining that he wished to demonstrate the need for governmental economy, after the extravagances of Lamar. A portion of the audience had thought him vulgar for costuming himself. Yet it was not all show with the new president. The executive mansion was boarded up and abandoned; the president cut his salary in half, and at that would be fortunate to receive his five thousand dollars for that year of 1842. He appointed Ashbel Smith minister to France on the condition that Smith pay his own expenses. If France recognized Texas, then Smith was to hasten to London and represent Texas there. Times were tight indeed. Houston wrote from his cramped hotel room, which overlooked the mud flat Lamar had envisioned as a grand boulevard and named Congress Avenue. At least Margaret had firewood, back on the coast.

In the winter of 1842, heavy psychological pressures built in the minds of the Texans over the likelihood of a Mexican effort to reconquer the country. A part of the public wanted to anticipate the Mexicans by immediately recruiting a Texas army to send to the Río Grande. Sam Houston was afraid of what domestic dangers such an army might create, and refused to co-operate, except to say that there would be a war only when there was a professional army available to fight it. The whole public was not pleased by the president's avoidance of the question. A wave of rumor charged that Houston had made a private arrangement with the United States. The president of the Republic of Texas made no move to discount the alleged collusion, and the whispers became more frequent. Margaret heard the stories in Houston City: "I am told they [the United States] only await your permission to send an army through Texas into Mexico. I hope you will not oppose it, but I know your course will be right."[62]

[62] Margaret Lea Houston to Sam Houston, Houston, January 12, 1842, Franklin Williams Collection.

Houston wanted Margaret to return to Alabama for a visit until the Mexican problem was solved. Having her in Texas was a risk, for in the event of an invasion, there might be no escape for her. Sam Houston knew the spirit of the Texas civilians very well. The population had fled previous to San Jacinto, notwithstanding its brave declaration of independence. Crossing into Louisiana, the people had hardly looked back to see the triumph of Houston's volunteer army. Doubtless Houston could imagine the Galveston docks and the mobs fighting to board the eastbound steamers and packets. Margaret would be lost in the scuffle to escape.

Mrs. Houston had no intention of going to Alabama. Naturally she had been afraid; the entire citizenry was afraid, and riots had broken out in the woodlands northward along the Sabine. But Margaret told herself it was gossip she was hearing and read books to distract her thoughts. A favorite book of hers was a romance about the lovers Giambelli and Cassilda. Giambelli cried, "I care not for the issues of the war!" And he was unafraid of the dark clouds that would make them "twin stars falling in the thick of night." Margaret copied passages of the dialogue for Sam Houston. "Dearest," she wrote, "is not that something like our own love?"[63]

Houston's dislike of poetry did not discourage the poetess in his wife. If her romances were curious sentiments to others, they touched Houston deeply. "I cannot be happy but where you are!" he wrote upon reading pages she had sent. "I must learn to write something else than love letters."[64]

On February 9, Houston tied his mule to the porch of the Houston City house. Bruin was the mule's name, and he was no comparison in beauty to the Tennessee mare, which Houston had

[63] *Ibid.*

[64] Sam Houston to Margaret Lea Houston, San Augustine, September 23, 1840, *Writings*, II, 352–53.

presented to Antoinette. But the mule was dependable. It was four days' hard riding west from Houston City to the capital; the mule achieved a certain immortality by effecting the same goal "in two hours less than four days." Houston laughed, "The *mule* did me honest service."[65]

Since Margaret's family was at the Bledsoes permanently, she and the general had the time to themselves. On February 22, they sailed to Galveston, where they spent the night. In behalf of some French expatriates he knew in the city, Ashbel Smith invited the general and Margaret to lunch with them. Galveston society was flavored by the presence of many foreign businessmen, who were the Texas agents for companies in other countries and brought a gay, European atmosphere to the balmy, tropical city. Ordinarily the Houstons avoided their entertainments, perhaps because liquor was so heavily drunk, both at private parties and at the several popular restaurants in Galveston. But on February 24, the Houstons sat down to luncheon with M. and Mme de Philibeauscourt, in company with Ashbel Smith, the Count de Narbonne, and the Baron de Montsabert. Smith was fascinated with Mme de Philibeauscourt, and the party went along pleasantly. It was not until several months later that the "Baron" and the "Count" were revealed to be swindlers and fled the Republic ahead of the Galveston County sheriff. M. de Philibeauscourt hid in a ship and shot himself to death. His destitute widow appealed to Ashbel Smith, whose many charities to her included passage back to France, where he went shortly afterward as chargé d'affaires from the Republic of Texas.[66] The February lunch was marred by none of the events later to come. When afternoon came, Smith and the lady went for a carriage ride alone on the beach, and the

[65] Sam Houston to Washington Miller, Houston, February 15, 1842, *Writings*, II, 484–85.

[66] Ashbel Smith's diary, February 24, 1842, University of Texas Archives.

Houstons went home, apparently never to see their hosts again.

A few days after the Independence Day celebration in Houston City, a rider brought a hurried note to the president's house. San Antonio had fallen to the Mexican Army.

The situation was unpropitious. Texas was still a poorly mapped wilderness between the Louisiana border and the ragged boundary of Mexico. Threadlike roads meandered to avoid wide creeks, thick woods, and bottomland mud. There were no adequate military facilities at Houston's disposal, yet emotional journalists stirred the cries for revenge. In the uproar, the president cast glances toward the United States. Mrs. Houston was frightened, as Houston indicated in a letter: "[Margaret] has some fears that I may take a fancy for the Río Grande and 'dodge' her until the war with Mexico is ended. Now, this is groundless, so far as my intentions are concerned."[67] Houston City's militant element made threats to the president. Friends saw figures moving about near the Houston house at night and implored the general to hire guards. Angrily Sam Houston lit candles and opened the windows and doors and brazenly paraded in the light. To complete his burlesque, he seated Margaret at her piano, ordering her to play, until the people of Houston City seemed convinced that the president was not afraid.[68]

Houston began emergency precautions for the Republic. On March 10, the Austin authorities were ordered to move the archives to Houston City for safety. Objections arose in Austin, culminating in a conflict between duty-conscious officials and the heavily invested business community led by a female hotelkeeper. Everyone knew Sam Houston preferred his coastal namesake. He seemed to be using the war as an excuse to abandon Austin, which

[67] Sam Houston to William H. Daingerfield, Galveston, April 27, 1842, *Writings*, III, 37–40.

[68] James, *The Raven*, 326.

the officials gladly did at once. Despite Houston's wishes, however, the archives remained in Austin.

General Houston's responsibilities increased. Public opinion tore his government into several camps, whose anger was fired by many ambitious men. Houston pretended to ignore them. He became a dictator, not particularly of his own choice, though he never objected, but through consent, out of fear, of the electorate. By May, Houston wrote that he was "literally worn down by continual labor."[69] Margaret complained of headaches and chills. Several days later Houston took her and Eliza to the *New York*, which was docked at Galveston preparing for its regular run to the United States. His law books revealed a law made in similarly desperate times that provided for financing a Texas agent in a foreign port to enlist support. Houston created the position, and appointed Martin Lea to fill it. In addition to his other duties, Martin was to escort Margaret back to Marion.[70]

And so they departed, leaving Houston in Texas to untangle the confusion of his government. It had been two years since Margaret had married Sam Houston. He was an alcoholic, but he had drunk only soothing bitters, and not excessively of them. As a husband he had been faithful and kind. Friends gave Margaret the credit for his conduct. Traveling with Houston had been hard. Three-day trips had taken six days when Margaret was along complaining of drafts and suffering fevers. But her presence on the Redlands tour had made sure that Houston did not touch liquor, and she had been pleased. When she was away from him, she always wondered if he was weakening because she was not there to watch him, but since she had not known him to fail her,

[69] Sam Houston to H. Washington, Galveston, May 1, 1842, *Writings*, IV, 91–92.

[70] Sam Houston to Col. Martin A. Lea, Galveston, May 2, 1842, *Writings*, IV, 93.

her anxieties began to relax. In Marion, Henry's white house presented familiar outlines to Mrs. Houston, and she would enjoy her vacation among her kin. Yet Marion, she knew, could never be home to her again.

3.

The Four-poster

Washington Miller was given the task of renting wagons for the caravan which would carry the Texas government to the new capital. He was presidential secretary, young and energetic, and a bachelor. The president had decided that the riverboats were undependable, so it would be a land journey to the town of Washington. Sam Houston had promised Margaret a coach, like Serena Lea's; however, the mercantile houses of Houston City provided no such vehicle. So Mrs. Houston traveled to the Brazos in a wagon that September of 1842. Eliza worried over making Margaret comfortable, hoping to ward off a return of the sickness that had plagued the visit to Alabama and the recent sea voyage back to Texas.[1]

The wagon rattled down Main Street and out into the forest westward. Washington-on-the-Brazos, at a distant place on the muddy road, was the compromise capital between Houston City and Austin. Lamar's town was only temporarily safe after the Mexican withdrawal from San Antonio. The archives were still

[1] Sam Houston to Anson Jones, Houston City, August 2, 1842, *Writings*, III, 138.

held in Austin by the citizens, who were determined that the seat of government would again be established there.

Margaret was not troubled by those details. The weeks since her return had passed slowly. General Houston's official schedule was interrupted once by a mild fever, and he resumed his normal routine as soon as he could get out of bed.[2] Margaret jealously implored him to go with her to Cedar Point to rest. The humidity activated his wounds until his ankle and thigh were so weak as to compel him to walk with a stick.[3] "My spirits remain unbroken and unbent," he wrote.[4] Margaret dreaded the isolation of Grand Cane, but she had nearly gone there for company during the last weeks the capital was in Houston City. The president had been impatient of her interruptions and her childish efforts to gain his attention.[5] Nancy Lea had been too busy in Galveston to spend time with her daughter. Accused of trespassing, the widow was being sued for twenty dollars. She fought the charge, and attracted an audience. The presidential caravan was gone from Houston City before the jury, following an all-night deliberation, was discharged at daybreak.[6]

The road to the new capital roamed deviously in forks and turns that got the executive party lost for two weeks. In some respects it was a fortunate delay for the president and Margaret. Both of them found time to reflect on recent events. Sam Houston, with a government peopled heavily with friends, was softening the

[2] Sam Houston to John C. Hays, Houston City, September 14, 1842, *Writings*, IV, 144–46; see also Sam Houston to William Christy, Houston City, August 14, 1842, *Writings*, IV, 134–35.

[3] Ashbel Smith, notes on Sam Houston, University of Texas Archives.

[4] Sam Houston to John C. Hays, Houston City, September 14, 1842, *Writings*, IV, 144–46.

[5] Sam Houston to William Christy, Houston, August 14, 1842, *Writings*, IV, 134–35.

[6] Ruth Lapham Butler and W. Eugene Hollon (eds.), *William Bollaert's Texas*, 150.

grip of his dictatorship and losing officers. George Hockley, for one, resigned the post of secretary of war and marine. When such dependable people returned to private business, the offices became the responsibility of the president. Margaret suffered deep worries over Martin Lea's mysterious financial problems, the nature of which escapes recorded history but which built quickly to a tragic climax.

The wagons' progress was slow. Joshua set up the tent at dusk, folded it down at dawn, and left the mound of leaves to the autumn rain. Although the trip was tedious, it gave the Houstons time together. Every household item that was not at Cedar Point was packed into the wagons. Margaret's furniture was greatly dissipated by its Texas journeys, but it would be many years before she would feel financially justified in buying more. The Houston City house was finally rented, and the piano was sent to Cedar Point. Only the most portable furniture was taken for use in the executive mansion promised by the city officials of Washington.

On October 2, the caravan stopped on the east bank of the Brazos, at the Washington ferry. The capital city presented more nearly the aspect of a crossroads than anything else. Two streets slanted up the yellow riverbank to one principal avenue, called Ferry Street, which bisected the village's ten or so lesser streets and continued a westerly rambling several days' journey into the Mexican danger zone. The twenty to thirty-five buildings of Washington were dwellings and stores. Paint covered none of the wooden surfaces greeting Margaret. Out beyond the town, ugly little camps of men dried their laundry and played cards, awaiting the gaiety the rowdy officials would bring. Chickens and cows drank from the mudholes and foraged in the streets. Cats basked in the windowsills until Major Hatfield cast his garbage out back of the saloon, whereupon they sauntered, with some of the population, to partake of the repast.[7]

Private family quarters had been provided for the president, but the rent was demanded in advance. General Houston did not have the required amount. He was forced to go to his friends, the John W. Lockharts, and ask for shelter. Mrs. Lockhart complied by setting aside a room and crowding her household into the remainder of the house. To please the youthful Margaret, Mrs. Lockhart decorated the room with personal belongings of which she was very proud.[8] The clothespress and the great high-posted bed of mahogany delighted Margaret, who was by now tired of cornhusk mattresses and crude furniture. It was probably the best room in Washington-on-the-Brazos, though Houston joked to a friend, "I will not attempt a description of the 'White House,' or the East Room, but I will wager you will say that it beats all the ravings of fancy and the decorations [of] poesy!"[9]

Margaret had expected a house. All her life she had shared houses with other people, and in spite of Mrs. Lockhart's efforts, she was disappointed at having to live as someone's guest. Besides, the first lady was not well. Sam Houston pulled the clothespress over the inside door and cut a new door to the outside. Apparently it contented Margaret, for the moment.[10]

If her demands irritated the busy president, he understood them by mid-October. Margaret was going to have a baby. General Houston was overjoyed. He quickly decided that the child would be a son.[11] The name was established: William Christy

[7] R. Henderson Shuffler, "The Signing of Texas' Declaration of Independence: Myth and Record," *Southwestern Historical Quarterly*, Vol. LXV, 310–32; also see John W. Lockhart, *Sixty Years on the Brazos.*

[8] Lockhart, *Sixty Years on the Brazos*, 119–20; see also *Bollaert's Texas*, 157.

[9] Sam Houston to Joseph Eve, Washington, November 6, 1842, *Writings*, III, 193.

[10] Lockhart, *Sixty Years on the Brazos*, 120.

[11] William Christy to Sam Houston, New Orleans, January 2, 1843, Houston Manuscripts, University of Texas Archives.

Houston, for the gentleman whose coach had taken the wounded hero of San Jacinto from the port of New Orleans for medical treatment.[12] Christy, a hero in William Henry Harrison's Tecumseh campaign, was an old friend of Houston and had been a friend to Texas during the Revolution.

Margaret bloomed under her husband's excessive attentions. He had an obsession for controlling situations, and to the best of his ability he controlled this one. Secrecy was established. Frontier women were rarely afforded the luxury of a pregnancy in seclusion. An appearance in public, such as Anna Raguet Irion had made, was not frowned upon, particularly in a rough place like Washington. Margaret, however, was reared in a part of Alabama where life was a full generation removed from the frontier. Her surroundings in Texas changed none of her attitudes about modesty.

A reason for the Houstons' secrecy is suggested vaguely in old letters and family tradition. Margaret, it is said, had suffered a miscarriage at Grand Cane the year before. Another story goes that she became ill en route to Grand Cane, at Liberty, where in a stagecoach station she miscarried twins. Two weathered gravesites are pointed out in a Liberty cemetery. The letters suggest that she was pregnant and that she was ill on several occasions while visiting Antoinette. If the story is true, the Houstons' reaction is understandable.[13]

"Mother-dear," which Houston insisted upon calling Nancy Lea, was informed by letter. Margaret went into seclusion at the Lockharts and left only for specific reasons, like the outings she

[12] James, *The Raven*, 337; see also *The Bee*, May 23, 1836.

[13] Author in conversation with Mrs. John L. Little, Sr., Beaumont, Texas, January 10, 1964; also conversation with Mrs. Jennie Morrow Decker, Houston, January 10, 1964; see also letters fall, 1840, through summer, 1841, Franklin Williams Collection and in *Writings*; also see R. Hudson to Ashbel Smith, Houston, March 1, 1841, Smith Manuscripts, University of Texas Archives.

and Eliza liked to make by buggy, into the Brazos countryside, whose swelling terrain Margaret grew to love.

Sam Houston had an office down the street from the Lockhart house. Washington was a town small enough to cross on foot; therefore the president walked and dressed for comfort. He packed away his good suits in preference to a cheap pair of breeches and a loose linsey-woolsey shirt, over which was buttoned a vest of leopard skin. His coat is best described as a duster, being nearly formless. His head bore his beloved wide brim beaver hat, set straight on a parallel with his shoulders.

Clothes were a personal passion with Sam Houston. Over all the fine silver and china presented to him as compliments for San Jacinto from all over the world, he is said to have been most pleased by a gaudy scarlet costume sent by a sultan. He never wore most of the garment for fear of looking ridiculous. There was a robe, however, that he considered magnificent, and he wore it in his office and on occasions wore it to meetings with the Indian tribes.[14]

Houston's demanding schedule merited some toleration of his excesses, for home and adornment were the only pursuits which might be expected to amuse him, considering the condition of the nation. Austin's archive trouble was still stewing and continued until New Year's Day. The Republic was weakened in that conflict. Yet people were much more anxious to send an army into the wild country between the Nueces and Río Grande than to settle the situation in Austin. Mexican raiding parties wandered about in the border lands. Hate was fanned by the frustrated efforts of Texans to filibuster, resulting in sensational executions and imprisonment in the interior of Mexico. Sam Houston's government had offices in sheds, and the debates of the senate rang out in an unfinished room above Hatfield's Saloon, or "grocery." Parts of the

[14] Lockhart, *Sixty Years on the Brazos*, 120.

story were brighter, though. The Republic of Texas was recognized by France, England, the United States, and Holland. Ashbel Smith was in France, writing back to tell how the court at Saint-Cloud was fascinated with Texas.

In time to interrupt the Houstons' quiet Christmas together, the Houston City stage deposited Nancy Lea on Ferry Street. She had received the letter, and had decided to return Margaret to the quiet life of Grand Cane to await the birth of the baby among her kin. Mrs. Lea would not be argued down. By early January, Margaret and her mother and Eliza entered the eastbound coach at its stopping place before Ramsey's Saloon. The weather was fair, and they expected that they would arrive at the Bledsoes' farm in five days.

Antoinette had done her best to civilize her surroundings. A distance from the house she had cleared a rectangle and enclosed it in wickets. Crepe myrtle, jasmine, and sweet olive trees from Mobile cuttings were planted in circles and rows.[15] She maintained the conviction that life could be happy under any conditions. Perhaps it was less innocence than selfishness that made her ignore her husband's crumbling health and fortune. Captain Bledsoe's life seemed to be ebbing away.

The brindled waters of the Trinity cooled none of the scalding heat of summer, nor did they warm the cold of the winter. Slowly the water slid toward the Gulf of Mexico, as deceptive in its movement as the moccasins and alligators that crawled through the vine curtains of the steep banks. Some of the wildlife had not yet learned the dangers men brought to new land. Turtles slept in regimental rows on half-sunken logs and let the sun dry their

[15] Site of Bledsoe-Lea-Creath residence in the Martinez Survey, Liberty County, Texas, visited in the summer of 1963; also, author in conversation with Mrs. John L. Little, Sr., Beaumont, Texas, March 17, 1965.

shells, and the same white cranes that had delighted Audubon tiptoed among them, hardly splashing the water.

It was not unpleasant for Margaret to be with her family. Other than for the companionship of Sam Houston, Washington did not really present an enjoyable society. Margaret found better company in books. Her favorite Texas history was William Kennedy's *The Rise, Progress, and Prospects of the Republic of Texas*. The Englishman who had written it, "a gentleman of fine intelligence and very superior manners," as Margaret described him, had visited in her home in Houston City. Margaret and the general had read the history and praised it.[16]

Houston made jokes about Margaret's reading habits. He thought reading about knights "and their Lady-Loves," was a waste of time. For "poesy" he had no use at all, though he had once fancied himself a clever rhymster. Once Margaret and Ashbel Smith had come into his room unannounced, to see him conceal a book under his pillow and act as though he were not reading.[17] Being able to forget herself by reading was a comfort to Margaret and would be all her life. Sam Houston, with little formal education, was suspicious of intellectuals and assumed an attitude of superiority toward creative people.

The Grand Cane circle filled the plain log house. Vernal and Mary made no plans to leave. They had moved their belongings there, and Vernal was directing the Negroes in the clearing of land as well as going to Liberty now and then to do legal work. He grew to love farming in his visionary way. Mary had suffered a miscarriage; that, with the memory of the child who had died in Marion, made her depressions acute. Vernal sought to amuse Mary

[16] Margaret Lea Houston to Sam Houston, Houston, January 12, 1842, Franklin Williams Collection.

[17] Ashbel Smith, notes on Sam Houston, University of Texas Archives.

with city pleasures on a trip to Galveston. His and Mary's attention was drawn to the plight of a little girl with brown eyes and chestnut hair. She was seven years old, and her parents had died in the yellow fever epidemic. The court was seeking a guardian, and Vernal and Mary accepted the responsibility of the child.

After a shopping spree they could ill afford, they took Virginia Thorne home with them, thinking the little girl was what the dreary house needed. Doubts came quickly. Virginia Thorne would not accommodate Nancy Lea, and the widow's gallic temper burst out. Children usually feared the sixty-two-year-old Nancy Lea. Virginia proved she could be insolent when she was annoyed. Nancy Lea took a youpon switch after her, but Vernal and Mary intervened.[18]

Margaret spent several weeks in this company at Grand Cane. In January she got a surprise. Sam Houston arrived, asking for her. When they were alone, he made a humiliating confession.[19]

A reluctant Houston had watched Margaret leave that day on the Brazos. He returned to his mounds of papers. Daily he rose early, walked to the office, worked until nightfall, and went to bed, after having dinner with the Lockharts. The passage of weeks spawned a hesitation in him to face the empty room.

One evening, in the course of his loneliness, he occasioned to acquire a bottle of wine, which he took to his quarters at the Lockhart home. The wine had been intended as a gift for Mrs. Lockhart, but the family was visiting elsewhere in town, so Houston took the wine to his room for safekeeping until Mrs. Lockhart returned. His old hunger got the best of him and he opened the bottle. Soon Houston was drunk, lying in the center of the bed, well through the wine. Vision became difficult for him, he later reasoned, as the evening progressed. He decided that one of the

[18] Henderson Yoakum diary, 1850, University of Texas Archives.

[19] Lockhart, *Sixty Years on the Brazos*, 119.

heavy bedposts obstructed his view. Out of bed he summoned a slave. The axe's chopping awakened the other occupants of the house, who, in the meantime, had returned home and gone to bed. With some trouble John Lockhart broke the door down and burst into the room, thinking an assassin was after the president. Houston was safely ensconced in the featherbed, finishing the last swallow of the wine, while his slave cut "even with the bed" one of the tall bedposts.

Mrs. Lockhart had been present in time to witness the last chops. She and her husband had been kind, considering they had already endured inconveniences because of the Houstons. Margaret had been demanding of comforts; the general had spat on the scrubbed porch. Now Mrs. Lockhart's bedstead, once one of the finest west of the Sabine, was no more. All the town was laughing at Sam Houston, and Sam Houston was uncomfortable and embarrassed. In the course of the next day he left for Grand Cane to find Margaret.

The Houstons returned at once to the capital. Margaret had been unwise in believing Sam Houston could be reformed so easily. Soon he would be fifty; he was set in his ways, and his reformation would have to come from within himself. Since their marriage, Margaret had competed with his political life. She knew that her efforts had been in vain, although she saw clearly that if she had no place in her husband's career, he needed her as an escape from his emotional uncertainty. Her competition, then, was not his political career, but his one other escape, liquor.

There was a poetic tone to the prospect of a contest between Margaret and alcohol. Margaret believed she had the advantage in her crusade. She had learned that she held power over Sam Houston, and she intended to use it. Because Sam Houston loved her, he subjected his private conduct to her judgment. Margaret's duty was to make him forever anticipate her verdicts, strict though they might be. She ceased trying to follow him in his travels in the political world. Her battle was not a physical one. Home, wherever it might be, must become to Houston an Arcadian vision of peace, always waiting. From afar he would long for Margaret's paradise and decry any substitutes, knowing her jealousy. In this way Margaret sought to effect the complete moral reformation of the president of the Republic of Texas.[20]

[20] Margaret Lea Houston to Sam Houston, Raven Hill, May 16, 1846, Texas State Archives; see also Margaret Lea Houston to Sam Houston, Raven Hill, June 20, 1846, New York Public Library; see also Margaret Lea Houston to Sam Houston, Grand Cane, December 5, 1846, University of Texas Library. Related references to Margaret's change of attitude appear as late as the 1860's, indicating its importance in her life.

4.

History's Hallways

The Houstons arranged for a house on the edge of Washington. It was one of many cheap little dwellings built of scraps for rental speculation, but Margaret was determined to make it pleasant. Her furniture needed new upholstery and fringe in order to draw attention from the pine tables and hide-bottom chairs.[1] The two-volume Bible, a present to Margaret from one of the general's admirers, was placed on the center table of the parlor, which also contained a bed.[2] Houston sent Margaret's upholstery orders to the Texas consul at New Orleans. While Mrs. Sam Houston's wishes were of national concern, the president had ideas of his own: "The firniture callico you [Mr. Consul] will select, but take care to select none such as will exhibit Gobblers, Peacocks, Bears, Elephants, wild boars, or Stud Horses!!! Vines, Flowers, or any figure of taste . . . you can select."

[1] Lockhart, *Sixty Years On The Brazos*, 119–20; see also Lester, *Life of Sam Houston*, 390–91.

[2] Items of furniture in the Sam Houston Memorial Museum and in the Franklin Williams Collection.

He added, "As I am so poor, if you can make a bargain for the freight, it might be well."[3]

The Houstons were comfortably settled in their house by Margaret's twenty-fourth birthday. Her pregnancy gave her no trouble, though the fact did not induce Houston to announce his coming parenthood. He requested of the consul, "1 bolt Linnen *Diaper for Towels*."[4] He wanted to be with Margaret more than was possible. "From my uprising to my down lying at night, I have rarely one hour thro' the day to pass in company with Mrs. Houston." Pressing business was endurable, but many of the president's callers came, "as they say, 'to spend the time.' "[5]

But even in the labors of his office, against a storm of public accusations of cowardice for not sending an army to Mexico, Houston mused, "Who can wonder at my happiness?" He wanted to be alone with Margaret, though he complained, "Of that pleasure I have been almost wholly debarred."[6] Margaret's requests interrupted the affairs of state. "CONFIDENTIAL!!!" he marked the letter to Dr. McAnelly. The doctor was requested to forward "Nipple guards" from Houston City for Margaret, for "she . . . expects soon to have to nurse. I hope you will pardon me for the trouble."[7]

Nancy Lea came to Washington in mid-April and was welcomed as an authority by a man ordinarily too vain to consult authorities. She arrived by river on one of the light-draft packets that had been making the regular run upriver from the coast.[8] She had embarked

[3] Sam Houston to William Bryan, Washington, January 24, 1843, *Writings*, III, 304–305.

[4] *Ibid.*

[5] Sam Houston to Tom Bagby, Washington, February 20, 1843, *Writings*, III, 323.

[6] *Ibid.*

[7] Sam Houston to Dr. Cornelius McAnelly, Washington, April 24, 1843, *Writings*, IV, 193.

near Grand Cane, a quick journey by Trinity steamer had taken her to the Gulf Coast, where she had sought out a boat bound for the Brazos. The trip was no longer an inconvenience of more than five days, though Washington's city fathers placed undue faith in the muddy, shallow Brazos as the advantage of their capital over Austin, which was, practically speaking, inaccessible to the sea.

Toward the end of April an unhappy dispatch, sent from the United States, found its way upriver. Martin Lea was dead. General Houston, who admitted that all Martin's traits did not "lean to virtue's side," was shocked; Nancy Lea and Margaret were disconsolate. Letters followed the dispatch that upset Nancy Lea. Houston wrote to a friend for details of Martin's death and thanked the friend for "defeating the mechanations of those fellows who sought to annoy mother. The malicious creatures will perish by their own poison." Martin's death has remained unclear. Family tradition intimates suicide, and while the family made every effort to gain "minute information in relation to the occurrence," that information was well hidden.[9]

So dismal was the financial situation of the Texas Republic that the salary of the president was not paid. Houston wrote notes on the treasury when necessities were called for at home, saying that the amount should be subtracted from his salary.[10] Nancy Lea managed the house and seems to have been a conservative spender, except when her children needed something. Then she often spent foolishly.

General Houston moved about nervously in the weeks that car-

[8] Andrew Forest Muir, "The Destiny of Buffalo Bayou," *Southwestern Historical Quarterly*, Vol. XLVII, 104–105.

[9] Sam Houston to James H. Cooke, Washington, April 22, 1843, *Writings*, IV, 180.

[10] See for example, Sam Houston to Treasurer's Office, Washington, April 10, 1843, *Writings*, IV, 180. In later political campaigns in Texas, Houston's "bills" became a topic of harsh criticism.

ried the waiting household into May. He wrote to the Irions, "Several old Ladies are at my house. It seems rather probable that there will be some *fuss* in a few days. I feel gratified, of course, but the idea of assuming the dignity of a 'daddy' rather throws me aback."[11]

On May 25, the child was born. It was a son, and the servants crowded near to comment upon the striking resemblance between the infant and his father. Propped against pillows, Margaret smiled at the baby: William Christy Houston was no name for him. She insisted upon Sam Houston, Jr., and the president of the Republic of Texas approved. Houston already had specific ideas about the boy's upbringing. He was not to be a poet or a "singer of songs."[12]

The general's critics in the Republic began to soften their tone. What had been bitter hatred for the president became in some quarters genuine admiration. Mexico had not been able to lure Texas into war. In spite of private filibustering and freebooting and their tragic rewards, Houston had kept his nation aloof, even though he was encouraged to do otherwise by public opinion outside Texas, through the Mississippi Valley of the United States and into every corner of backwoods America. New York and Mobile land speculators encouraged the war effort, but Sam Houston was not one to take glaring risks. He wanted a United States military commitment before he even considered a war. In the meantime, Houston mended fences at home. Lamar's defunct paper money was called in and new bills issued, and the Houston dollars were a small improvement.

Sam Houston dismissed his critics as impediments to progress. The excesses of his oratorical assaults on his opponents sometimes overcame his powers of reason, leaving him more vulnerable to

[11] Cited in Miles, "A Famous Romance," 149, from Irion unpublished papers.
[12] Sam Houston to Washington Miller, n.d., University of Texas Archives.

ridicule than the objects of his scorn.[13] But ordinarily that was not the case. Even those temper explosions were the cool calculations of a man who knew exactly what he was doing.[14]

General and Mrs. Houston displayed Sam to friends in Washington. Letters of congratulation began to arrive. Secretary Miller wrote to Ashbel Smith in Paris: "You will have heard ere this that General Houston has been blessed with an heir; and a fine fellow he is too. There is a very striking favor between father and son. . . . You would suppose the General is proud of his boy—and you would not be far mistaken!" Both parents were devoted to the infant. "His name is *Sam*—Sam junior."[15]

An awaited letter arrived:

Paris, Rue Cartiglione, No. 10.
November 27, 1843

My Dear General,

I learned . . . for the first time, the good news that there is a *scion* of the House of Houston. I had indeed been led to hope for such an event by an intimation in a letter I got . . . from Mr. Miller. Allow me, my dear General, to offer you on this occasion my very sincere felicitations; and I hope you will present the same together with my most respectful compliments to Mrs. Houston. . . .

ASHBEL SMITH[16]

In Washington the baby was in a sense public property, though Margaret would probably not have admitted it. From the first she was overly possessive of Sam. Her mother was called on to rid her of overstaying guests, for she had, by virtue of her experience as

13 Ashbel Smith's notes on Sam Houston, University of Texas Archives.

14 *Ibid.*

15 Washington Miller to Ashbel Smith, Washington, July 21, 1843, Smith manuscripts, University of Texas Archives.

16 Ashbel Smith to Sam Houston, Paris, November 27, 1843, University of Texas Archives.

a minister's wife, an easy manner with people. Indians—whom Mrs. Lea distrusted—came to call with presents. Beaded moccasins, a belt, and feathers took their places beside silver cups and jars of preserves. Little girls brought nosegays of Indian paint-brush.[17]

The summer was spent at Washington. Vernal and Mary Lea visited briefly, and Varilla and Robert Royston were in Texas investigating land opportunities. There was news of Alabama, and plenty of leisure on sunny, comfortable afternoons in which to discuss old times. Margaret's health was improved, though little Sam suffered a malady in July which nearly took his life. Nancy Lea seems to have been happy presiding over the presidential household. Her efforts to discipline Sam Houston were more successful than ever. She had warned him, "I will make a good tempered fellow of you yet!"[18]

Washington was small and ugly in spite of the pretty white and yellow flowers that grew over its hills. This was the town where Texas' declaration of independence had been signed seven years before. The building where the event had taken place was in the middle of town, gaping, windowless, erected as a store and rented for the convention. Not far from Independence Hall was the town well, a subscription facility to which the Houstons contributed fifteen dollars during their tenure in Washington. The well was protected by a latticed shed, whose wisteria runner was the only sign of civic beautification to be found in the Texas capital.

Except for "floaters," as the men who camped beneath the trees were called, Washington's people were like those Margaret had

[17] Author in conversation with Mrs. Jennie Morrow Decker, Houston, February 22, 1964; also with Mrs. James A. Darby, Houston, February 22, 1964; also see items in Sam Houston Memorial Museum.

[18] Margaret Lea Houston to Sam Houston, Galveston, December 7, 1840, Franklin Williams Collection.

known in Alabama, though prosperity was not so evident. There seemed to be more old ladies in Texas than at home in Marion, maybe because even the women young in years were aged by experience to look old. Their black dresses smelled of camphor; the lace collars had yellowed with the years. After church the dresses were folded into a little iron-banded trunk until some other event, a wedding or a ball, warranted using the best. In death, the woman, wearing the dress, was placed in a crude coffin, her hands together under a paper fan to hide the callouses. Through her church work, Margaret knew many of these women and their husbands. Since her own life was eased by slaves and her mother, she sensed little identity with the Texans who had come west from some other place to labor for economic betterment. Yet as time passed she would enter more and more into their anonymity, in reaction to her dislike of the publicity associated with Sam Houston's career.

From New Orleans the general had ordered, "a carriage or double Barouch . . . the usual width of waggons, for the road . . . 4 Seats with shafts, tongue and double harness with whip!"[19] Margaret and little Sam went to Grand Cane in September, and Houston planned for her to return overland in the "tolerably genteel barouche," which had arrived in Galveston, because the Brazos was low and not navigable.[20] After some difficulty, Margaret, the baby, Eliza, and Nancy Lea returned to Washington in the coach in time for Christmas. Remembering Serena's fine carriage, Margaret could only have been disappointed in the coach Houston bought for her. It was a wagon, with a lightweight wooden frame permanently fixed to the bed and stretched over with heavy canvas. Two doors admitted what air and light—and

[19] Sam Houston to William Bryan, Washington, January 24, 1843, *Writings*, III, 304–305.

[20] Sam Houston to Charles Elliot, Washington, October 5, 1843, *Writings*, IV, 224–26.

cold wind—the interior enjoyed. The Houston coach resembled the Marion-to-Selma, Alabama, carryall more than the carriage of a president's lady. But Margaret seems not to have complained, and she even became sentimental about the color which Houston himself had it painted: bright yellow.

On New Year's Day, Margaret and her mother attended church at Washington. General Houston resolutely refused to go to church, even though his wife insisted he had much to be thankful for.[21]

It was true that things were looking better. Houston had sent Hockley to a peace conference at Laredo, and as a result the pressures of war were lessened, and the future looked more secure for the Texas Republic.

Margaret seldom complimented him for public achievements. She approved of his efforts for peace, but other aspects of their lives interested her more.[22] The president described his son as a "hearty brat, robust and hearty as a Berkshire pig," but in his letters he more typically wrote of politics.[23] The question of annexation to the United States had become a major one again. Was Texas' best prospect as a state in the union or as an independent slaveholding republic, extending to the Pacific and possibly to the Isthmus of Tehuantepec? Houston's preference was unmistakably the latter. "The Pacific alone," he said, "will bound the mighty miracle of our race and our empire. From Europe and America her soils to be peopled. In regions where the savage and the buffalo now roam uncontrolled, the enterprise and industry of the Anglo-

[21] Author in conversation with Mrs. John L. Little, Sr., Beaumont, Texas, March 12, 1964; see also Margaret Lea Houston to Sam Houston, Raven Hill, June 20, 1846, New York Public Library.

[22] Sam Houston to Margaret Lea Houston, Washington, September 28, 1844, *Writings*, IV, 373.

[23] Sam Houston to William Murphy, Washington, January 23, 1844, *Writings*, IV, 223.

American are yet to find an extensive field of development."[24] The issues within the United States puzzled Sam Houston. Abolition was beyond his conception. "It is a palpable scandal of the 19th century, that Statesmen should be prating about the emancipation of persons born, and their race held in slavery, but by the custom and consent of nations for centuries, while they permit Santa Anna to forge and rivet chains, upon eight millions of people who were born free."[25]

To nobody's disappointment, the Congress of the Republic adjourned in February, 1844. Ill tempered and hostile, the Congress had opposed Sam Houston on everything. Houston had in turn displeased most of his officials, and Margaret had lost friends among their wives, particularly Mrs. Anson Jones, wife of the secretary of state. But politicians could forget small differences perhaps better than their wives, and Houston endorsed Anson Jones for the approaching presidential election. On the question of annexation both Jones and Houston were undecided. Houston did not want to make a mistake in his decision. The drama of Texas history and the name of Sam Houston belonged together. Houston was not going to dissociate the two by taking an unpopular course, and the public at that point was difficult to understand. Sometimes it seemed that there was more proannexation sentiment in the United States than in Texas. The situation tensed, and the territorial plum south of the Río Grande ripened and hung heavy on the stem. If the United States would not pluck it, then the Texas Republic might do so and be certain that abundant volunteer companies would flood in from the United States, as they had done at San Jacinto.

[24] Sam Houston to the Texas Congress, Washington, December 9, 1844, *Writings*, IV, 401–405.

[25] Sam Houston to J. Pinkney Henderson and Isaac Van Zandt, Houston, April 16, 1844, *Writings*, IV, 298–301.

At Margaret's dinner table, the diplomats of England and France listened intently to Sam Houston's conversation, analyzed it later, and wrote the analysis to their superiors back home. Charles Elliot, the British agent, felt encouraged. The French agent Cramayel and his predecessor "Count" Saligny, who assumed the position for a second time that spring, also found a willing ear for France's proposals. Intimations of Houston's attitude drifted eastward, and the aged Andrew Jackson wanted to know where his protégé stood. Houston sent Washington Miller to The Hermitage with a letter in which the Texas president was noncommittal. Texas, he wrote, had been rejected twice by the United States; she would not suffer the humiliation again. Now she was "presented to the United States as a bride adorned for her espousal." A third rejection would be final, should it take place, and after that, negotiations with the United States on annexation would, in the opinion of the Texans, be "forever terminated."[26]

At the end of the letter he spoke of himself and Margaret. "In the event [annexation] speedily takes place, I hope it will afford me the opportunity of visiting you at the Hermitage with my family." It was his and Margaret's "ardent desire to see that day when you can lay your hand on our little boy's head and bestow upon him your benediction . . . an event so desirable to us."[27] Sam Houston remembered how much he had loved Nashville. Retirement from the presidency would come soon, and knowing the end of life was close for Andrew Jackson, Houston considered taking Margaret and Sam to Nashville and showing them off in the scene of his first triumphs and deepest hurt. Probably the Houstons would have gone to Nashville sooner than they did but for the president's indecision on the question of annexation. He

[26] Sam Houston to Andrew Jackson, Washington, February 16, 1844, *Writings*, IV, 260–65.

[27] *Ibid.*

knew that he would attract attention in the United States and would be asked for a statement, and he was not ready to make that statement.

Margaret was excited at the prospect of the trip. In April, she, Sam, and Eliza took the boat to Houston City, where they made fruitless efforts to find a steamer headed up the Trinity. Houston's friend Tom Bagby made room for them in his house, and there they waited, stranded because of impassable roads in the interior and low water on the river.[28] On April 11, Mary Rhodes, an old friend of the general's, gave a birthday party for Margaret. The first lady was twenty-five.

May rains elevated the rivers and the boats began to move. Little Sam's first birthday was spent at the Bledsoes' with his parents. Houston left the next day on business of state, and Margaret faced the dreary quiet of the country. Sickness and poverty hung over the occupants of Antoinette's house. To ward off howling creditors, the property was transferred into Nancy Lea's name, and during a particularly trying period, it was held by Houston. The family economized in an effort to keep from losing its slaves, and the dreaming Vernal cultivated Bledsoe's vision of the sugar plantation he did not have the money to establish. Mary was a semi-invalid whose days were spent happily instructing Virginia Thorne. In a moment's emotion Margaret promised to take and rear Virginia if Mary died before the girl came of age.[29]

An obvious course was for Houston to buy the Bledsoe farm on extended credit and move there after his retirement. Margaret's asthma ended any discussion of that idea. Houston, "as soon as practicable" sought a "change of residence for her."[30] That spring

[28] Sam Houston to Mary Rhodes, Houston, April 7, 1844, *Writings*, IV, 296.

[29] Henderson Yoakum's diary, 1851, University of Texas Archives.

[30] Sam Houston to Charles Elliot, Washington, n.d., 1844, *Writings*, IV, 288–92.

of 1844, he began negotiations on a large unimproved tract up-country in the vicinity of the town of Huntsville, one hundred miles northwest of Grand Cane by twisting river, into the timberland. He drew house plans and showed them to Joshua, who was a good carpenter.

During the summer, Margaret traveled no farther from Antoinette's than the village of Grand Cane. Houston visited his wife when he was in the area, which was seldom, for he was covering much of settled Texas campaigning for Anson Jones. Riots over land speculation had erupted in the Redlands so fearfully that plows had not cut the earth for three years. Houston rode there, established a riot force, and calmed the danger. In the election month of September, Sam Houston heard the news of Jones's election. That month he made his way back to Grand Cane, where he arrived exhausted and was put to bed violently ill.[31] On the eighth day of his sickness, however, he mounted his mule and was off to Washington-on-the-Brazos.

Margaret made the best of her stay in the country. She made friends among other residents of the Trinity banks and had the Negroes row her down to the Ellis place, Pleasant Lawn, to picnics. At the Ellises', she, her mother, and Antoinette liked to hear Mr. Ellis read the scriptures. Margaret played the guitar, and they all sang hymns. It was evident to Nancy Lea that there were enough Baptists there to form a congregation, and this soon became a topic for discussion. Frequent meetings increased the likelihood of such an organization, and Margaret was enthusiastic.

The new interest was reflected in Margaret's exuberant letters to Sam Houston. She mentioned illness only occasionally now. When Etheridge, the Houstons' courier, arrived with a letter from the general, Margaret finished another for him to take back

[31] Sam Houston to J. C. Neill, Grand Cane, September 10, 1844, *Writings*, IV, 368.

to Washington-on-the-Brazos. Houston was curious about life at home. His replies to her letters were tender: "I will not tell you of my regret at your illness and sorrow. My heart bleeds. Duty and necessity alone compel my absence." The meetings with the Indians required long weeks at the falls of the Brazos or at the treaty grounds. Houston especially wanted the treaties made during his administration. What he remembered of Lamar's administration led him to fear that they would not be made at all if not by himself. So he was compelled to communicate with his wife through letters: "Press our dear boy to your bosom and tell him it is for me. . . . My hand is so faulty that I can hardly write a legible hand."[32] The scourge of pneumonia and the autumn chills made him fear for Margaret's well-being, and for that of Sam. "You may fancy what I felt, and feel for poor Sam at our separation. I thought when I told you adieu, that I had felt the last pang of parting, but I was mistaken. . . . Your last letter, Love, I will take with me, and peruse it often!!!"[33]

Anson Jones took office December 9. Sam Houston left Washington at once and spent Christmas at Grand Cane with Margaret and Sam. Homecoming was "joyous" and Margaret was jubilant knowing that her husband's "probation" had ended.[34] For his Christmas present she wrote a poem:

Dearest, the cloud hath left thy brow
The shade of thoughtfulness, of care,
And deep anxiety; and now
The sunshine of content is there.

32 Sam Houston to Margaret Lea Houston, Washington, September 28, 1844, *Writings*, IV, 373.

33 *Ibid.*

34 Sam Houston to Anson Jones, Grand Cane, December 21, 1844, *Writings*, IV, 408–10.

Its sweet return with joy I hail;
And never may thy country's woes
Again that hallowed light dispel
Thy bosom's calm repose.

Thy task is done. The holy shade
Of calm retirement waits thee now,
The lamp of hope relit hath shed
Its sweet refulgence o'er thy brow.

Far from the busy haunts of men
Oh! may thy soul each fleeting hour
Upon the breath of prayer ascend
To him who rules with love and power.[35]

She was eager for Houston to hear about her new friends and the church they were going to form. Houston was not interested. He had sent Joshua and the hands from Cedar Point upcountry to the new land. For the moment Houston was occupied opening presents he had brought to his son. Among them was an "antelope vest" trimmed with gold braid.[36]

In February, the United States Congress made a proposal for annexation and sent it to Texas. The offer had not been expected. Foreign ambassadors hurried through winter's mud to the capital. Letters were forwarded to Grand Cane from Washington, Houston City, and Galveston. The letters went unanswered.

Andrew Jackson Donelson, General Jackson's nephew, a powerful figure in the Democratic party and presently the United States chargé d'affaires to the Republic of Texas, had known a younger Sam Houston. That fact gave him a certain priority with the

[35] Margaret Lea Houston, "To My Husband," December, 1844, Franklin Williams Collection.

[36] Sam Houston to Margaret Lea Houston, Washington, September 28, 1844, *Writings*, IV, 373.

general and certainly an advantage over the other diplomats. He wanted to interview Houston in person, since his letters had obviously been ignored.

Houston, Margaret, Sam, and some of the slaves were traveling north with a wagon train into the pine-covered highlands of East Texas. Even the piano was along, after having been stored at Cedar Point. The yellow coach got a coat of Texas mud from the rain-moist road. Fourteen miles outside the little town of Huntsville, the coach climbed a raw trail that encircled a hill covered with trees.

The Houstons stopped before Joshua's interpretation of the house plans Houston had drawn the fall before. For the Texas frontier, it was a good house. It was similar to Cedar Point, only bigger. Axe-squared logs comprised the sole material, and the windows were mere openings, protected by slab shutters. Two large square rooms under a board roof flanked an open hallway and were warmed by wide, reddish chimneys built of native rock. The kitchen was in the yard, with various farm buildings still in construction. There was a splintery floor of puncheons, and a yard had been fenced in front for Margaret's flowers.[37] From the hill's peak, which, strangely enough, was a distance behind the house instead of beneath it, one witnessed a spectacular vista of the land. Far away the pines fused into a blue haze, and the wind blew with a lonely constancy. Sam Houston liked the domineering quality of the land; he planned to clear meadows for his horses and otherwise to tame the land into a gentle place, as Timber Ridge had been. The name of the plantation bore a personal stamp: Raven Hill.

The piano, candlesticks, chairs, tables, and mosquito bars were

[37] *Houston Chronicle*, December 11, 1948; author in conversation with Mrs. Jennie Morrow Decker, Houston, April 3, 1964; visits to the site of Raven Hill, summer, 1965.

arranged in the two rooms. By the time that work was done, Raven Hill's look was settled. Soon the Houstons had slowed to a routine which belied the political urgency of the day. They were involved in a domestic existence heavily centered in Sam, who would be two that year of 1845. Houston had previously written to a friend, "Mrs Houston . . . bids me say to Madam, 'Sam has no less than four teeth,' and I say, 'Sam's mother has recovered from her ecstasy at the discovery of his first tooth.' "[38] Washington Miller first observed that, "Never was [a] child more thoroughly the pride of his parents."[39]

There is record of only one caller at Raven Hill in the rainy spring of 1845. Tracing paths, Andrew Jackson Donelson urged his mule up the steep road. Houston had deliberately avoided his old friend because he knew Donelson would solicit his support on annexation. The general was thinking about his political future. Uncertain of the public's sympathies, he had no intention of committing himself to a point of view which might ultimately be unpopular.[40] Donelson stayed at Raven Hill several days talking to Houston, and in Louisiana a short time later he reported that Houston "seemed to be under the influence of Elliot and Saligny."[41]

When Donelson was gone, the Houstons discussed the possibility of a trip to the United States. From Donelson they had learned that Andrew Jackson could not live much longer. Newspapers in remote places were already announcing his death.[42]

[38] Sam Houston to James Reily, Washington, March 18, 1844, *Writings*, IV, 280.

[39] Washington Miller to Ashbel Smith, Washington, July 21, 1843, Smith manuscripts, University of Texas Archives.

[40] Ashbel Smith, "Reminiscences of the Texas Republic," University of Texas Archives.

[41] E. G. M. Butler's report, cited and quoted in Crane, *Life and Select Literary Remains*, 250–51.

Meanwhile, the general and Margaret decided to go to Grand Cane for a visit, which they did, taking the yellow coach, in the last days of April. It was as though they were emerging from hiding, for the country in which Raven Hill was located was hardly settled at all.

At the Bledsoes', Houston read newspapers which shocked him. He was being denounced as a traitor who was in collusion with the British. Quickly he boarded the steamboat *Oriole* on the Trinity River and left for Galveston. In his cabin he wrote letters to the newspaper editors, saying that they were printing lies.[43] Additional letters, sent to the right places, scheduled speaking engagements in Houston City. At Galveston, Houston booked passage for himself and his family to the United States, then hurried up the bayou to Houston City.[44]

Houston had been elected to represent Montgomery County at a summer convention which would consider the annexation question. But there was no longer any question in Houston's mind about sentiment in Texas toward annexation: he knew it would take place. Now he envisioned his political field broadening beyond the Sabine. While the other Texas politicians were still contemplating the coming convention, Sam Houston knew that he would not be there.

In mid-May Houston sailed back to Grand Cane to fetch Margaret and Sam. He was in a hurry to reach the United States, but Margaret was not ready to leave. She had business to attend to. On May 18, boats from other farms along the Trinity tied to the Bledsoe landing on the riverbank. In the afternoon, Margaret,

[42] Culver H. Smith, "The Funeral of Andrew Jackson," *The Tennessee Historical Quarterly*, Vol. IV, 195.

[43] Sam Houston to Hamilton Stuart, Grand Cane, April 22, 1845, *Writings*, IV, 420.

[44] Sam Houston to Thomas Jefferson Rusk, aboard the *Oriole*, April 26, 1845, *Writings*, IV, 422.

"Sister Nancy Lea," and "Sister Antoinett Bledsoe" were among the seven founders of Concord Baptist Church. A piece of land back from the river was contributed for a church house and graveyard. The founders "sung and prayed" and obliged themselves to acquire a "Church-book."[45]

Six days later, in the evening, the *New York* docked at New Orleans. Margaret and Sam were taken to the William Christy residence in Carondelet Street. Houston went elsewhere. As he left the steamer, a messenger handed him a sealed letter from a guest at The Hermitage. In the American business section of the city, Banks' Arcade glowed with light; an "immense crowd" awaited General Houston.[46] By the time he took the platform Sam Houston was able to express his views. He had felt the pulsebeat of the public since his emergence from Raven Hill. The newspapers' fever was matched by that of the people. Houston read the letter given to him at the dock. "My Dear General . . . it can not be possible that a native of Virginia and a citizen of Tennessee can have so far forgotten what is due to himself and his country as to lend himself for an instant to the representatives of England and France."[47] Sam Houston had not doubted the benefits annexation would bring to the United States. As for the good it would do Texas, and himself politically, he had been uncertain and perhaps still was.[48]

The crowd cheered enthusiastically at Banks' Arcade. More people gathered, and the room got so stuffy that one of the news

[45] Minutes of the founding meeting of the Concord Baptist Church, May, 1845, Margaret Lea Houston manuscripts, University of Texas Archives.

[46] *New Orleans Tropic*, May 25, 1845, as quoted by the Nashville *Union* for June 10, 1845.

[47] E. G. M. Butler's report, cited in Crane, *Life and Select Literary Remains*, 251.

[48] Sam Houston to Andrew Jackson Donelson, Huntsville, April 9, 1845, *Writings*, IV, 410–17.

reporters left even before Houston's speech began.[49] Houston orated about the rich land west of the Sabine. He described the Texas drama, that of the Anglo-American penetration, and he scathingly criticized the liars and hacks who had called it filibustering. Then, according to his usual pattern, he talked extravagantly of himself. After a glorious account of his triumphs: "I have been accused of lending myself to England and France; but . . . I have been only coquetting with them."[50]

On June 4, the Houstons' riverboat had climbed the Mississippi to Memphis, where they boarded the Nashville stagecoach. At six-thirty in the evening of the fourth harrowing day, they arrived in Nashville, which was quiet and somber in expectation of Jackson's death. Margaret and Sam were hurried into a carriage, which in the fading daylight moved out the Lebanon Pike toward The Hermitage. Several miles into the country they halted at a bridge, where they met the doctor returning to town. Andrew Jackson had died about three hours before.[51]

Within an hour, Margaret, holding Sam, stood with General Houston in the death room. Houston closed the eyes of the dead man.[52] Old and withered by his long, agonizing sickness, the hero of New Orleans in death was a small form in the tall, curtained bed. Houston held Sam in his arms and said, "My son, try to remember that you have looked upon the face of Andrew Jackson."[53]

The coffin arrived, and the bedroom was cleared. An overflow of guests filled The Hermitage, and Margaret and General Hous-

[49] *New Orleans Tropic*, May 25, 1845.

[50] Crane, *Life and Select Literary Remains*, 251.

[51] Sam Houston to James K. Polk, Hermitage, June 8, 1845, *Writings*, IV, 424–25.

[52] *The Nashville Union*, June 10, 1845.

[53] Author in conversation with Mrs. Jennie Morrow Decker, Houston, June 1, 1964; James, *The Raven*, 357.

ton accepted an invitation to stay at Tulip Grove, the residence of the Andrew Jackson Donelsons across the road. Houston, at midnight, in The Hermitage, wrote a letter notifying President James K. Polk of Jackson's death. Of all the famous people involved with Jackson, some of whom were at The Hermitage when he died, the most publicity went to Sam Houston, who very clearly seemed in quest of it.

Margaret was probably glad to leave The Hermitage, and in the following days welcomed the peace of Tulip Grove. Over at The Hermitage the threadbare chairs were occupied by mourners, who also paced the old-fashioned carpets and wandered through the dark house. Margaret knew some of the guests by name, others she knew by reputation, a number of them known to her as professionals in soliciting favor. Jackson's remains lay in state in the parlor.

From the upstairs gallery of Tulip Grove, Margaret could see the Lebanon Pike. On the morning of June 10, a Tuesday, a ribbon of vehicles and horsemen extended from Nashville. There had been memorial services in town on the day before. Crowds poured over the park of The Hermitage and into an adjoining pasture to see the celebrities and pay honest tribute to the man the younger ones of them had seen in public only a few times.

The minister spoke: "And one of the elders answered, saying unto me, What are those which are arrayed in white robes? And whence came they?" His sermon was brief and told of Jackson's conversion to Christianity. The coffin was carried across the yard to a fenced garden, where it was placed in the classical pavilion beneath which Rachel Donelson Jackson was entombed. Sam Houston, at the peak of his Tennessee career, had walked over a path of cottonbolls as one of Mrs. Jackson's pallbearers. Andrew Jackson had specified that no pomp accompany his burial.[54]

[54] Smith, "The Funeral of Andrew Jackson," 195–97.

While the coffin was lowered into the grave, the Nashville Blues fired three volleys into the air. The spectators, numbering thousands, watched the dirt shoveled back into the opening. By dark The Hermitage was quiet, except for the guests whose candles glowed in the louvered shutters they closed against the summer night.

Margaret was overtaxed by the strain of the trip and the heavy social schedule. Houston's appearance had created excitement. At Tulip Grove, Margaret went into retirement for most of the duration of the stay in Tennessee. Houston was extensively entertained by his old friends. He had not been in Nashville since 1839, after he had met Margaret. People found him "more reserved" than previously, and they noticed traces of pallor from his illness.[55]

Now and then Margaret accompanied Houston on his excursions. On one such trip she met a preacher who commented later that she was "an intelligent and apparently pious lady—a member of the Baptist Church." The minister told Margaret about his proposed missionary work in Texas and presented her with a five-volume set of religious books. She thanked him and promised that when she had read all the books she would write him a critique. That night the preacher notified his superiors in the church—"You may remember this incident so that any young man who may go out [to Texas] as a missionary may remember I have prepared a welcome for him at the General's."[56]

The barbecues for Sam Houston continued into August. Margaret accompanied him sometimes, but she was usually unwell, so she visited with the Jackson and Donelson women, who were in mourning and unable to attend public functions. When Mar-

[55] *Niles' Weekly Register*, Baltimore, July 12, 1845.

[56] David Christy to Rev. William R. Hemphill, Lincoln County, Tennessee, June, 1845, Duke University Archives.

garet's condition seemed to be improving, Houston took her and Sam to Blount Springs, Alabama, for mineral baths. On September 1, they arrived by stage in Marion, well recovered and in good spirits.[57]

They stayed with Henry and Serena. General Houston obliged the townspeople by speaking on annexation, a subject he had spoken on continually since the previous May. In his absence, a special session of the Texas Congress had rendered a positive vote, and in the fall the people would express their opinions at the polls. That September in Marion, a dinner party was held for Houston, whose speech was anything but humble in describing his genius in effecting annexation. The newspapers wrote the kind of reviews he had counted on. "Nature," raved one paper, "intended him for distinction among his fellows." His manner "is eloquence itself." He "moves with the firm elastic tread and erect carriage of the young Indian Chief."[58]

Margaret remained with her family, and Houston went to speak at Greensboro, Alabama, then journeyed to Mobile, where he boarded a boat home to Texas. There were things to interest Margaret in Marion. Martin's widow and children were there; Judson Female Institute was building new buildings; Mr. and Mrs. Goree were preparing to move to Texas and hoped to open an academy of their own. Sam had spent his second birthday in New Orleans on the way to Nashville, and Margaret felt that it was important that he know his Alabama kin.

Houston was busy with politics and work at Raven Hill. So Margaret did not return to Texas until soon after New Year's of 1846. At Galveston she took a Trinity steamer to Grand Cane. During the summer, William Bledsoe's suffering had come to an end. He was buried in the clearing in which the framing for

[57] *Alabama State Review*, September 17, 1845.
[58] *Ibid.*

Concord Baptist Church had been raised. On November 1, Mary Lea had died of a heart attack, and her grave was beside that of Captain Bledsoe. The log house was no longer crowded. Nancy Lea opened the shutters and filled the vases with greenery. Feeling responsible for the household, Vernal took the job of postmaster in the town of Grand Cane to insure an income and continued his efforts at farming.

Only Mrs. Bledsoe seemed not to adjust to her new life. Even mourning was becoming to Antoinette. She pitied herself for weeks, a widow at twenty-five, with no prospect of change. Steamboats passed on the Trinity as if to taunt her. Then one afternoon, ignoring the outrage of her mother, she ordered the Negroes to flag a boat. In a pile of bandboxes and trunks, Antoinette waved from the deck of the departing steamer. She was going to Galveston.[59]

Sam Houston joined Margaret late in January. He had missed her and little Sam in the four months of their separation. Just a year before, he had written to Anson Jones describing a reunion with his family: "It was indeed a joyous meeting, and strange to say, I find my mind falling back into a channel, where the current flows in domestic peace and quiet, without one care about the affairs of government, and only intent upon domestic happiness and prosperity."[60]

On the Sunday after he came to Grand Cane, services were held at Concord Church, which had been completed across the clearing from the graveyard where Bledsoe and Mary Lea were laid under

[59] Author in conversation with Mrs. John L. Little, Sr., Beaumont, Texas, January 10, 1964; also in conversation with Mrs. Dan O'Madigan, Beaumont, Texas, June 1, 1964; see also clippings in Mrs. Little's collection, though most of them are from twentieth century newspapers.

[60] Sam Houston to Anson Jones, Grand Cane, December 21, 1844, *Writings*, 408–10.

bare, earth mounds. That morning the household rose early and dressed for the meeting. From her room stepped Margaret, on the general's arm. Sam Houston was going to church.[61]

[61] Ellis, *Sam Houston and Related Spiritual Forces*, 67.

5.

Raven's Roost

On February 21, 1846, Sam Houston was elected to the United States Senate from the state of Texas. His victory was not a surprise. General Houston had covered the tracks of his indecision and emerged with most of the medals of the old Republic. The other participants in the event would try to discredit him in their memoirs, only to create a perpetual controversy.

Margaret was not told that Houston was returning to Texas to become a candidate for public office. Probably in consideration of her grief over the deaths of Bledsoe and Mary Lea, Houston did not wish to multiply her anxieties and ruin her stay in Marion. Back in Texas, she and Houston remained on the Trinity for a week before returning to Raven Hill to await the results of the election. They had been away from home for nine months.

During that period Houston for the first time articulated the changes Margaret had engineered in his life. While she was still visiting in Alabama, he wrote to a Tennessee cousin, "It has been my lot to be happily united, to a wife that I love, and so far we have a young scion of the old stock. My wife is pious, and her great desire is, that Sam should be reared, in the fear and admonition of the Lord. It is likewise my desire. Not because my wife desires it and controls me (as the world has it) but, for sundry weighty reasons."

Houston continued: "You, have, I doubt not, heard that my wife controls me, and has reformed me, in many respects? This is pretty true." Margaret deserved the "full benefit of my character," but "she gets all the credit for my good actions, and I have to endure all the censure of my bad ones."[1]

Raven Hill was the beginning of an agrarian dream anchored in the Texas wilds. The country was like piedmont Virginia, and with continued improvements, Raven Hill would be a place in which to rear a dynasty in the grand manner, with more land and maybe a bigger house some day. Experimental farming and cattle breeding were included in Houston's plans. Raven Hill itself was a manifestation of his visions of aristocracy, visions expressed in a letter to William H. Letcher: "There is one matter which I wish to learn something about. . . . It is our family. Aunt Gillespy often wished to write down our *genealogy*, but I always neglected it. . . . Now I know only my Grand Father Houston['s] name, if it was Robert. I wish you to let me know all the information, which you have, on the subject of our family."[2]

A rider came out from Huntsville with the news that the state legislature had elected Houston to the United States Senate. Most of a lifetime had passed since Houston had moved in the scene of national affairs. The Senate and the feeling of urgency in being there appealed to him, for the Texas government had returned to Austin, where it was of course reduced to the pedantic details of a

[1] Sam Houston to William Houston Letcher, Galveston, November 25, 1845; see also F. N. Boney (ed.), "The Raven Tamed: A Sam Houston Letter," *Southwestern Historical Quarterly*, Vol. LXVIII, 90–92.

[2] *Ibid.*

local system. Houston's pride demanded that he be involved in major issues. His ambitions could best find an outlet in Washington, D.C., in national pursuits. He knew that when he crossed the Sabine into the United States, the factions in Texas would become inaudible behind him, and San Jacinto, annexation, and his closeness with the late Andrew Jackson would unlock important doors, if used judiciously.

When Houston won an election, Margaret was always a little disappointed. She had convinced herself that Raven Hill would insure his retirement, though she must have suspected that his political life was not over. A war with Mexico seemed inevitable. Houston had freely made an issue of using such a war as a means of acquiring territories westward beyond New Mexico as well as a border established at least at the Río Grande. The project had seemed unrealistic for the Republic; but the United States could effect it very easily, and Houston eagerly imagined political advantages that would come from his part in it.

Margaret halfheartedly began packing to leave for Washington. Houston allowed her three weeks in which to close Raven Hill.[3] Early in March, she found that she was pregnant, and her plans changed. With vague arrangements about Margaret's following later, General Houston departed on March 8, down the steep road to the Trinity, thence to Galveston, where he and the other senator, Thomas Jefferson Rusk from the Redlands, would sail for the Mississippi's mouth.

Margaret moved quickly in delegating responsibilities. Housekeeping's only reward for her was in pleasing the general. When he was gone, Eliza attended to the house and Joshua managed the farm. The senator's lady did not want to be bothered with either

[3] Margaret Lea Houston to Sam Houston, Raven Hill, May 16, 1846, Texas State Archives; see also Sam Houston to Major Vernal Lea, Raven Hill, March 6, 1846, Liberty County, Texas, Historical Society.

problem. She took up her needlework, chorded on her piano, and played the guitar. In the rough-fenced yard she had ordered plowed, she made a flower garden with slips of crepe myrtle, cape jasmine, and iris bulbs she brought from Marion. The front hallway opened into the garden by means of steps. Every morning the ground of the garden between the flower beds was swept with a brush broom.

Loneliness quickly enveloped Margaret. The file of days and the wind in the pine tops had a melancholy repetition. To make a farm of Raven Hill's little clearing would mean a war against the most abandoned of forests. It was a war Margaret did not want to fight.

One Saturday each month, Joshua hitched the coach and drove Margaret, Sam, and Eliza to the little town of Huntsville. Margaret spent the night with friends, either Mrs. Merritt or Frances Creath, and attended the all-day Baptist Sabbath service, which began early. On Monday they drove the difficult fourteen miles back to Raven Hill, where Margaret returned to her sewing, her music, and Sam, to labor at amusements which might make her forget the slow tick of Nancy Lea's clock, which was kept on the mantel.

A part of Margaret's days were spent writing letters at the squat, cupboard-like secretary in her bedroom. The gold and crystal inkwell was a gift from a Houston admirer; the silver pen was Margaret's own.[4] Pastel stationery, which she preferred, was stacked in the pigeonholes. Margaret's letters were verbose ramblings covering sometimes four or five pages. They were composed as though she were conducting a conversation with Sam Houston. "I have been anxiously expecting the daguerreotype you

[4] Margaret Decker Everitt, notes on the Houston furniture, Huntsville, Texas, May 5, 1965, author's collection; item, Franklin Williams Collection; items, Sam Houston Memorial Museum.

promised me. A true picture of my beloved would be quite a companion to me. If his image would be so sweet, what about his real presence?"[5] At Huntsville the mail was taken once each week, unless a rainy season delayed the stagecoach.

News came slowly to Raven Hill, and Margaret awaited it impatiently. Nancy Lea and General Houston were her most faithful correspondents. Vernal called on Margaret, staying long enough to see that her crop was in the making. Later in the summer, Varilla visited, bringing her youngest child, Martin, who was Sam's age. Antoinette had promised to come and spend the summer.

The widow Bledsoe's plan changed when she very abruptly eloped. In Galveston, her beauty and good humor became the fascination of Captain Charles Power. He was a widower, a wealthy Englishman living in Galveston as agent for a Liverpool mercantile company, and was considered one of the major merchants in town. Antoinette responded to his attentions, and in a short time they were married, reportedly at dusk, aboard a wrecked schooner in Galveston Bay. Nancy Lea was humiliated. Margaret's feelings were hurt, but Charles Power "makes so many pretty promises to *love honor and obey*" that Margaret was willing "to forgive their youthful indiscretion."[6]

When letters failed to free her from the oppressive quiet of Raven Hill, Margaret returned to her poetry. Senator Houston, on a speaking tour, had met Mrs. Eliza Allen, editor of the *Mother's Journal of Philadelphia*. They had discussed the possibility of publishing some of Margaret's poems.[7] Margaret sent

[5] Margaret Lea Houston to Sam Houston, Raven Hill, June 12, 1846, Franklin Williams Collection.

[6] Margaret Lea Houston to Sam Houston, Raven Hill, May 16, 1846, Texas State Archives.

[7] The Eliza Allen here is not to be confused with Houston's former wife, who had married Dr. William Elmore Douglas in Tennessee.

manuscripts to Mrs. Allen under a pseudonym which is lost. The pages and pages of poems in these ladies' books of the mid-nineteenth century remind one of Margaret. Sunsets, roses, and tombs were Margaret's delight, and the delirium of several hundred more lady poets. Mrs. Allen was a critic as well as a publisher, though she seems to have required a subscription before she would publish Margaret's work—"Dearest I enclose you my letter to Mrs. Allen, which I wish you to read and forward to her, enclosing *if you please love* one dollar for the years subscription. It is a poor price for all the aid she will give me." Besides the money, "a few lines from you accompanying my letter I know would be very gratifying and encouraging to her, but I do not require it of you darling. . . . I know you have few moments of your own, and I am almost selfish enough to claim them all."[8]

The publication gratified Margaret little in her isolation. From her desk she rose and tried to interest herself in the farm, as Nancy Lea had always done. "The two mules have done all the plowing as we gave up Black Hawk and the Tennessee Mare. . . . I expect we will have a fine crop of potatoes. Your wheat has been my especial charge. The rabbits [ate] it down once and I then had it staked so closely that they could not get to it."[9]

Sam was with her all day, rather than playing with the Negro children of the slaves. Margaret thought the "little negroes . . . so corrupt that I do not suffer him to play with them at all."[10] In a while Houston responded to Margaret's complaints by offering to send a housekeeper, a girl whose name survives merely as "Anna."[11] Anna came to Texas, and like the others in a seemingly

[8] Margaret Lea Houston to Sam Houston, Raven Hill, May 16, 1846, Texas State Archives; see also Eliza Allen to Sam Houston, Philadelphia, n.d., Sam Houston Hearne Collection.

[9] Margaret Lea Houston to Sam Houston, Raven Hill, June 12, 1846, Franklin Williams Collection.

[10] *Ibid.*

Margaret Lea at the time of her marriage.

University of Texas Library

The Engagement Cameo.

San Jacinto Museum of History, Hearne Collection

Sam Houston as a United States Senator from Texas, 1846.

Sam Houston Memorial Museum

Henry Lea and Serena stand behind the seated Varilla.

Sam Houston Memorial Museum

Galveston as Margaret knew it.

Archives Division, Texas State Library

Margaret at thirty.

University of Texas Library

Ashbel Smith. Oil attributed to George Catlin.

Texana Collection, University of Texas

Antoinette Lea Bledsoe.

Sam Houston Memorial Museum

Loggia of the Huntsville house. Here, in the hot Texas summers, the Houstons' dining table was set, to capture the breezes from the pine-land hills of their farm.

Hickey and Robertson, Photographers

Nancy Lea, painted at Huntsville by George Allen.

Harris County Heritage Society, Katherine Hume Seymour Memorial Collection, Houston

Three little Houstons: Maggie, Mary William, and Nannie.

Sam Houston Memorial Museum

Sam Houston wearing his linen duster.

University of Texas Library

George W. Samson, pastor of the E Street Baptist Church, Washington, D.C., and Houston's minister. Photograph by Mathew Brady.

Library of Congress

Independence.

Texana Collection, University of Texas

Margaret Lea Houston at forty.

Sam Houston Memorial Museum

Sam Houston as governor of Texas. Sketched in his office in 1860 by Gustav Behne.

Collection of Paul Adams

Margaret Houston in 1860, when Sam Houston was the governor of Texas.

Houston Museum of Fine Arts, Bayou Bend Collection

Capitol of Texas (right) and Baptist church (left) at Austin in the 1860's.

Austin Public Library

Sam Houston after the departure from Austin.

University of Texas Library

Nannie at fifteen, a student at Baylor.

Sam Houston Memorial Museum

Nettie stands beside Mary William in this daguerreotype ca. 1865.

Sam Houston Memorial Museum

Nannie commissioned this portrait after Margaret's death and closely consulted with the artist on its details. It is as she last saw her mother.

Collection of Mrs. Jennie Morrow Decker

endless list of employees, found Margaret difficult to please, and departed after a short stay. One suspects that the tiny houses of the Houstons were crowded enough without the addition of another woman, particularly a woman whose life had perhaps been harder and who might eye with disgust Margaret's constant self-indulgence.

Margaret's pregnancy advanced. Waists were loosened and maternity garments were unpacked. Margaret wrote to Houston, "The hope of seeing you . . . makes my heart thrill with delight. I was about to say—makes me almost *dance with joy*, but you know dearest, I *never* was a very elegant dancer, and now from some cause or another it would be a most *ungraceful* exercise."[12]

There were still plans for moving to Washington. Margaret was hesitant about living in the city because social obligations would interrupt her life. Public appearances would require fashionable clothes, and Houston's salary presently afforded her too small an allowance; his bills at his Washington hotel, together with the cost of travel, were substantial. Her presence would merely increase expenses, for besides living quarters, they would have to purchase vegetables and meats, hats, bonnets and shoes, all of which were costly in the city. But Margaret insisted upon going, for she was determined to be with Sam Houston.

Delays frustrated her. The pregnancy began to present problems, which part of the time confined her to bed. When she had carried Sam, soreness in her breasts had worried her. Now the aches and rawness had returned, and she asked Sam Houston to send protective cups "of india rubber or the skin of a cow's teat."[13]

[11] Margaret Lea Houston to Sam Houston, Raven Hill, May 16, 1846, Texas State Archives.

[12] Margaret Lea Houston to Sam Houston, Raven Hill, June 12, 1846, Franklin Williams Collection.

[13] Margaret Lea Houston to Sam Houston, Raven Hill, June 20, 1846, New York Public Library.

Pain brought gloom over her inability to make the trip to Washington. She wanted Houston's sympathy. In a letter he had mentioned seeing a former lady friend of his. Margaret wrote, "Well, darling, I know that she loved you devotedly, but oh her love does not deserve to be mentioned in the same day with what I feel for you now! . . . But why do I speak of my feelings at all! I cannot describe them. Oh my love if you could look into my heart at this moment, I know you would never leave me again!"[14]

The vast separation of miles of rugged land and long water voyages was bewildering. Formerly Houston had ridden over Texas, stopping at least once a month at home, if only to spend the night. Margaret anticipated his visits and had been understanding of his absences. In Texas the Houstons had been thankful that they were seldom more than five days apart. The journey to Washington required a month, under favorable circumstances. Though Margaret was too far away to know the difference, Houston was not drinking, and he no longer mentioned bitters in his letters. He had attended church with Margaret and Sam and the servants. At home he had led daily prayer services. Still he was away from the surroundings Margaret had designed for him, and the possibility of his weakening presented itself ominously in Margaret's mind.[15]

In Washington, Sam Houston moved across the parade ground of his past. Nearly fifteen years were gone since he had known the United States capital. Long ago he had walked along Pennsylvania Avenue in the costume of a Cherokee ambassador, nostalgic even then over an earlier time of beaver hats and gold-mounted canes, of a young man on the rise. In 1846 he had come back not as the romantic Cherokee or the prodigal favorite of Andrew Jackson, but as the man whose name was synonymous with Texas.

[14] Margaret Lea Houston to Sam Houston, Raven Hill, May 16, 1846, Texas State Archives.

[15] *Ibid.*

"Sam Houston's Republic," they had called it. He was the foremost celebrity of the West, in a time when the western territory already owned and the want of more territory were the topics of Senate debate.

James K. Polk's Washington retained physical associations from Andrew Jackson's days. Gas lights now lit streets that Sam Houston remembered as being dark in old times when a galaxy of young politicians, himself a bright star, had caroused late. Grand avenues still swept to nowhere; geese and hogs wandered about in the streets' emptiness. Hotel bars stayed open long after midnight, and curious people sought there the famous figures of the capital. It was Sam Houston's destiny to be a great national personage, or at least he believed it was so. Considerably more than a fighting chance for great fame had been laid before him. By going to Arkansas and then Texas, he had abandoned his national chances, midstream, while men he had known before and now saw again every day had remained and risen within the system. Now Sam Houston was back with brazen demands. He wanted his place again, as though he had never been away. Political maneuver was the means by which he intended to get what he wanted. He was received with marked coolness from some of the young, ambitious Democrats. The Texan believed in his personal abilities just as much as the new politicians believed in their intricate organizational mechanisms. At fifty-three, Sam Houston calculated the best approach for his comeback.

It was invigorating to be in Washington again, except for the loneliness that came with the night and Sundays. For the first time since his personal renaissance he was so far away from Margaret that he could not reach her in time of weakness and doubt. Still, in a manner of speaking, she was with him, for he knew precisely how she felt on pertinent subjects. Monotonous evening sessions at the Capitol were stuffy with the smell of whisky and tobacco. In few places was liquor more available or more accepted than in the capital. As General Houston went from his hotel to his Senate desk, he was taunted by memories from which he had once fled in drink. A shuttered window, a faded sign, a street corner, a scent in the air, and he found himself on the dangerous rim of remorse.

Margaret was honest about her own fears. She wrote to him: "You can imagine my state of mind, for a few weeks past. It amounted almost to desperation, and I often longed 'for the wings of a dove, that I might fly away and be at rest.' " Houston urged her to join him. "Never have I," she wrote, "been so strongly tempted, to act in opposition to the dictates of my judgement. . . . I felt willing at first to risk my life in the attempt rather than be longer without you."[16]

She would have gone if Houston's sister had not "prevailed against it." Eliza Houston Moore and her husband and children were in the Huntsville vicinity on a farm Houston had rented for them. Their stay was temporary, but Eliza Moore spent considerable time at Raven Hill with her young sister-in-law, and Margaret respected her opinions. Eliza was surprised that Margaret would think of going on a trip to Washington. Margaret's health was too precarious, and now she carried a child. As they talked one evening a hailstorm broke out. Eliza spent the night in the safety of Raven Hill. The next day Margaret felt "much cheered by her visit." For her health's sake, she would not go to Washington.[17]

But she was lonely. At Raven Hill she sought ways to end the terrible silence. "We have great excitement throughout our country about the war. A large number of volunteers are preparing to set off . . . as usual on such occasions, a perfect mania is abroad on the subject." Eliza's son Houston Moore "is crazy to go." A rider came out from "Colonel Woods," who "expects to set off with his

[16] *Ibid.*
[17] *Ibid.*

company on Thursday. He sent up today to request my presence at his house on next Monday to direct the making of his flag." Sam Houston was a principal spokesman favoring the war, and he had become something of a national newspaper favorite because of his views. Margaret wrote that she was invited to sew the flag because "[the colonel] thinks my connection with you will give it some charm." She attended the flag making and brought guests home with her.[18]

Raven Hill became, for a time, a place of entertainment. As many as eight people spent three and four days at once there. They fished in a lake at the foot of the hill. Mrs. Merritt played the piano and they sang popular songs and hymns. Young Sam—according to his mother—was usually the center of attention: "He was seen struggling hard to ascend a little dog-wood tree, which he finally accomplished, and I do wish you could have seen his bright triumphant eyes peering through the leafy boughs, and heard his silvery voice ringing joyously through the wild-woods."[19] Rural pleasures, however, soon bored the guests. Huntsville itself was smaller than some of the coastal sugar plantations, so a farm presented a limited novelty to the Huntsville guests, and Margaret found herself alone again at her desk.[20]

The smoke of the first shot still drifted in the South Texas air when General Zachary Taylor rode his horse across the Río Grande. War drums lured volunteers from the newer of the United States to join in the invasion. There were no other topics of talk, nor any other subjects about which to read. López de Santa Anna had broken his promises to President Polk and slipped into Mexico from Cuban exile. There, he gathered up an army and marched out to meet the Yankees. Sam Houston schemed for a

[18] *Ibid.*

[19] Margaret Lea Houston to Sam Houston, Raven Hill, June 20, 1846, New York Public Library.

[20] *Ibid.*

military commission, imagining the great theatrical possibilities of his again being pitted against the old enemy of San Jacinto. Raising the Stars and Stripes at Mexico City would bring more glory to Houston than the same had done for General Jackson at New Orleans thirty years before. There was almost a certainty that Polk would commission Houston. San Jacinto's hero would be the best one to tarnish Taylor's glory and his delusions of Whig candidacy for President of the United States.

The subject that was discussed at the White House caused sleepless nights at Raven Hill. Margaret was hurt. Houston wrote and asked her if she thought he should go to war. "Dearest," she replied, "you tell me that I should decide whether or not you are to go out with the army. Alas, what has always been my decision, when my own happiness or the good of the country was to be sacrificed? . . . I . . . invariabl[y] ascertained your views, and then coincided with them, let my own sacrifices be what they might. . . . And even now, though your personal danger will be far greater than it has been on any previous occasion, since our marriage, I will not express one word of opposition."[21] She did oppose, however. It was cruel to shoot Mexicans, "poor deluded creatures! Born to wretchedness, and compelled to die for a country which has never cared for their happiness . . . if they must be slaughtered, why may not some other hand than yours perform the bloody deed?" She begged him to consider little Sam: "I cannot look around upon my widowed hearth and hear my poor boy's plaintive cry, 'what makes Pa stay so long?' and then tell you that I am willing for you to go. . . . But I have said that I would not express one word of opposition, nor is it my design to bias your judgement by what I have said. I wish you to be governed entirely by your own judgement." Whatever his decision might be, she would "try to bear it without a murmur."[22]

[21] *Ibid.*

[22] *Ibid.*

Until Houston wrote of his desire for a commission in the army, the war had seemed very far from the placid life at Raven Hill. Summer flowers had bloomed in the woods, and Sam had plucked them and presented them to his mother and her friend Frances Creath. Margaret sometimes pressed the flowers in her books of Burns's poems and her Shakespeare. When they dried she mailed them to the senator.

The summer passed, and Margaret began to expect Sam Houston to return home. Beside her window that looked over the treetops to the horizon, Margaret turned the pages of her Bible. At her desk she wrote, thinking each time that she was writing the last page she would write before Houston was home again. When the rider came out from Huntsville with the mail, there seemed always to be another letter, telling of another delay. Margaret wrote a note and sent it as a postscript to the package she had already handed the rider:

> My Beloved Husband
>
> I was awakened this morning by your letter, and a most welcomed one it was. Sam and I kissed it with great delight, but I could have bestowed the kisses with much more pleasure on the *writer*. However—though it is a cloudy and rather gloomy day I am very happy because I hope in a few hours to be clasped to the noblest heart that ever beat. I was delighted at your taking the temperance pledge. This sacrifice of pride for the sake of your fellow beings I trust will be followed by happy results and spiritual blessings upon yourself and many of them. I am still all impatience to see you.
>
> Farewell my beloved
> Thy devoted wife
> Master to Me MARGARET LEA HOUSTON
> Written standing and in a great hurry.[23]

[23] Margaret Lea Houston to Sam Houston, Raven Hill, n.d., Franklin Williams Collection.

She had more monotonous weeks to watch the sunlight on the unchanging pines and the rain make gullies in the bare dirt of the yard. "I often reproach myself severely," wrote Margaret, "for wishing to hurry the moments of your absence, the precious moments given me to prepare for eternity, and I have no excuse for this sinful impatience, except that my husband is so inexpressably dear to me that I cannot be happy without him."[24]

Margaret was troubled thinking Houston might fall victim to old temptations, and she felt helpless to fight any tendencies he might have. She would not be able to go to Washington until the condition of her health changed and, of course, the baby was born. Houston must not lose the progress he had made toward God. "The time is short," she wrote to him, "and in that day nothing will serve as an excuse, for having defrauded our Heavenly Father of a single moment that was his due. Should we meet again, oh may the main business of our lives be to prepare for Heaven."[25]

Houston dismounted at Raven Hill late in August, in time to see the hospital Nancy Lea had made of his house. Margaret, who had waited so painfully for him, awaited now the coming of her second child. On September 6, Nancy Elizabeth Houston was born. She was named for Nancy Lea and Elizabeth Paxton Houston, who had died in Tennessee years before. Within a few days the guests had left except Nancy Lea. Eliza Moore and her family moved to Galveston, and the rest returned home. Margaret was out of bed in a week. In a letter she had imagined Houston's return. "I shall be sitting, as in bygone days, on your lap, with my arms around your neck, the happiest, the most blest of wives."[26] In spite of the war, and the various complications that prevented

[24] Margaret Lea Houston to Sam Houston, Raven Hill, June 20, 1846, New York Public Library.

[25] *Ibid.*

[26] *Ibid.*

Margaret's removal to Washington, the Houstons were together.

Sam Houston's interest in the war was high. He endorsed the establishment of a United States protectorate over Mexico. The plan was an adaptation of the old idea of expanding the Texas Republic to the Pacific and the Isthmus of Tehuantepec. President Polk felt obliged to commission Houston, but he was slow and cautious about effecting it, probably because he suspected Houston's political ambitions. Margaret realized that Houston's chances of going to war would be the same with her in Washington as at Raven Hill. She had never lived in a city. At least with the productive farm she was able to provide for the slaves, herself, Sam, and baby Nancy Elizabeth. Eight of the twelve Negroes were hired to Captain Frank Hatch in Huntsville in exchange for Hatch's services as overseer of Raven Hill. A commission in the army for Houston would not make financial matters worse, but it would increase Margaret's worry and her desperate feeling of separation from him.

With so much war talk, the question of death began to torment Margaret. Should Sam Houston be slain, what of Margaret and the children? "I have none of that Spartan spirit that can equip for the battle-field the dearest object of my affection, not knowing that he will ever return." She would not "exchange one hour of happiness such as we have had, for all the glory that may be won from the present contest." The comforting words with which she reassured herself "found no echo" from General Houston. In her anxiety, Margaret said "the hand of God alone can support me."[27]

God's protective hand seemed to her a long way from Sam Houston. He sneered at the church services he attended with her. If he met death on the battlefield, his soul would be at the mercy of the devil.

Margaret watched him descend Raven Hill on October 4, not

[27] *Ibid.*

knowing how many months it would be before she saw him again. She was left with the servants and Sam and Nannie, which was what they called Nancy Elizabeth. Joshua's split-rail fences ran deep into a partially cleared forest south of the house. He was working on a new building, set in the midst of Margaret's flower garden. It was an office for the general, to house his books and papers.

So Raven Hill was growing, even if the process was slow. The sound of the axe could be heard through the log rooms where the children napped beneath the brush fans of Eliza and Charlotte. Nancy Lea returned to Grand Cane. Margaret wrote letters to Washington and to relatives on the Trinity and wiped the autumn humidity from her brow.

The weather cooled, and Margaret ordered fires built. Sharp pains in her breast grew intense. She tried at first to ignore the pains; she attempted to drown her fright in responsibilities at Raven Hill. After a week of cold endurance, her hand traced a lump in her right breast. In panic Margaret told Joshua to hitch the yellow coach. She did not want to live at Raven Hill, though she did so. But she was not going to die there.

Early in December, Nancy Lea watched the Houston coach draw to a halt. It was a cold, rainy season on the Trinity and hardly the time for a woman to travel. Margaret was weak and pale and Nancy Lea put her to bed. Tender attention satisfied Margaret for a while. On December 5, she wrote to General Houston, having apprehended a letter from him on a Trinity steamer the day before. He had written to her while setting sail for New Orleans. "I did not like your letter," she wrote. "I could perceive that it was a very hurried thing, yet . . . it . . . pained me exceedingly. After reading it again and again I [have] . . . come to the conclusion that it may possibly have originated from the omission of that very important expression 'I love you.' "[28]

Being pampered by her mother and Vernal, Margaret was able to languor in bed with her guitar and letter box.[29] Doubtless she seemed out of place in that frugal, sometimes penniless household. The only one in the family with money to spend was Antoinette. Money complemented Antoinette. Expensive New Orleans modistes, and reportedly some London ones, fashioned her dresses in greens and the becoming blues which flattered all the Lea women. Charles Power's Matagorda Bay sugar plantation paid profits. His commissions from the home office in Liverpool brought cash for his wife to spend. Antoinette possessed two necklaces, a chain of alternating diamonds and sapphires and a second, similar chain of emeralds.[30] She was building a big house on Matagorda Bay and importing some of its furniture from England through Power's mercantile connection. The Houston children grew up in a more conservative world. During childhood, they would gaze in wonder at "Auntie" and "Uncle Charlie" and their glamorous lives.[31]

The children were probably not aware that Antoinette, perhaps at the instigation of her husband, sought to use her family connection with Sam Houston to gain political favors for Power and his brothers in Washington. General Houston reprimanded Antoinette strongly, both in a letter and through Margaret.[32]

Seclusion and rest from the problems of Raven Hill eased Margaret's fears about her breast pains, but the soreness was still

[28] Margaret Lea Houston to Sam Houston, Grand Cane, December 5, 1846, University of Texas Archives.

[29] *Ibid.*

[30] Author in conversation with Mrs. Dan O'Madigan, March 20, 1964, Beaumont, Texas; see also the O'Madigan collection, Grosse Point, Michigan.

[31] Author in conversation with Mrs. Edward A. Everitt and Mrs. Jennie Morrow Decker, Houston, January 30, 1965; see also clipping dated 1869, collection of Mrs. John L. Little, Sr.

[32] Sam Houston to Antoinette Power, Huntsville, November 4, 1849, Liberty County, Texas, Historical Society.

with her. Houston's letters showed his concern over her indisposition. His helpless removal in Washington kept him writing letters home and sending sentimental presents which would amuse Margaret. One of her old love letters was among the surprises, and Margaret recorded her reaction: "I received my old letter to you with melancholy pleasure. Ah how different are my feelings now, from those of girlish romance, that dictated that letter. I loved you then with all the enthusiasm of my nature, but my heart was free from care."[33]

Her cares were mostly happy ones: Sam and Nannie. "The Lord has given them to me, that I may train them for a higher and never ending existence and I shrink not from the task." Nannie looked like Margaret. "Our sweet babe with her violet eyes raised to Heaven hath drawn my heart thence more than ever." At Grand Cane "I received . . . that first look of recognition which stamps itself upon the Mother's heart, never to be erased." General Houston must miss little Nannie. "She preserved a melancholy silence for several days after your departure." And "Mother says I must tell you that when you left us, she was just half as beautiful as she is now." Houston's son "also grows more interesting. . . . He is truthful, generous, affectionate, and magnanimous."[34]

Houston advised Margaret to write to Ashbel Smith and have him come and examine her breast. It was after the first of February before Margaret told Charles Power to summon the doctor, as her pain had become insufferable.[35] Soon afterward the Powers packed to leave for their sugar plantation. Margaret became hysterical,

[33] Margaret Lea Houston to Sam Houston, Grand Cane, December 5, 1846, University of Texas Archives.

[34] *Ibid.*

[35] Charles Power to Dr. Ashbel Smith, Grand Cane, Trinity River, February 3, 1847, Smith Manuscripts, University of Texas Archives.

and the Powers postponed their departure. The tumor within Margaret's breast swelled daily. During February it broke, discharging small quantities of its liquid. Power and one of the servants rode to Liberty, twenty-five miles away, and returned with a doctor before whom Margaret refused to expose herself. Hardly had the doctor gone when the tumor began to drain blood.[36]

A riverboat deposited Ashbel Smith on the high bank. After examining his patient, who was in intense pain, Smith told Nancy Lea to set aside a place where he could operate. Everyone but Antoinette was ordered from Margaret's room. Charles Power brought the whisky Smith had requested, but Margaret refused to drink it. When Smith shrugged and began to prepare his instruments, Antoinette began to weep, saying her sister must not be cut upon without painkiller. Margaret watched Ashbel Smith bicker with Antoinette. Tiring of the contest, Mrs. Houston took a silver coin and gnashed it between her teeth until the tumor was removed.[37]

Once the opening was dressed, Ashbel Smith rolled down his sleeves, packed his bag, and drove to Liberty with the Powers, thence home to his farm. Antoinette had become so ill at the sight of blood that she leaned against the wall and gagged during Margaret's operation. Significantly, however, she was the wife of Charles Power, who had provided what in those hard times was perhaps the only silver coin on the Trinity River.[38]

Margaret was able to take short walks along the riverbank when Houston arrived home April 5, 1847. He was saddened over her

[36] Charles Power to Ashbel Smith, Grand Cane, February 24, 1847, Smith manuscripts, University of Texas Archives.

[37] Author in conversation with Mrs. Edward A. Everitt, Houston, January 15, 1965.

[38] *Ibid.*; see also author in conversation with Mrs. John L. Little, Sr., Galveston, April 5, 1965.

condition but happy to find her "on the recovery."[39] The senator was not immediately re-elected to the Senate when his term expired. His colleague Rusk had drawn the long term in 1846, and to Houston had fallen the short term, so that an election for the full term must now be held. Houston was in the race, but complications in the state legislature facilitated his enemies in blocking his re-election. The affair fell into dispute.

At Grand Cane, Houston whittled toys for Sam and Nannie and visited with Margaret. Word came upriver that Ashbel Smith was sick with a fever. Houston wrote a note: "It has been told to me, that you were dangerously indisposed. . . . Now in your case I really do think, if I could see you, and thereby induce you, to court, and marry some fine woman, that you would recover by a most rational treatment."[40] Smith had maintained since that summer they all lived on the bay that the principal advantage of being a bachelor was that one could ride a stud horse, and he stood by his preference.[41]

By the spring of 1847, both Houston and General Rusk were no longer being considered for commissions in the army. There was time for Sam Houston to think about his family's residence. Margaret refused to return to Raven Hill without him, saying that if she could not go to Washington, Houston would have to make an arrangement more suitable for her than the forlorn hilltop.

Late in April, Margaret suffered another swelling in her breast. It was followed soon by similar swellings on her stomach. Houston wrote to Ashbel Smith that Margaret suspected these later developments were indications of "the root of the cancer."[42] Smith

[39] Sam Houston to Ashbel Smith, Grand Cane, April 12, 1847, *Writings*, V, 10–11; also Charles Power to Ashbel Smith, Grand Cane, March 20, 1847, Smith manuscripts, University of Texas Archives.

[40] *Ibid.*

[41] Ashbel Smith, a short note, ca. 1839–40, Smith manuscripts, University of Texas Archives.

could not leave Galveston. After several days' wait, Houston rode to Liberty and returned to Grand Cane with a doctor Smith had recommended. Margaret this time voiced no objections, and was cured by the end of May.

With his election still pending in the legislature, Houston left frequently during May to make speeches. In the first days of June he rode ahead of Margaret's coach, bound back to Raven Hill. There was little chance that Margaret's last months at Raven Hill would be lonely ones. Inside the coach with her were her mother, Eliza, Sam, Nannie, and Virginia Thorne, who, in accordance with Margaret's promise to Mary Lea, would now live with the Houstons. Already Margaret had experienced a conflict with Virginia over an unexplained "poisoning" involving little Sam.[43]

The family had been absent from Raven Hill for six months, during which time Frank Hatch rode out from Huntsville at intervals to conduct the operation of the farm. There was a vegetable garden and a field of corn, and very likely a small cotton crop had been planted. Although the house had been closed, at least one family friend had spent the night there in the early spring. The agrarian progress at Raven Hill did not soften Margaret's determination to move nearer to town. The general made every effort to please her, and ultimately he exchanged the Raven Hill residence and a parcel of land for Captain Hatch's house and some of its surrounding land near Huntsville. On June 12, Sam Houston sat at his desk and wrote to a Grand Cane neighbor: "I have traded for another place within two or three miles of Huntsville. It is a bang up place! What you say to a look at it?"[44]

[42] Sam Houston to Ashbel Smith, Liberty, April 27, 1847, *Writings*, V, 10–11.

[43] Henderson Yoakum diary, University of Texas Archives; see also Margaret Lea Houston to Sam Houston, Grand Cane, December 5, 1846, University of Texas Archives.

[44] Sam Houston to Joseph Ellis, Raven Hill, June 12, 1847, *Writings*, V, 13–14.

The new house was a small cabin with a chimney of mud and sticks. It stood on a hillside that sloped down to a creek, and on one side of the house the land spread rather flat to a natural pond. A public road a short walk from the house, over the rocky creek, led one to Huntsville's town square in a walk of an hour or so. It had all the privacy of the country with few of the features Margaret had disliked about Raven Hill.[45]

During the summer of 1847, the Houston "family," as Margaret called the slaves, expanded the log house to accommodate the sizable household.[46] The Houstons themselves remained at Raven Hill in domestic peace, worrying about such small matters as what to name the new farm. Sam and Nannie had nurses, Eliza and Charlotte, the latter of whom Margaret later sold to a planter in the country, for she caused trouble among the other Negroes.

The last days on the isolated hill passed pleasantly. In the early autumn the Houstons first occupied the new house, of which Sam Houston himself is said to have been the architect. An open hallway was added to the original house, and a second log room was attached to the end of the hallway or "dog-trot." A porch was

[45] Architectural evidence substantiates the apparent fact that the Houston house began as a one-room cabin; Captain and Mrs. Frank Hatch, who occupied the original house must have lived in one room. The deed records of Walker County (which was settled at about this time) and a letter, Sam Houston to Joseph Ellis, Raven Hill, June 12, 1847, *Writings*, V, 13–14, show that there was probably an existing house on the property when the Houstons got it in trade from the Hatch family. It would have been unlikely for the Houstons to have built the one-room cabin, since their household was big and growing. Unmatching materials in the existing structure are the keys to the house's evolution into what it ultimately became. Much remodeling has been done in the course of its use as a museum, and at one time it was moved, then returned to its present site. There is no architectural study of the house, though it is mentioned, and pictured, in Drury Blakely Alexander, *Texas Homes of the Nineteenth Century*, 37–38, 237.

[46] Margaret Lea Houston to Sam Houston, Grand Cane, December 5, 1846, University of Texas Archives.

built across the front, and above the two rooms was a loft, probably for the house servants until quarters were finished. Plank doors and flat-nail floors were the sole details of the Houston house. In the yard stood two log buildings which were mirror images of the rooms of the main house. One was Houston's office, while the other housed the kitchen. Behind the main house was a fenced yard for Margaret's flowers.

December brought an end to the happy life the brief interruption from politics had allowed. The disgruntled legislature elected Houston to the Senate on December 18, and he rode to Austin for the swearing in, then returned to Huntsville. Christmas was spent in the company of familiar people. Soon after Christmas Day the happy months ended with Margaret's waving the eastbound stagecoach out of sight.

Before her fireplace on New Year's Eve, Margaret began a period of loneliness. There would be another child in the coming spring. Pregnancy would temporarily stop her efforts to improve the house she had demanded Houston buy for her. But there was abundant promise in things as they were, and she seems to have believed that life would be better in the new house than at Raven Hill. It would have been wrong to force herself or her children to endure the loneliness of such a place. In moments of solitude Margaret recalled disquieting questions that had tortured her as a girl in Marion. The volumes in Henry Lea's library had not produced answers, and she had come away then, as now from her own books, frustrated. "I have spent much of my time," she wrote, "in the study of my own heart . . . of its different emotions . . . endeavoring to cherish the good and reject the bad." But light seemed never to come. "I am often enveloped by clouds of gloom, which I cannot understand."[47]

When it seemed that she could bear no more, she found welcome

[47] *Ibid.*

escape by turning her thoughts to Sam Houston. "I have never borne upon my heart the weight of immortal souls," she said, upon realizing her religious responsibilities as a mother.[48] In a true sense Houston's soul too was in her hands. Her prayers and her life itself were dedicated to guiding her husband on the right path. What if she were not there to guide him? And what if she should die and leave him with the responsibility of her children? There must be more strength in him than that inspired by a mere mortal. Sam Houston must experience a spiritual rebirth through belief in Jesus Christ. Margaret decided that the general must not only profess religion, but must be baptized in the Baptist church. From the shadows that had nearly smothered her, Margaret stepped into the sunlight of purpose.

[48] *Ibid.*

6.

Sweet Rocky

On the morning of April 13, 1848, Eliza held a pale infant before the windowpanes of Margaret's bedroom. The Negroes who crowded outside to see must have wondered what the baby girl's name would be. Long before his departure four months before, the general had convinced himself that the child would be a boy and had established a name, Andrew Jackson Houston. It was some months before he would admit defeat. They finally named her Margaret and called her Maggie, which was Houston's nickname for his wife.

The uncomplicated childbirth occurred two days after Margaret's twenty-ninth birthday. Improvements were still in progress on the new property, which covered 173 acres of hilly woodlands, with meadows around the house. Margaret had decided to stay in Texas. Only a few times more would she consider going to Washington, for she believed her place was at home, and home for Sam Houston must always be Texas. The necessities for a growing family were more readily available in Texas than they could ever be in Washington, where the Houstons would have neither a smokehouse nor a vegetable garden nor unlimited credit at the stores. It would not have been in harmony with Margaret's manner of dealing with Houston for her to have followed him to the capital. Her place was at home.

Joshua cleared a pasture for the general's horses and plowed a very large vegetable garden. His projects would have been completed more quickly had he not been assigned duties at the part of Raven Hill the Houstons had retained, as well as at Cedar Point. Since some of the slaves were still hired to Frank Hatch, Margaret, as was often the case, was left with only house servants, who were under Nancy Lea's careful supervision.

By summer Margaret complained that she needed rest. She was weary of the crowded house, whose two rooms and loft housed six, not counting the children's nurses. The Leas seemed to have a way of clustering together, and the more crowded the happier. To relax herself, Margaret decided to go to Cedar Point for a stay in the healthful salt air. The supreme court had finally settled Cedar Point's land title, so the property was safe to use again.[1] On June 1, the coach headed south to Galveston Bay.

Margaret had left her mother with every responsibility she could possibly abandon. Two servants went along to the bay with her. Sam had never been to Cedar Point, and he was five. Leaving

[1] Sam Houston purchased Cedar Point from Tabitha Harris, common-law wife of John Jiams, both of whom were former residents of Kentucky, where their illicit romance began and where they had families, and later residents of Bayou Sarah, West Feliciana Parish, Louisiana. Mrs. Harris was never legally divorced from her Kentucky husband, nor was Jiams divorced from his wife. Therefore, Jiams' son by his legal marriage denounced Mrs. Harris' right to inherit from his father and, upon the death of the elder Jiams, declared Sam Houston's title by purchase from Mrs. Harris void. John Jiams, Jr., sold the property to Andrew J. Yates, who promptly ran cattle in the meadows and groves around the house. Infuriated, Sam Houston exchanged threats with Yates and took the final battle to court, when he discovered some of the oak grove had been cut down. See Sam Houston to William Duncan, Huntsville, December 6, 1847, *Writings*, VI, 16–17; for a good account of the trial and the various legal points see *Texas Reports* for 1848.

the noisy house must have pleased Margaret. Nancy Lea was not always amiable, particularly around little children, whose upbringing was an area in which she claimed supreme authority. And Virginia Thorne was not compatible with anybody but "Sammy," as she called Sam. Sam was also Margaret's favorite. Before he could walk, Margaret was composing manly letters to the general and signing them "Thy Son, Sam Houston, Jr." He was a precocious boy, possessed of his mother's sensitivity. As long as his father did not know it, Margaret permitted him to draw pictures of animals and characters from the Bible and maybe write a rhyme or two.

Margaret and the servants tied the shutters back and turned the horses into the oak grove, which had grown taller in the years since Houston planted it for her. She had never surrendered her idea of the bay house as a retreat for herself and Sam Houston, though her romantic visions about Ben Lomond were gone. The name Cedar Point had prevailed. Ashbel Smith had built a handsome story-and-a-half house of lumber on his bay land. Cedar Point had remained rather primitive, because the Houstons used it in the summers only. Late in June, Margaret decided to leave the bay and go to Grand Cane for a visit with Vernal, who was contemplating remarriage. She was back in Huntsville in mid-July.

At once she set out to improve the situation at home. She hired a youth named Thomas Gott as overseer, to be in charge of the Huntsville farm. Gott took up residence in the house and managed everything about the farm but the horses, which were to be maintained by Joshua, at the general's request.[2] The house itself was enlarged, out of necessity.[3] Additions of milled lumber ex-

[2] Henderson Yoakum's diary, University of Texas Archives.

[3] The Houston house in Huntsville survives in more or less the form described in the text, though it has undergone many changes since its use as a museum. Investigation from an architectural point of view must include an observation of

panded the existing house of logs. The loft was converted into two bedrooms, separated by a low hall, whose ends were open and barred, so that the children would not fall out when they used the breezy hall as a playroom. Each of the bedrooms upstairs had heating facilities but no wooden sheathing to insulate them. A steep, enclosed stair rose in a closet in the lower hall. Dark, weathered logs butted against gables of new lumber, which, because of its expense and scarcity, was used judiciously. Two windowless rooms were partitioned at the opposite ends of the front porch, leaving between them a loggia for summer dining. The front of the house seems to have become the back at this time. Now facing the creek and a pretty, sloping meadow, the house gained a feeling of style. The open back of the hall was embellished by the addition of a pediment, which sheltered the upper hall, and a crude portico to shelter the lower one. Latticed and supported by four plain columns, the stoop was a comical attempt at a classic veranda.

---

other houses in similar locales and of the same period. This has been extensively done. The architectural historian Drury Blakely Alexander has pointed out that the house evolved from a single cabin. If this was the case, work was apparently done on an existing building before the Houstons could move in, for they occupied Raven Hill for several months prior to actually living in the new house. The second floor was there at Christmas, 1849, and it was partitioned into two bedrooms and a hall, which was open (see Henderson Yoakum's diary, University of Texas Archives). I am convinced that the house was expanded from a log cabin, both because the logs were deliberately finished for appearance's sake and because it would have been unusual to have built a squared-log house for the sole purpose of covering it up. All the windows on the front of the house date from the Houstons' occupancy, though the rest are since that time. Undoubtedly there were unglazed openings, if any, in all but the two principal rooms of the house. The bulk of the lumber siding is of a later date than that of the gables and might never have been known by the Houstons. White paint is always conjectural in frontier houses, but inevitable in a restoration of one. The Houston house is painted. Houston's campaign biogaphy, written shortly after the family moved to the new house, describes a "log cabin."

Near her church and her friends, Margaret created an idyllic environment. The county of Walker, which had just been officially organized, was not a populous place but one that expected great prosperity from cotton. One visitor to Huntsville during that period said it was "a town of growing importance . . . rivaling in growth and prosperity other towns in the State of older standing."[4] The citizens were farmers dedicated to having a fine city some day. Stores and saloons stood in proximity to houses and barns over the several hills of the town. At a high place the courthouse commanded the center of the square. The streets were mud washes with the usual roots and stumps impeding passage, clutching wagon wheels, and enduring because they were strong. Austin College was new, and money was being raised to build a good building for it; the Huntsville Male Academy opened with optimism. Phrasemakers called Huntsville the "Athens of Texas." Cincinnati, fifteen miles out on the Trinity, also claimed the title, as did some other places. But Huntsville was so pleasantly the possessor of its hilly domain that none of the townsmen seemed to know the difference.

Several congregations were organized locally. Margaret joined the Baptists, led by Reverend J. W. D. Creath, whose wife Frances was Margaret's closest friend. There was no church building in Huntsville because of dissension among the believers.[5] Small Texas towns usually built one church where various denominational services were scheduled on alternate Sundays and open to everyone. Creath fought with the other church people over fundamentalist doctrine. "My heart," wrote Margaret, "is deeply grieved for my beloved church." There had been a conference for the purpose of dismissing Creath. Houston told his wife to stay at home. "I had forgotten," Margaret replied in a letter, "to notice

[4] Melinda Rankin, *Texas in 1850*, 138.
[5] *Ibid.*, 138–42.

your request not to interfere in Mr. Creath's case, a request from you is second to a duty injoined by my Heavenly Father, but your letter came after the conference was over."[6]

It was important to Margaret that the church exist calmly. When Sam Houston was at home, he attended services with her, and she knew that religious controversy would only drive him away, for he was impatient with bickering preachers. To help matters, Margaret offered her house for meetings. She had Thomas Gott enlarge a pool in the creek for purposes of baptism, which the church practiced there. Through her bedroom window she saw the pool and was continually reminded of the goal she had set for the hero of San Jacinto.

Her letters to Houston contained religious notes. "Have you heard of Lucy Ann Lea's conversion?"[7] Lucy Ann was Henry's oldest child. If Christ could come to a young girl, then the same could be true of anybody. Sam Houston's children said their prayers and daily heard Bible stories. Virginia Thorne had already been baptized by Brother Creath.[8] "You have nothing but the great world about you, with its heartlessness and mockery of joy . . . but I am enjoying the sweet belief, dearest, that you will draw from the word of God, from prayer and meditation, rich consolation."[9]

Margaret's religion was emotional. In her excitement her pen sometimes recorded curious scenes: "Today while reading my precious Bible, the words seemed so sweet that with child-like fondness involuntarily I pressed it to my heart and buried my weeping eyes in its hallowed pages."[10] She begged Houston not to

[6] Margaret Lea Houston to Sam Houston, Huntsville, December 19, 1848, Franklin Williams Collection.

[7] *Ibid.*

[8] Henderson Yoakum's diary, University of Texas Archives.

[9] Margaret Lea Houston to Sam Houston, Huntsville, December 19, 1848, Franklin Williams Collection.

be cynical about the Huntsville Baptists. "The Lord will not suffer the cloud to rest upon us always. Ah no, there are too many praying spirits amongst us."[11]

General Houston was kept reminded of the happiness he was missing by being in Washington. His wife sent letters to his desk in the Senate. "Long before this I suppose you have entered upon your arduous duties. I feel deeply for you, when I think of the tiresome routine that awaits you day after day. How much happier you might be with your little band at home."[12]

He was in Texas for a short stay in September of 1848. Always a popular speaker, he was now more in demand than ever, and he seldom refused an invitation. The Mexican War had extended the United States to the Pacific. Sam Houston's San Jacinto was one of the events of the era. The senator, through speeches and letters to the editor, wove his name as brilliantly as he could into the fabric of recent American history. Audiences cheered him from New Haven to New York City to Baltimore. The general's showmanship seemed overwhelmingly unaffected. He was in his mid-fifties and stood straight, even when the painful wounds made a cane necessary. An anguished expression emanated faintly from his face, giving the romantic effect of an old gallant reflecting on his experiences. While his attitude did not betray the fact, he suffered from chronic nervousness, which sometimes made it difficult for him to sleep and manifested itself elsewhere in his habit of whittling. Recipients of his whittled creations took them home and treasured the precisely cut corners and smooth surfaces of crosses and toy hearts. A man of courtly manners, Sam Houston

[10] Margaret Lea Houston to Sam Houston, Huntsville, March 4 [18?], Texas State Archives.

[11] Margaret Lea Houston to Sam Houston, Huntsville, December 19, 1848, Franklin Williams Collection.

[12] *Ibid.*

was attractive anywhere, and to insure the fact he costumed himself to draw attention, in rawhide boots, Mexican shawls, and leopard-skin vests and cuffs. In the eastern United States he fulfilled the popular vision of the Texan, a wild, irreverent man, yet one blessed with common sense unpoisoned by devious organizations of politicians.[13]

At home, Margaret worried lest some detail not be correct in Houston's sojourn with her. As hostess she made abundant recompense for her laziness as a housekeeper. The gray-haired mutton-chopped senator sat down at one of the most famous tables in all of East Texas. Eliza operated the kitchen and cooked the cakes that brought compliments to Margaret. Houston's friends never hesitated to stop by for a meal, according to the custom of a day when there were insufficient means of preserving food and quantities of it had to be cooked and eaten or thrown to the hogs. Henderson Yoakum, a prominent Huntsville attorney, met with Houston, spending entire days talking business in the office. At mealtime, Houston and his guests walked to the house, where in the summertime they were served at the cherry banquet table Margaret placed in the loggia. She set her table with monogrammed silver and surrounded it with homely mule-ear chairs whose cowhide seats, the general liked to note, retained their animal hair.

Houston invited friends from all over Texas to visit him at home. A great talker, the general missed the company of men when he was with his household. He had few close friends, for he

[13] My description of Houston is from portraits and verbal descriptions contemporary with him. Houston was very aware of his public appearance; each account, whether photographic or verbal, bears some pretention. The best portraits are found in the San Jacinto Museum of History, the Sam Houston Memorial Museum, the Eastman House, Rochester, New York, the collection of Mrs. Jerome Head, Terrell, Texas, the collection of Mrs. Cade Downs, San Augustine, Texas, and the University of Texas' Barker Texas History Center.

was rarely sympathetic toward the frankness in others that he prized in himself. His sarcasms could be offensive, unless the beseiged party could reply in a manner sufficient to end the conversation in laughter. Sam Houston alluded frequently to his own place in history. He believed himself to be a man of destiny, and he was concerned over what the future would say about him. Perceptive people had known all along that time would look with disfavor on those who opposed annexation. Houston, always cognizant of public opinion, had realized the fact before most, and he had cleverly made himself appear to be the lone designer of annexation. Anson Jones, in bitter retirement, was writing to vindicate himself, believing that he deserved the credit and that Houston deserved condemnation as a liar. In his many speeches endorsing Lewis Cass for President of the United States, Houston gave extravagant attention to his part in the annexation negotiations, denying that he had ever opposed Texas' joining the Union.

During that period, the late 1840's, Houston felt his first failing before the public. His popularity in the eastern United States grew while his stature in Texas declined, and his speeches show his mind turning more to national interests than ever before. He believed his greatest future would be achieved in a national office, but the individualist in him began to resent the regimentation and the hierarchy within the Democratic party. Sensationalist talk of breaking up the United States alarmed Houston. His political philosophy was based in the concept of a strong Union. Obscure figures in the Democratic party banded together under radical banners, and their respective states, conditioned by economic situations that had long bred an insular form of patriotism, cheered them on to greater daring. The circumstances of Houston's career were different from those of the newer people. He had gone to Washington well clothed in fame and prestige. Though he was of moderate national importance politically, he was associated with a past generation of distinguished statesmen. Certainly he was the closest thing to a Texas version of Henry Clay or Daniel Webster. As death reduced the number of the venerable ones, light shone brighter on Sam Houston, who welcomed its warmth and, able politician that he was, exerted himself to increase his appeal to the American people.

In his occupation with his own national career, Houston had permitted new political material to grow on Texas soil. While as yet the new politicians were no formidable enemy, the foundation they had laid was mighty. Yearly they would stand taller before him. Their ideas of disunion were Houston's favorite targets, and when he shot at them, his bullets were dependable Jacksonian principles, which, to the majority of the Texans, were indisputably true, if elsewhere in the country they evoked only nostalgia.

Back in Washington the memory of home rang in Houston's mind. The Houstons did not like the original name of their farm, Bermuda Spring, and the general suggested changing it to "Woodland Home," though he said, "You are free, My Love, to select a better name."[14] Margaret, in the new year of 1849, had concerns more serious than the naming of a house. Her retreat seemed violated by a growing attraction between Virginia Thorne and the overseer Thomas Gott. When Margaret had hired Gott, there had seemed nothing questionable about having him in the house. Virginia was fourteen, and Gott was about twenty-six. What was happening was Virginia's fault.

The girl had been an uncomfortable addition to the Houston household, though Margaret felt that it would be unfair to return her to Grand Cane. Vernal was her real guardian, but his farm was remote and far from schools. The attachment to Gott began more easily when Virginia lied and told him that she was nineteen. She

[14] Sam Houston to Margaret Lea Houston, Washington, D.C., February 9, 1849, *Writings*, V, 74.

began following him in his duties around the farm, and at night they sat on the porch and talked, infuriating Margaret with their procrastination when she ordered Virginia to go to bed. Gossips in town began to whisper of an intimacy between Virginia and the overseer.

Margaret heard the gossip and the whole aspect of her paradise seemed endangered. She went to Frances Creath, Melicia Baines, and the wife of Dr. Evans, asking if the problem should be brought before the Baptist church. The ladies protested that the church was the last resort because its investigation would merely increase the public's curiosity. They advised Margaret to handle her domestic difficulties at home. Mrs. Creath offered to ask Virginia to visit her in town for several weeks. Since the women seemed to know what they were talking about, Margaret complied and sent Virginia to stay with the Creaths, who believed that an absence from Gott would cause the girl's fascination to cease.[15]

On Sundays, Houston took leisurely afternoons to write long letters home. He called them "Sunday Replies" to Margaret's correspondence.[16] His letters had gained a new interest for his wife when she learned he was attending services at the E Street Baptist Church of Washington, D.C. The cogent young minister George Whitfield Samson stood challenged by the tall man who ambled into his church and sat before the pulpit whittling little toys as he listened to the sermon. After the service, Houston, "draped in a Mexican blanket," waited to speak to the preacher. He said he would not ordinarily have been in church, but that respect for Mrs. Houston, "one of the best Christians on earth," drew him there.[17]

[15] The details of the Virginia Thorne affair are recorded in the Henderson Yoakum diary, University of Texas Archives. Unless otherwise stated, the details of the Thorne incident are from that diary.

[16] Crane, *Life and Select Literary Remains*, 242.

[17] *Ibid.*, 241.

Margaret heard the news with joy. It was progress in the "divine life" she so zealously wanted for him.[18] Her labors took on new meaning; she had been given a sign to go forward more passionately into the wilderness. "We are all in good health," she wrote. "Dear little Maggie had been very low with the winter fever, but through the blessing of God she is now a convalescent. Nannie says 'I want my Pa to come home.' Sam says I must tell you he will do as you say."[19]

Houston's replies were tender and directed frequently to the children, whose remarks about their father Margaret preserved. To Sam, Houston wrote, "Your letter made me very happy. You are a dear boy to send your Pa a pretty letter. You tell me that you are a good boy and . . . I know you would not tell any thing but the truth." Sam Houston was lonely for his children. "Many people talk to me every day about your Ma and yourself. They all want to see you both and say that they hear your pa has the best wife and best son that any husband and father has in Texas."[20] Sam was his father's special pride, and the general expressed pleasure at signs of character Margaret recorded when she described the boy's development.

"I think much about Nannie and Maggie," Houston wrote to Sam. "You say Maggy looks very smart. You did not tell me who little Maggy looks like."[21] It gratified the general to hear that his children resembled him. After the comparison was made, he usually discoursed on the particular child's superior intelligence. He wrote to Sam: "I am glad to hear that the hogs do well and

[18] Margaret Lea Houston to Sam Houston, Huntsville, January 28, 1850, Texas State Archives.

[19] Margaret Lea Houston to Sam Houston, Huntsville, December 19, 1848, Franklin Williams Collection.

[20] Sam Houston to Sam Houston, Jr., Washington, D.C., February 16, 1849, Sam Houston Hearne Collection.

[21] *Ibid.*

that matters are all in a fair way." The boy's interest in the farm indicated Margaret must let him have a taste of important duties. "I think I was seven years old when I began to work," the general wrote, though he believed Sam was yet "too small to drop corn. I hope my son I will be with you to show you how to work when you have to learn."[22] But Houston's most affectionate remarks were to Margaret: "Today I could only tell you I passed another lonesome night, and that my hopes soon to be with you brighten, as the sands of time run."[23]

Margaret's own loneliness would not have been as great if her house had been closer to the activities of the town. Nancy Lea could not understand why her daughter had permitted Houston to buy a place two miles out in the country. Mrs. Houston knew, however, that her husband derived pleasure from open fields and woodlands, that he liked to own creeks and springs where children might swim and fish, and that he had a vision of himself as a country squire. Even when Margaret, for fleeting moments, fancied that she might take the children and go to Washington to live, she prescribed "a pleasant boarding house . . . about 8 or 10 miles from the city," where "I would have your company, without being so much interrupted by visitors."[24]

Faithfully the letters from home arrived on Houston's desk in the Senate. The Texas senator escaped momentarily into the blissful world described by the dainty handwriting and picked up the pressed wildflowers that might have tumbled from the envelope into his lap. "It always creates in my heart the greatest pleasure to read your epistles . . . as the reception of a Bogart by a lady from

[22] *Ibid.*

[23] Sam Houston to Margaret Lea Houston, Washington, D.C., February 9, 1849, *Writings*, V, 74.

[24] Margaret Lea Houston to Sam Houston, Huntsville, February 8, 1851, Texas State Archives.

her devoted lover. Such a feeling as once existed in an old ladies garden *near* Mobile! My Love do you recollect everything about the incident? I do!"[25]

His letters reflected his efforts to please Margaret with his piousness. "They cannot get me here, *by urgency*, to attend the theatre, tho, I hear there are two in the city. I assure you my Love, that I have not ever seen the buildings, to know them! It is . . . regard for the feelings of my Dear that keeps me away, tho I have no earthly wish to go." To Margaret he gave credit: "Were I otherwise situated, I have no doubt but what I might attend them."[26]

Early in May, 1849, Houston was at home, with plans to spend the summer. His house was crowded, and he could not have failed to understand that some of the company was invited on his behalf. Most of the preachers in the region found places at the Houston dining table. The Creaths were frequent guests as was the Reverend George W. Baines, husband of Margaret's friend Melicia and a particular favorite of Houston. Baines was a clever, alert minister with a good education and a sense of independence not commonly found among the pitifully underpaid Baptist preachers. Houston liked to talk with him. Over the years a friendship developed that pleased Margaret more than Houston's relationship with anybody else outside the family.

Dinner was served to sometimes as many as twenty-two people. Besides guests, the Houston household, including the servants, comprised nineteen people. There were often occasions when fifteen guests sat down with the family to a meal. Traveling ministers, political friends, and people with letters of introduction

[25] Sam Houston to Margaret Lea Houston, Washington, D.C., March 7, 1849, Sam Houston Hearne Collection.

[26] Sam Houston to Margaret Lea Houston, Washington, D.C., February 19, 1848, Sam Houston Hearne Collection.

from all parts of the United States were company at the log house on the hillside. Nancy Lea's silver and cutlery supplemented what the Houstons lacked. Blue and white china tureens and platters, inexpensive purchases at Tom Gibbs's store, were placed on damask tablecloths that had been brought from Alabama. The monogrammed punch bowl was a gift sent by the Sultan of Morocco. If there were not enough chairs, young Sam sat on Santa Anna's mahogany medicine chest, a trophy from San Jacinto. William Christy's julep cups had seen their last whisky, but they served well for soup and fruit juices.

Prayer services followed breakfast and the evening meal. When the servants had removed the appointments from the table, Joshua placed chairs in rows on the porch. Margaret and the guests and the children sat on the front rows and all the servants sat behind them. General Houston, standing before the assembly, read the Bible and delivered a short explanation of what he had read. A hymn and a prayer ended the service. If Sam Houston was away from home, which was usually the case, a male guest or Margaret herself took his place.[27]

The house seems to have maintained the air of a carnival when Houston was at home. Curious people drove along the picket fence of Margaret's flower garden, and visitors came from various places. The children most vividly remembered the visits of the Indians. Houston had befriended several Indian tribes besides the Cherokees, and the Indians felt at home when they came and camped at the Houston farm. The meadow beyond the creek, in front of the house, was sometimes occupied by several hundred Indian men and women. A beef strung on saplings was cured for cooking. For days General Houston and special friends, like Henderson Yoakum, met in council with the Indians. They sat in

[27] Temple Houston Morrow to Mrs. Grace Longino, Lubbock, Texas, January 17, 1957, Sam Houston Memorial Museum.

a circle around a washtub, into which they tossed bones from the meat the women brought them to eat. The Indians sang and danced, and people walked out from Huntsville to see the performances. Before the Indians broke camp and left, they presented gifts to Houston and Margaret, who participated with reluctance, for she disliked the Indians' coming to her home. She was repulsed by what she must have considered a casual attitude toward sanitation, and all her life she had heard terrible Indian stories from Nancy Lea, who remembered Indian trouble in her Carolina girlhood.[28]

Houston and Margaret took the leisure to enjoy their family that summer of 1849. The comfortable expansion of the house was successful, and Houston took an interest in its interior decoration. Pictures of selected Texas heroes were hung on the log walls. At the time they sold the Houston City house the general had lent several of his pictures to Tom Bagby and to Major Nathaniel E. Kellum. Now he wanted one of two favorite portraits of himself to hang with at least three others of himself in the parlor: "What has become of those Portraits of mine? One was in military green dress, and one in citizen dress, Green also."[29]

Company was plentiful and Houston invited more. Ashbel Smith got a "hearty welcome" with the promise of "no great fuss." The lure was irresistible to the bachelor. "On the fourth of July, we are to have a Temperance blowout."[30] Smith's visit lasted two weeks, and he witnessed the meeting of the Sons of Temperance, to which gathering Sam Houston spoke. It must have strained propriety for Ashbel Smith not to laugh, for at the close of Houston's speech a coffin was borne into the hall by the town's bar-

[28] *Ibid.*; author in conversation with Mrs. Jennie Morrow Decker, Houston, January 15, 1964.

[29] Sam Houston to Tom Bagby, Huntsville, May 7, 1849, *Writings*, V, 92–93.

[30] Sam Houston to Ashbel Smith, Huntsville, May 31, 1849, *Writings*, V, 95.

tenders, and Drink was symbolically consigned to the earth in the graveyard outside. Margaret found the ceremony deeply moving.[31]

In mid-November, the visitors and Sam Houston were gone. Margaret received a letter Houston had written at a stagecoach stop the first night out on the eastward road. "I do pray that you may be cheerful in my absence, and not repine at what is unavoidable. . . . Nothing on earth can make me more happy than to know that you are happy." She was pregnant again. This time they anticipated there would be an Andrew Jackson Houston to add to the perfect existence she described to Sam Houston. He missed the children already. "Tell Sam, Nannie, and Maggy that I have preserved all the roses and chrysanthemums which they gave me. I will keep them."[32]

The mild winter brought Christmas uneventfully. Vernal married a Polk County girl named Catherine Davis, and they moved to the old Bledsoe place near Grand Cane, where Nancy Lea traveled in January to meet the bride. Houston's salary made life a little easier that new year of 1850, though he gave her money only when he was at home, and he spent too heavily in Washington. Margaret, having not the slightest concept of her financial condition and even less interest in finding out, saw her own inheritance, except for the slaves, slip through her fingers in the form of unrepaid loans to her family and general extravagances on the part of her husband.[33]

Margaret's efforts to correct Virginia Thorne aroused the girl's indignation, and even Captain Hatch felt that Margaret was harsh

[31] Undated newspaper clipping, files of Sam Houston, Sam Houston Memorial Museum.

[32] Sam Houston to Margaret Lea Houston, Douglas, November 18, 1849, *Writings*, V, 108–109.

[33] Margaret Lea Houston to Sam Houston, Grand Cane, November 27, 1848, Texas State Archives.

with her.[34] Virginia and Thomas Gott were quite open in their relationship. Since Gott disliked Mrs. Houston anyway, he seemed to find a certain pleasure in flaunting his indiscretions in her house. It became the delight of Huntsville's tongues. Margaret tried to ignore the town's maliciousness, but she could not.[35] The explosion came around Christmas. From Grand Cane, Nancy Lea had gone west to Independence to visit Varilla. Margaret and Virginia were upstairs one evening putting Sam and Nannie to bed.[36] Nannie would not sleep, so Margaret asked Virginia to get her out of bed. Irritated with Nannie, Virginia jerked her from the bed to the floor. Across the hall Margaret cried, "Don't hurt the child."[37]

"I am not hurting it," Virginia replied. She dragged the weeping child toward Margaret.[38]

Hurrying into the room, Margaret took Nannie, then turned on Virginia, who screamed, "Don't kill me." Margaret took a cowhide and struck Virginia twenty times on the shoulders, back, and arms. When she drew away, Virginia was slumped on the floor, sobbing. There were cuts on her right elbow and her wrist.[39]

The next evening Margaret called down from the upstairs hall to Virginia, who was sitting with Gott on the porch. "Virginia, be careful how you behave, remember what you got last night. That cowhide is still there."[40] From then on, Margaret and Virginia got along "finely," with Margaret remarking that Virginia was "happier and more cheerful . . . than I ever saw her."[41] Late Sun-

[34] Margaret Lea Houston to Sam Houston, Huntsville, January 28, 1850, Texas State Archives.

[35] Henderson Yoakum's diary, University of Texas Archives.

[36] *Ibid.*

[37] *Ibid.*

[38] *Ibid.*

[39] *Ibid.*

[40] *Ibid.*

[41] Margaret Lea Houston to Sam Houston, Huntsville, January 28, 1850, Texas State Archives.

day night, January 27, 1850, Margaret made a shocking discovery. With the knowledge fresh on her mind she wrote to General Houston the next morning.[42]

> You may prepare yourself for an astounding piece of news. On last night Virginia eloped with Gott, as I suppose to marry him, but today I learn that he has taken her to Cincinnati to go to school to Miss Rankin one session and then they are to marry. You may form some idea of my astonishment by your own, for I was totally unprepared for it.

Margaret was glad Virginia Thorne was gone. In Margaret's haven, Virginia had held nothing sacred, so there was no regret at her leaving. In her letter regarding Virginia, Margaret said that she had "the sweet assurance that I have been faithful to my trust."[43] Virginia had worried her and caused her to lose sleep. Margaret had prayed about it, and "truly the Lord has delivered me out of my great troubles."[44]

Nancy Lea returned to Huntsville with glowing reports of Independence and its Baptist inhabitants. She seems to have been renewed by her visit. "Mother," wrote Margaret, "never interferes in anything at all pertaining to the farm, but reads and meditates a great deal. I told her a short time ago that I believed the Lord sent old Mr. Hatch that she might be forced to give up her earthly cares and prepare for another world."[45] On the parlor wall hung a portrait of the widow Lea.[46] The limner had painted a stern countenance under a lace cap. His subject pointed her finger to the pages of an open Bible and looked back, lips pursed, her expression one of determination. Her occupations were few,

42 *Ibid.* 43 *Ibid.* 44 *Ibid.*

45 Margaret Lea Houston to Sam Houston, Huntsville, January 29, 1850, Texas State Archives.

46 Item, Kellum-Noble House, Harris County Heritage Society, Houston, Texas, gift of Mrs. Ben Calhoun; see also Pauline Pinkney, *Painting in Texas: The Nineteenth Century*, 23–27.

except for Bible reading and the pet pig, which amused her and the smallest grandchildren. To insure Nancy Lea's leisure, General Houston hired another resident overseer after the departure of Thomas Gott. The new man's name was Daniel Johnson, aged forty-nine. He had a son, Joe, who was nine and also lived in the house during his and his father's two-year residence with the Houstons. Nancy Lea's days became dedicated to preparing for death and the life thereafter, and, being a good businesswoman, she questioned ministers and sought appropriate Bible passages which might assure her in advance of the direction of her journey.

Soon winter came to an end. Margaret was proud of the home she described to General Houston in her letters. She knew he was susceptible to "our little rose buds and their noble brother." The children spoke often of their father: "I often sigh when I look at them and think how much happiness you are losing . . . I send you a boquet from your far off home. It bears a kiss from each of your little band and a message from one who loves you fondly, Ever Thine Own, Margaret."[47]

On April 9, Mary William Houston was born. General Houston had promised to be at home in time, but Margaret wrote for him not to hurry if his absence would harm the "democratic cause."[48] Antoinette came up from Matagorda to assist her sister. She snipped a lock of the infant's hair and sent it to Sam Houston with a note. A reply came in May. "I would tell you if I could how happy Sister's letter made me. My solicitude had been as great as you can imagine. Well, I am very happy to hear that it was a little daughter, tho' I would have been equally gratified if it had been a son." Remembering six-year-old Sam's amusing remarks about Margaret's pregnancy, Houston wrote, "Poor Sam, he will feel

[47] Margaret Lea Houston to Sam Houston, Huntsville, February 6, 1850, University of Texas Archives.

[48] *Ibid.*

the apparent injustice, I fear, and think he is not treated with justice or fairness . . . This looks but little like giving him the six brothers, tho' it appears something like the six little sisters." The senator took Antoinette to task. "Well, I was surprised to see the sweet little lock of hair and have it called *black* by Sister, for I assure you, when it reached me, it was a beautiful auburn or pretty golden lock. It certainly is not black."[49]

That spring Margaret sat in the hall and read Bible stories to the children, then followed them to pick flowers in the pastures. She wrote that she thought often of Houston's divine life on earth and how he must accept Christ in the symbolic ritual of the Baptist church. Progress only whetted Margaret's thirst for reaching her goal. She wrote long letters recommending discourses she had read or discussing religious books Houston might purchase for her in Washington.

Early in the summer Margaret's tranquillity came to an end. Thomas Gott and Virginia Thorne appeared in Huntsville and filed charges of assault and battery against her. Though she was assured that some political enemy of Houston's had instigated the suit, Margaret was terror struck. Vernal had been ill with malaria, and Eliza Houston Moore had died. The general's beloved sister Mary had gone insane, and the fact had so tormented Houston that he asked Ashbel Smith to go to her in Tennessee and save her from madness. Considering the problems already weighing on Houston's mind, Margaret feared that the public humiliation of his wife might have dangerous effects upon his stability.

Sam Houston was unable to come home because of commitments in Washington, so he wrote to Henderson Yoakum, who was involved with Austin College and research for a history of

[49] Sam Houston to Margaret Lea Houston, Washington, D.C., April 30, 1850, *Writings*, V, 145–47.

Texas. Yoakum engaged H. Gadknew and A. P. Wiley, himself remaining in an advisory capacity. A preliminary hearing was set for September 30, 1850. Mrs. Baines, Mrs. Creath, and Mrs. Evans stayed close to Margaret. In her letters Margaret acknowledged their concern but attributed her survival to God.

Houston comforted her. Even letters to the children bore words for Margaret. "Bad men and bad women," wrote Houston to Sam, "are the only beings that will not return good for good and kindness for kindness. . . . Bad or wicked people cannot be happy, and they are bad because they are the children of the Devil, and not the children of light. . . . You have a kind mother to teach you to be good and pray with you."[50]

The hearing was called to order on the scheduled Monday morning. It took place in private in a room on the first floor of the courthouse. Henderson Yoakum was refused admittance, but to keep his promise to Mrs. Houston, he sat on the ground beneath the courthouse windows. The day was hot, and, as he had calculated, the windows were raised, so Yoakum had no trouble hearing the proceedings, which he paraphrased in his journal.

Many people testified in Margaret's behalf, Frances Creath and Vernal Lea among them. Virginia related to the grand jury the events of that evening upstairs in Margaret's house. When Gadknew and Wiley asked her age, she said she did not know it. She said she had been told about the hearing only two days in advance, and that Gott and some other men had made all the arrangements. Finally she showed the scars on her elbow and wrist.

Thomas Gott gave a more certain testimony. The girl was nineteen, he said. He told of the evenings on the porch. Margaret's attorneys, in questioning Gott, found that he was "not

[50] Sam Houston to Sam Houston, Jr., Washington, D.C., September 23, 1850, *Writings*, V, 258.

always treated kindly" by Mrs. Houston and might bear a grudge.

The witnesses for Margaret praised her "mild and forbearing" manner with the children. Virginia's defiance was explained, and Mrs. Baines quoted Virginia as saying Margaret was a "lady and a Christian." A question was raised about Virginia's "setting up late at night" with Gott. Although the judge overruled the question, the subject was obviously an important factor for discussion. Someone asked that the windows be closed, and Henderson Yoakum's diary necessarily stopped. At sundown, Margaret and her friends left the courthouse. The grand jury was deadlocked, and the case was recommended to the Baptist church. Early in November, the church completed a "lengthy investigation." Margaret was fully acquitted.[51]

General Houston arrived home one week later, greatly disappointed that in spite of his rush from Washington he had missed the trial. He agreed with Yoakum "that the matter has been urged on & brought to court at the insistance of some of his enemies for the purpose of affecting him."[52] Knowing Margaret's feelings of guilt, Houston seems never to have sought revenge of any kind, although it is clear through his laughter that he was angry over his enemies' attack upon his wife.

The unhappy Virginia Thorne disappeared from the lives of the Houstons. Margaret never again mentioned the girl who had interfered with the sanctity of her home. More than ever, Mrs. Houston directed her energies toward the day on which Sam Houston would accept Jesus Christ. Houston had written to her from the Senate: "I attended church today, as usual, and as I intend to do every Sunday. . . . I have not lain down a single night

[51] Henderson Yoakum's diary, University of Texas Archives.
[52] *Ibid.*

. . . that I have not read a portion of the New Testament. . . . I feel more pleasure and instruction in reading the scriptures than I ever did."[53] Soon afterward she wrote, "Go on my beloved . . . and the Lord will give you more and more light."[54]

But Margaret's day was slow to break in Sam Houston. "My Love," he wrote, "I do not feel that holy and gratified devotion that I ought and wish to do. The time I pray for is when you with many other pious persons will find in my conversion an answer to your prayers."[55]

In the windy January of 1852, Nancy Lea found things to complain about, probably more because of the bitter cold than the fact that she had to remain in Huntsville until Margaret's fifth child was born, which would be at any time. Temple Lea's widow had aged remarkably. White hair framed her deeply wrinkled face. She talked and wrote about the nearness of her own death to her children and to her twenty-four grandchildren in Alabama and Texas. No wonder the family was surprised when Mrs. Lea announced that she had already begun construction of a new house for herself. It was in Independence, where Varilla lived, near Washington-on-the-Brazos. The Baptists' Baylor College was there, and the town was another "Athens of Texas," with civilization, a good climate, and abundant clergy.

Margaret's pregnancy had not been as easy as the four prior pregnancies. Since Christmas she had remained in bed, writing daily long letters to Sam Houston. The general would not be at home for the baby's birth. Early one wintery morning Margaret

[53] Sam Houston to Margaret Lea Houston, Washington, D.C., January 20, 1850, Franklin Williams Collection.

[54] Margaret Lea Houston to Sam Houston, Huntsville, January 28, 1850, Texas State Archives.

[55] Sam Houston to Margaret Lea Houston, Washington, D.C., January 20, 1850, Franklin Williams Collection.

was awakened by little Sam. He told her he did not want "any more sisters, but a little brother to play with." Margaret, in relating the incident, said she was puzzled why he was so bothered, but she "did not question him about it."[56] The prospective mother wanted only for the childbirth to be over with. Her pain was increased by the chill wind that came between the log walls of the house. She stayed in bed to keep warm. "I had an uncomfortable night, and it is so cold today that I can hardly hold my pen."[57] Isabella, the housekeeper Houston had hired in New England and sent to Huntsville, kept great fires burning in the fireplaces, which terrified Maragaret because of their danger to the wooden roof.

Winter's smells and the frost on the tall glass windows were far removed from the past summer when Sam Houston had been at home. "I am farming in a small way," he had then written to a friend, "and am as busy as a 'bee in a tar barrel,' planting peas, corn, rice, and millet." He had bought more cows. "I love milk and butter and they are fine for children." Farthest from his mind, he insisted, had been politics. "I do not talk of them, I have not written of them, and if you will believe me, I think but little about them!"[58]

Against her pillows that winter, thinking of the summer, Margaret wrote, "My time will pass pleasantly with the hope of seeing you soon."[59] There had been talk of his running for president on the Democratic ticket. The talk was strongest in Texas, but it was not exclusively a Texas idea. Houston was impressed by the ap-

[56] Margaret Lea Houston to Sam Houston, Huntsville, January 7, 1852, University of Texas Archives.

[57] *Ibid.*

[58] Sam Houston to Nicholas Dean, Huntsville, May 8, 1851, *Writings*, V, 297–99.

[59] Margaret Lea Houston to Sam Houston, Huntsville, January 7, 1852, University of Texas Archives.

plauding audiences on the East Coast, at dinner engagements and speeches which he made to conservative Democrats. His flock of young admirers did not make him forget the irony that some of his obstacles to the presidency were ambitious young members of the Democratic party. Political parties themselves had changed since the old days. Personality meant less than it had in Sam Houston's earlier political career. He remembered a time of stump speaking, when a lively orator with a penchant for drama was the man likely to capture the most votes. The political scene was not noticeably changed in Texas. In many other places, however, the emphasis upon independent political personalities was dying out. The political party became a more dominant feature, its carefully groomed candidates introducing sensational emotional issues on the platform, while the machine connived in private to make political alliances. Sam Houston found himself alien less to the technique than to the powers behind the system. When he began to fight for his own advancement, his only course was to seek the support of the people through a direct confrontation. Enough thousands of people responded to Houston's bravo that he rallied a flattering national following.

Margaret knew her husband's career faced brighter prospects in Washington. As for his coming to Huntsville for the baby's birth, "It is my wish," she wrote, "that you should weigh the matter well, and not do anything that can properly militate against your interest, or take any other step that you may hereafter regret."[60] In her generosity Margaret was not playing the martyr, for she was no sacrificial lamb. But she was jealous of the capital that took Sam Houston away. "I can imagine but one attraction that the great city of Washington would permit me, and that is my husband's society," and that "would be far sweeter in some wildwoods shade, for there I could have it all to myself."[61]

[60] *Ibid.* [61] *Ibid.*

The hardship of their separation was made easier for Margaret by knowing that Houston was cognizant of his responsibilities to God. "I rejoice to find," Margaret praised him, "that in the midst of your many cares, and surrounded as you are by gay company, you still find time for your religious duties and for good books. I am not surprised that you see the nothingness and vanity of all around you."[62] Margaret wrote as confidently as though she had visited Washington in person. Houston accepted her criticism of the capital and admitted to a warm sentiment about home: "Tho' my life has been one of strange vicissitudes and dark clouds have often shrouded my horizon in deep gloom, almost bordering upon despair . . . [when] I am at home in my woodland residence with my wife and brats, I feel no disposition to return again to the scenes of official conflict."[63]

Antoinette Power Houston was born on January 20, 1852. The birth was wrought with complications, and Margaret was still confined to her bedroom when Houston arrived at home in February. From Washington he brought "bonnets" and "dresses" and toys for Sam and "My pretty little flock of *girls*."[64] For Margaret he had a gold locket engraved "Mrs. Sam Houston, Texas."[65]

The Texas Democratic Convention had sent Houston's name to the Democratic National Convention as a favorite son candidate for President of the United States. General Houston's enthusiasm was not matched by any joy on Margaret's part. Even a remote possibility of having to move to Washington, particularly as first lady, frightened her. She would have been a young hostess,

[62] *Ibid.*

[63] Sam Houston to Nicholas Dean, Huntsville, May 8, 1851, *Writings*, V, 297–99.

[64] Sam Houston to John R. Burke, Huntsville, July 19, 1851, *Writings*, V, 302–303.

[65] Item, Franklin Williams Collection.

nearly thirty-three, and she would have been a pretty one. Illness and childbirth's toll was slight. Her violet eyes and pale white skin were youthful looking and accented by her mahogany-colored hair, which she liked to part in the middle and sweep up over Spanish combs, then allow to hang to her waist in finger curls.[66] She liked to dress in clothes that pleased Sam Houston, in purples or maroon, but the idea of being a lady of fashion in the national capital did not interest her.[67]

Sam Houston was happier about his career than he had been since the Mexican War. The isolation of Huntsville seems to have bored him in his stay at home. He worried about Margaret's slow recovery from Nettie's birth, and the education of the children was not being conducted entirely to his liking. Isabella had the children "bewitched," but perhaps a governess was not sufficient, especially for Sam.[68] The general listened with interest to Nancy Lea's praise of Independence as a great center for Christian educations.

Houston departed for the East in April, and soon Nancy Lea moved to Independence. Margaret's asthma attacks had sent her to Cedar Point the summer before in hopes of finding relief in the salt wind. The whole family was afraid that the humid, pollen-laden air of the pine country would be bad for her health. In July, Margaret and four of the children rode to Grand Cane in the yellow coach to visit Vernal and Catherine Lea. Laboring to support his wife and their child, Vernal had wrecked himself physically. Consumption had developed, and he had to stop working at a time when his land was at last operating successfully and when

[66] Shuffler, *The Houstons at Independence*; see also portrait, Texana Collection, Undergraduate Reading Center, University of Texas.

[67] Author in conversation with Mrs. Jennie Morrow Decker and Mrs. F. S. Baldwin, Houston, January 20, 1965.

[68] Sam Houston to Nicholas Dean, Huntsville, May 8, 1851, *Writings*, V, 297–99.

he was only thirty-seven years of age. His only alternative to save his health was to go to nearby Sour Lake and bathe in the mud springs.

Back in Huntsville, Margaret missed her kin. She had no idea when Houston would appear, but her family seemed settled, with Nancy Lea and Varilla at Independence, Antoinette at Matagorda, and Vernal on the Trinity. Houston wrote of coming home. "I want you to tell Joshua to have the filly in good order and well rubbed."[69] He obviously had no intention of staying at home when he returned to Texas.

Margaret was otherwise lonesome. Dr. and Mrs. Baines had moved to Anderson; Dr. and Mrs. Evans now lived on a farm in the country. Besides Frances Creath, Margaret had few friends left in Huntsville. She had some comfort from Houston's attendance at Brother Samson's Baptist church in Washington. Houston sometimes sent her abstracts of Samson's sermons in his Sunday replies. She read the abstracts and penciled them as a schoolmaster might do and discussed salient points with her husband.[70] Huntsville's world was one of hard-working and usually narrow-minded farmers, who had little time, and sometimes no respect, for books. Margaret Houston's scholarly interests were an exception to the local way of life, and she found herself starved for intellectual companionship.

The children's schooling was a subject Margaret and General Houston discussed with increasing concern. Margaret reported that the children were "more and more interesting," that Nannie was the most clever of all, her mind a "mighty Niagara that rushes impetuously over every obstacle." One day Nannie asked what was the sin that caused the devil's fall. "I told her it was pride. She

[69] Sam Houston to Sam Houston, Jr., Washington, D.C., July 19, 1852, *Writings*, V, 347–49.

[70] Crane, *Life and Select Literary Remains*, 242.

then asked how pride could get into the heart of a pure angel, and if God had not put it there." Sam Houston must realize that these were not ordinary children. They required special treatment: "Nannie is a strange child and although her intellect is so masculine, her nervous system is so exceedingly delicate that she cannot bear the least harshness." Margaret was sometimes specific. "If she should ever be deprived of a mother's care, and thrown upon your hands, my dear husband, let her always be controlled through her affection and judgements."[71]

The old brooding about death had come over her again. If Margaret should die, then Sam Houston would control the children's upbringing. Was Houston strong enough to lead the children in the Godly path? Margaret was obsessed to know that her works on earth would be permanent, should she go to the grave. In Christ, she believed, was the only assurance. And General Houston had not accepted Christ.

In the last months of 1852, Margaret reflected on a sad year. Henry Lea had died in his sleep in Marion. When Margaret heard the news, she went to Independence to comfort her mother. A letter announcing Vernal's death arrived before she returned to Huntsville. It was otherwise a year she would not forget. A mighty hurricane swept the Gulf Coast. In its wake, the Charles Powers' sugar plantation was destroyed. Power was left nearly penniless. He hitched his oxen to fallen cypress trees and his family and slaves moved to Independence. With the cypress they built an unpretentious house.[72] At Independence, Antoinette gave birth to Margaret Houston Power, a sickly baby whose needs gave new life to the bereaved Nancy Lea.

[71] Margaret Lea Houston to Sam Houston, Huntsville, January 7, 1852, University of Texas Archives.

[72] Clippings in collection of Mrs. John L. Little, Sr.

Houston was at home for three days in February, 1853. He was re-elected to the Senate in a satisfactory victory over Texas' infant party organization, whose campaign, though localistic, was tinged with the ideas of the radical branch of the national Democratic party. The general had sold himself and his conservatism with gusto. He accepted his office in Austin and returned from there to Washington.

By the time of his return in early June, he and Margaret had decided to move to Independence. Ostensibly the reason for the move was Sam's education.[73] The boy was enrolled by his father in the new Male Department of Baylor University that July. Two months later Houston acquired a house. "I bought the premises of Mr. Hines on the hill to the left as you go out of Independence, consisting of two-hundred acres timbered land adjoining the town tract—all for $4,000, in short payments."[74]

The house in Huntsville was rented to Professor and Mrs. L. J. Goree, who had resigned at Judson College and had accepted positions in Huntsville. Exactly why the house was not sold is puzzling, for Houston wrote that at Independence, "I intend . . . to spend the residue of my days should Heaven be pleased to give me more."[75] The plain country furniture, for the most part, stayed in Huntsville. Margaret ordered new tables, chairs, a sideboard,

[73] Houston was an active supporter of Austin College at Huntsville. Early in 1853, he and Samuel McKinney, president of the college, had a disagreement which resulted in McKinney's resignation on June 29, 1853. Undoubtedly this had something to do with the Houstons' removal to Independence and the decision to enroll Sam in Baylor. Any speculation that the Gorees were brought to Huntsville by the Houstons is tempting but has little support in the manuscripts. See Dan Ferguson, "Austin College," *Southwestern Historical Quarterly*, Vol. LIII, 398.

[74] Sam Houston to Washington D. Miller, Washington, D.C., September 13, 1853, *Writings*, V, 456–58.

[75] Sam Houston to Washington D. Miller, Huntsville, August 24, 1853, *Writings*, V, 185.

wardrobes, and bureaus sent to her house in Independence.[76] Latrobe stoves were bought to replace the open fires Margaret feared. Margaret bade farewell to her friends and to Isabella, who, over the objections of the family, returned to New England. The Houstons moved west, sadly perhaps, for they had loved Huntsville.

On October 25, 1853, the coach rolled into Independence. Nurses, babies, and luggage filled the coach and the accompanying wagons. General Houston rode ahead with Nannie in his black buggy. The spectacle of Independence must have made Margaret feel as though she had been a prisoner in the woods. Independence was not much larger than Huntsville, but it was grander. Dominating the landscape were the two divisions of Baylor, regularly planned arrangements of yellow limestone and wooden buildings in the Greek Revival fashion. White board fences enclosed each structure at the college and most of the houses, inns, and shops that lined the several avenues leading from the college's high hills. Gnarled, dry-looking oak trees shaded the streets. Some of the houses were of stone; fewer, like Antoinette's and Nancy Lea's, were wooden.

The Houston house was near the college end of the longest avenue. It was a pleasant old place set back from the road, with an orchard, a spring, and a small log house with an open hallway and a wing of rooms to the rear.[77] Mrs. Lea was two long blocks away, beyond the Baptist church. Antoinette and Varilla lived in the country, eastward, toward Washington-on-the-Brazos. Houston left his family in Independence and began traveling in Texas, making speeches against anti-Union men and the new party organization in Texas. The furniture arrived broken and poorly

[76] Sam Houston to William Sarla, Independence, November 28, 1853, *Writings*, V, 463–64.

[77] Photograph, collection of Mrs. F. S. Baldwin.

mended with wax. "I would not accept [it] as a gift," wrote Houston to the coastal dealer.[78]

The Houstons liked Independence from the start. While the air did not improve Margaret's asthma, it was more enjoyable to live near Nancy Lea than to live so far away in East Texas. Sam and Nannie walked to school. Joshua or Eliza climbed the hill to take their lunch pails to them at noon. In the evenings after the children's bedtimes, Margaret and the general walked over to Nancy Lea's house to drink coffee and talk in Mrs. Lea's long parlor.

Nancy Lea still spoke often about death and had even ordered her coffin, a metal one, from New Orleans. On the back of her property, immediately across the side street from the church, she had built a tomb of plastered limestone with a heavy iron portal. There was space inside for her and Varilla and Antoinette and Margaret, but no husbands.[79]

One could walk to the Baptist church from any place in Independence. It was a plain structure without a bell or a stove. Services there, however, were known as the best Baptist services in Texas. There was little of the loud testimony here that Margaret had witnessed in Huntsville, and while it seems to have pleased her less, General Houston became fond of the church.

Rufus Burleson was the president of Baylor College, and he occupied an octagonal house on the edge of town. More realist than dreamer, more aggressive churchman than preacher, the young Burleson controlled the college and thereby controlled a substantial part of Independence. Sam Houston tolerated him, though they rarely agreed on anything. It was important to Mar-

[78] Sam Houston to William Sarla, Independence, November 28, 1853, *Writings*, V, 463–64.

[79] Document dated 1886, collection of Mrs. John L. Little, Sr., describes the tomb; see also Margaret Lea Houston to Sam Houston, Jr., Independence, February 16, 1864, Sam Houston Hearne Collection.

garet that Houston would consent to discussing his personal philosophy with Burleson, for the preacher, who enjoyed associating himself with the famous Texan, would give the general sage advice in spiritual affairs. Houston seems to have had a layman's familiarity with the Bible. Often he livened the conversations and infuriated Burleson by insisting that birds brought divine revelations of the future. Christianity was more difficult for Houston to accept than for a man of less experience and fewer convictions. Rufus Burleson argued with him until late at night. At times neither he nor Houston could drop a topic when they parted. On one occasion Houston became so irritated when Burleson's sermon in church continued an argument of a previous date that he stood up, interrupted the sermon, and attempted to correct the speaker.[80]

Independence assumed a special significance to Margaret when she found that its pious population was an inspiration to General Houston. The Baineses lived at Anderson, a short buggy-ride away. Margaret sometimes drove to Anderson with Burleson's beautiful wife Georgia Jenkins and visited the Baineses. Brother Baines was a patient adviser, and he remained Sam Houston's strongest friend in religious matters.

When Senator Houston rode away at Christmas, 1853, he knew Margaret would have another child in the summer. She faithfully wrote to him, telling family anecdotes and including notes from the children. All the family letters were important to Sam Houston. A child's neglect of the father was often felt sharply. Of Sam he wrote, "I do not intend to send him any more [newspapers] until he writes me and asks for them. He has made my heart *sad*; I am fearful that he is too *selfish* either to be happy himself or to try to make others happy"; to Nannie, "I delight,

80 Mrs. Georgia Burleson (ed.), *The Life and Writings of Rufus C. Burleson, D.D., L.L.D.* (privately printed, 1901), 114.

my Daughter, that you try to make others happy and thereby make yourself happy. . . . If Sam is *penitent*, you *may* kiss him for me!"[81] Houston gave advice: "Kindness is so beautiful in children that all should while young learn to be kind and look upon the smiles which it lights up in pleasure."[82]

Houston had been in Washington a short time when he made a dramatic political move. He rose and opposed the Democrats' Kansas-Nebraska Bill, which was political grandstanding in the form of a proposal to destroy the limitations set on slavery by the Missouri Compromise. Houston thought the idea dangerous, and he loathed the bill's radical creators. He shrewdly endorsed the extension of slavery, but only southward into territories yet to be possessed, perhaps over the Río Grande, where he thought it feasible. The Kansas-Nebraska Bill was, as Houston knew it would be, very popular in Texas among politicians, powerful businessmen, and newspapers. By opposing the bill, Houston opposed his party. The act was fatal so far as his affiliation with the party was concerned. Yet he had faith that because of his act his name would increase sufficiently in national popularity to sustain him. His reasoning seemed sound. The White House was not entirely an impossibility in his future. He knew that a vast pool of voters were dissatisfied and might unite behind one dynamic man who promised optimism and stability. The time for such a hero to step out before the public had to be perfectly opportune. Sam Houston was a master of good timing, though his stage had previously been smaller. Kansas-Nebraska had been his first cue, and he had answered it.

The senator scarcely heard the vicious attacks from Texas, so

[81] Sam Houston to Nannie E. Houston, Washington, D.C., February 2, 1854, *Writings*, V, 374.

[82] Sam Houston to Sam Houston, Jr., Washington, D.C., January 15, 1853, Sam Houston Hearne Collection.

sweetly did New England's praises fall on his ears. He swept his Mexican blanket over his shoulders and straightened his beaver hat. While touring the cities and hamlets of the East Coast, he bowed to a thunder of applause. On jerking railroad cars he wrote notes to his little girls and his son.

In the spring he was at home in Independence. Margaret, pregnant and confined to some degree, jealously watched him in the capture of controversy. Rufus Burleson took him to Brenham to speak to the Baptists there, and after a week's interrupted visit at home the general was gone. Margaret went to bed, complaining that she was ill.

June was the ninth month. Margaret lay in her high-post bed depressed and uncertain about her fourteen years of marriage. She admitted to happiness, but also to frustration. "As usual," she wrote to Houston, "I have serious presentiments with regard to my situation, but I am striving hard to attain a perfect resignation to the will of God." It was the finest triumph of life to believe in the Heavenly Father, "and if it should be his blessed will to call me away at this time, I trust I shall be enabled to confide our little ones and their dear father to his care."[83]

Death was all around Margaret. Nancy Lea wandered to the tomb and poked at its walls with her stick, then walked to Margaret's bedside, to keep Margaret company in the days approaching childbirth. The old lady seemed sad to Margaret—"It is a mournful thing, particularly as I think she does not realize . . . she is talking every day about arranging her temporal matters for death."[84] Antoinette's little girl died of pneumonia, and Antoinette came to Margaret to pour out her sorrow. Death's frightening prospect disturbed Margaret's sleep. Her idleness

[83] Margaret Lea Houston to Sam Houston, Independence, June 14, 1854, Sam Houston Hearne Collection.

[84] *Ibid.*

gave her time to worry. Eliza operated the household, and Charles Power consulted with Joshua about the farm. Margaret was able to enjoy her children but was not obliged to be near them if she did not want to be. Of the children she wrote, "They cannot sympathize with me in my trials and sufferings."[85] Her longing was for personal peace. This she was able to satisfy to some degree with bright thoughts of Sam Houston's conversion.

On June 21, the women stepped back from the bed and Nancy Lea and Eliza smiled at Andrew Jackson Houston. The sixth one was a boy. Sam Houston was not there to appreciate the fact, nor had he stated a possibility of his coming soon. During the last months Margaret had written, "If you were with me, I am sure I could be cheerful, but without you . . . my spirit . . . shrinks into its . . . solitude."[86] The letters from Washington were for all the family. "I send now apple seeds," he wrote to Sam, "which you may plant. . . . I hope my dear son, you will not let your love of drawing interfere with your studies or your plans."[87] And he said to Nannie: "I know you say your prayers, and I hope you will never do anything which the Savior forbids in his teachings to his disciples. I must look out for some pretty present for you as well as the other *little fellows*."[88]

Houston was back in Texas in October, and by the time of his arrival at home, October 17, Margaret had resolved that he would not leave her again before he was baptized. She had been encouraged. He was a hero among the godly for his Senate floor championing of 3,050 New England preachers who had filed a petition protesting the Kansas-Nebraska Act and had been intimi-

85 *Ibid.*

86 *Ibid.*

87 Sam Houston to Sam Houston, Jr., Washington, D.C., January 15, 1854, Sam Houston Hearne Collection.

88 Sam Houston to Nannie E. Houston, Washington, D.C., June 16, 1854, *Writings*, VI, 28.

dated by the clever orator Stephen A. Douglas. Houston pronounced ministers in general the "harbingers of peace to their fellow men" and hoped that no insults to them would again blacken the Senate chamber. Before he had left for home, a New Hampshire convention had nominated him for President of the United States. Proudly Houston wore his laurels home to a Texas which was less sympathetic now, if still fascinated by his style.

Margaret's neighbors, the preachers and the professors, conferred with her on her plan. Judge R. E. B. Baylor would be in Independence in November to hold a four-day revival. Margaret was superstitious; maybe it was a good omen that back in Marion, years before, Baylor had rescued her from drowning. Now she was plotting a rescue of another kind. The judge would deliver his famous "Jesus Wept" sermon as the feature of the revival. It would be a splendid meeting, a gathering of devout Baptists from all over Texas.[89]

No sooner were the Houstons alone than Margaret implored her husband to consent to being baptized. Houston readily dismissed her request by saying he would think it over. He underestimated her zeal. She would no longer be put off, and filled his every waking hour with talk of religion. Armed with her Bible, she read to him and discussed selected passages. The weeks passed into November, the month of the great revival. Sam Houston stood firm in refusing to be baptized, yet, one evening at sunset, as Margaret spoke to him over her open Bible, he made a profession of faith. She was suddenly helpless to proceed. At that moment Brother Baines passed down the public road on horseback, and Margaret saw him through the window. She ran

[89] Dayton Kelley, "BU Hourglass," *The Baylor Line*, Vol. XXX, 13; see also Ashbel Smith's notes on Houston, n.d., Smith manuscripts, University of Texas Archives.

to the front gate and called him. Being told the situation, Baines dismounted and agreed to do what he could. Margaret had no intention to allow Sam Houston peace until he promised to be baptized. Houston, however, could be imposed upon only in a limited sense. He had a firm way of dealing with Margaret, so the religious discussions ended, and the household prepared for bed. Margaret begged Baines to stay.

After breakfast, George W. Baines, doubtless glad for the chance to leave a tense situation, excused himself, saying that he must go to Brenham on business. Houston asked if he might accompany him. Out on the road Houston spoke: "My wife and other friends seem anxious for me to join the church, and I would if I could."[90]

In that way the conversation began, as the horses ambled through the open land.[91] Houston described attending a Presbyterian meeting with his mother when he "was quite young." It was a "communion season," and "the great Dr. Blackburn" officiated. That same minister quoted Corinthians, "which sets forth the fearful danger" of unbelievers' taking communion, wherein they hopelessly "seal their damnation forever." Sam Houston said his hesitation to be baptized or participate in any other sacred rite was a fear of making a "sad and awful mistake."

Baines stood challenged. He replied that the Presbyterian had not known what he was talking about and had "missed entirely the true teaching of the inspired apostle." Among the Corinthians the complaint was against those who succumbed to feasting and drinking to satisfy animal yearnings and thereby mocked holy symbols. When Baines finished talking, Houston said, "Your

[90] Crane, *Life and Select Literary Remains*, p. 244.

[91] See clippings from Houston newspapers reprinted in Ellis, *Sam Houston and Related Spiritual Forces*; see also, Crane, *Life and Select Literary Remains*, chapter on Houston's religious life, wherein Crane reported Margaret and Baines's story.

views are new to me. I will return home and read that chapter carefully."[92]

There is every indication that Baines's visit was the turning point. Houston had held ministers in scorn for many years. While he was still in Tennessee and Eliza Allen had gone, Houston had asked for a Presbyterian minister. Two of them refused to attend him, saying that the "respectable connections" of the young lady would be offended.[93] He had been hurt by his rejection on the part of the Presbyterians. Margaret elevated somewhat his low opinion of people, but her task in getting him to respect any church was a more ambitious one.[94] His excuses were myriad and she and her compatriots attacked them one by one. The last of Houston's theological barriers was finally drawn into the open that autumn day on the road to Brenham. His rereading of Corinthians satisfied him, and he offered no more obstacles to his wife's wishes.

Margaret, in tearful excitement, sent riders to inform the relatives in the area. The news spread elsewhere very fast. Soon Rufus Burleson, completely ignoring Baines, had gathered up a team of slaves for the purpose of building a coffin-shaped baptistry in Kountz Creek. Even Judge Baylor would have trouble matching the spectacle of the famous sinner's submergence into the water, and the symbolism of the coffin as the burial place of past weakness.[95]

People came from Washington-on-the-Brazos, from Brenham, from Austin, and from the scattering of little towns in between. Had the news gone faster, more would have come, entering Independence on the road that passed before the Houston house.

[92] Crane, *Life and Select Literary Remains*, 244.

[93] Shearer, "The Mercurial Sam Houston," 8–9.

[94] Ashbel Smith's notes on Houston, n.d., University of Texas Archives.

[95] Burleson, *Life and Writings of Rufus Burleson*, 165.

It is told that there was not a vacant pallet or bed in Independence the night before. To amuse themselves, people walked to Kountz Creek to admire Reverend Burleson's coffin-shaped creation.

A bright sun lighted the morning of November 19, 1854. The Houston household awakened early, for Margaret required everyone to attend the service. Some of the citizens of Independence looked suspiciously toward the Houston house when they heard that during the night ruffians had outraged Burleson's pool with tree limbs and stones. General Houston's baptism was held in another stream.[96]

Outside the town in a broad meadow, Rocky Creek commanded Margaret's vision. Crowds of onlookers lined the water's edge, awaiting the Texas Baptists' most unbelievable triumph. A passage cleared, and Burleson and Sam Houston walked to the creek, through the now silent throng. At noon the hero of San Jacinto stumbled from the cold water into the cheering conflux that swept forward to congratulate him. Margaret could hardly see him for all the people. But it was her custom to stay back. She never interfered with Sam Houston and his public. Experience had taught her to wait until the people were gone, when he would come to her of his own accord.

[96] *Ibid.*, 166–67.

7.

A Lady Waiting

Margaret and her children were in Huntsville, confined to the house. Even old Texans could not remember a worse winter than that of 1856. The freeze had begun on Christmas Day, soon after the general's departure for Washington, D.C., and the cold had killed the fruit trees. Clothed in as many shawls as she could bear, as well as two pairs of woolen stockings, Margaret hovered before the fire in her bedroom. She wondered if their orchard in Independence would survive the bitter weather.

Sam Houston had been at home for six months during the previous summer. He quickly became bored with Independence and moved the family to Cedar Point, where they spent the hot months and were healthier for doing so. Then the Gorees moved to Madisonville and the Huntsville house was suddenly vacated. A delighted Senator Houston re-established Margaret and the children there in the fall.

Again Margaret faced the wind that blew between the logs and up through the cracks in the floor. There were three Houston houses now: the Huntsville house, Cedar Point, and the house in

Independence. They were not elaborate—in fact, very plain places—but they were kept furnished and ready for occupancy. Houston did not hesitate to move from one house to another at any time. Margaret was agreeable, if it made Houston happy, and he seemed happier than ever. He was a gentle father and an understanding husband. These good things Margaret attributed to his baptism, a subject on which she sometimes became sentimental.

Sweet "Rocky!" of what hallowed joys
Shall mingle with my dreams of thee!
On Sabbath eve, beyond the noise
Of village life removed I see
Upon thy sloping banks in cadence low
Ascends the soft baptismal song.[1]

Margaret Houston had reason to be proud of her accomplishments. Yet they did not bring her the peace she had expected. She was afraid to be alone with her own thoughts. Independence had presented more diversions than Huntsville. Her kin lived in Independence, and she was close to all of them; debates and recitals made Baylor University an interesting place to go. Huntsville provided too much idle time for introspection.

Seldom did Margaret have a reason to leave the farm in Huntsville unless it was to go to church or to see Frances Creath. The people of Independence, on the other hand, were usually exuberant about something. There was Nancy Lea's bell, for example. The widow had worried over the fact that the Baptists of Independence were without a bell to celebrate marriages and to toll the dead. She decided to sell the Moffette silver and use the money to buy a bell, and having already given most of the

[1] "Farewell to Independence," by Margaret Lea Houston, Huntsville, November 10, 1855, collection of Mrs. F. S. Baldwin.

silver away, in the process of preparing for death, she made a quick inventory and sent her servant Bingley out to gather it up, assuring each person that he would be "more than repaid in the hereafter" for his losses. The bell was cast in New York. On its side was an inscription chronicling the good deed of Nancy Lea.[2]

Margaret loved Huntsville, however. Three of her girls had been born there, in the very house in which she now lived. Before the house was the garden she had planted with cape jasmine, iris, phlox, pinks, and ivy, some of which Houston had brought to her from Washington's tomb. Houston had planted the pecan trees himself. Their Huntsville friends varied from retired military officers, preachers, farmers, storekeepers, and lawyers to the seamstress who lived on the square and made most of Margaret's clothes from bolts of cloth the general brought from Washington. Huntsville friendships seemed enduring. Tom Gibbs carried the Houstons' credit at his store as long as the general needed it, and Henderson Yoakum made a weekly visit to Houston's office in the yard and examined business papers and pertinent mail.

Margaret's best friend was Mrs. J. W. D. Creath, the thirty-five-year-old wife of the Baptist minister. Life with Mr. Creath had sometimes been difficult. There was little money, and Frances Creath was no Nancy Lea, to invest her own money and make more. Her inheritance from her family in Virginia had quickly disappeared. There were two Creath children, a boy named Luther, aged six, and a younger girl. Margaret lavished sisterly affection on Frances Creath in return for the sympathy Mrs. Creath gave when Margaret felt insecure. They met frequently and talked for long hours, discussing and trying to help each other understand confusing passages in the Bible.

[2] Temple Houston Morrow, a statement regarding the bell, collection of Mrs. F. S. Baldwin; see also Olive Branch White, "Margaret Lea, Wife of General Sam Houston," *Naylor's Epic-Century Magazine*, Vol. III, 30.

"My dear love," Margaret wrote to Sam Houston. "Tuesday has come again, a cold raw day, so cold that the children can not go out to play and I am shivering over the fire, in the midst of playblocks, doll-clothes, & c & c."[3] On writing days she told news of the children. Sam was twelve; Nannie was nine; Maggie was eight; Mary Willie was five; Nettie was soon to be four; and during the summer Andrew would be two. "Maggie is beginning to learn very well . . . and Mary Willie will soon begin to spell . . . Sam is . . . learning a great deal, but I am sure he will not impair his health by hard study. Andrew is crazy about Sam's gun. He saw a buzzard flying over the yard yesterday and pointed to it and said 'pow'. . . . Nannie intended to have answered your letter on Saturday."[4]

Margaret's letters were minutely written, the lines close together and immensely monotonous in appearance. She filled the margins with postscripts about life at home: "Dearest perhaps you may suppose from the multiplicity of things I have had on hand, that I find no time to pine for you. Then you are mistaken for there is everywhere a void, which nothing can fill, but the presence of my darling husband."[5] She made some effort to become excited over his political fortunes. But that interest did not lessen her personal religious doubts or keep her mind off herself for very long. Margaret was running from questions from which she had fled intermittently throughout her life. Now she wanted Sam Houston with her, because she did not worry when he was there. In a letter he indicated that he might be home in the spring. "Oh do not disappoint me if you love me," she wrote.[6]

If Houston realized the extent of Margaret's growing fright, he left not even an impression of concern. When he was in Texas,

[3] Margaret Lea Houston to Sam Houston, Huntsville, February 5, 1856, University of Texas Archives.

[4] *Ibid.* [5] *Ibid.* [6] *Ibid.*

he thoughtlessly pulled her and the children from house to house in the uncomfortable coach; then, just as the household was settled again, he was bound for Washington. Left alone, Margaret sought an outlet in the children, or on cold days she wrapped herself in her cloak and wandered in the field, along the rail fences.[7] She played her piano and read books. Still, "some dark cloud hung over me," she wrote, "threatening to fall upon me and extinguish the feeble light of my soul."[8]

One day after mid-January, 1856, Margaret was at her desk writing a letter to General Houston when a messenger came to her door and said Mrs. Creath was sick and calling for her. As she found Frances Creath seriously ill, she did not return home but remained to nurse her friend. Eliza ran Margaret's household anyway, and Eliza had promised that even if Margaret died, she would never leave the children.[9] At Frances Creath's side, Margaret kept a relentless vigil Monday and Tuesday. By Wednesday morning the patient was worse, and the doctor told Margaret that Frances Creath would die. Margaret coldly dismissed him and administered medicines herself. As Frances Creath sank, Margaret's anxieties rose. In the tired eyes of Mrs. Creath, Margaret saw herself dying and Sam Houston far away. "You will see, my Dearest," Houston had written, "that my enemies assail me for my late profession of religion. . . . This does not mortify my feelings in the least. . . . To God only am I account-

[7] See particularly Margaret Lea Houston to Sam Houston, Galveston, December 7, 1840, Franklin Williams Collection; see also Margaret Lea Houston to Sam Houston, Huntsville, January 28, 1850, Texas State Archives; see also Margaret Lea Houston to Sam Houston, Huntsville, March 11, 1856, University of Texas Archives.

[8] Margaret Lea Houston to Sam Houston, Huntsville, March 11, 1856, University of Texas Archives.

[9] Author in conversation with Mrs. Jennie Morrow Decker, Houston, January 10, 1965.

able."[10] Margaret never understood why he stayed among those who seemed to hate him so much as to criticize the noblest act of his life.

Poor Frances Creath had not been so blessed as to find Christ. And Frances Creath was dying. Margaret took up her Bible and began reading at the bedside. On Sunday morning, Frances Creath seemed to understand what Margaret was reading and "had a glorious manifestation of her acceptance with God and shouted aloud for half an hour." That afternoon Margaret bent over the bed and Frances Creath put her arms around Margaret's neck. "My way was so clear this morning!" she said to Margaret.

"Is it not still so, Sister Creath?" Margaret asked.

Frances Creath mumbled no, that she could not have borne the ecstasy longer. She slept "very sweetly" and "her mind seemed to rest quietly upon Jesus." At twilight Mrs. Creath was not moving at all. People filed by her bed to say goodbye. Preacher Creath, "crushed beneath the mighty blow," came to her, and she kissed him, saying "Farewell my husband! Oh will we not be happy one day!" He said yes, and with the others left the room.

Margaret watched the scene silently, but she was tense and frightened. She opened her Bible and read aloud. "The Lord is my shepherd I shall not want . . . ." Frances Creath repeated the verses after her and fell asleep. Kneeling at the bedside Margaret whispered, "Jesus can make a dying bed feel soft as downy pillows are."

"As on his breast I lay my head and breathe my life out sweetly there," said Mrs. Creath. Two hours after midnight she died.[11]

[10] Sam Houston to Margaret Lea Houston, Washington, D.C., January 6, 1855, Franklin Williams Collection.

[11] Margaret Lea Houston to Sam Houston, Huntsville, January 19, 1856, University of Texas Archives.

Margaret opened the door to her room at home. The unfinished letter to Sam Houston still lay on the desk. She sat down and resumed her writing. "Oh if the prayers of the church could have saved her, and the tears and sleepless watchings of friends she would have been with us still." Margaret wrote that Mrs. Creath's death must not be questioned because the "Heavenly Father has taken her." But it was terrible that a woman so good must die. "Oh how I loved her!" Sister Creath had remembered Sam Houston: "I love Gen'l Houston," she had said among her last words, "although I do not make any great parade over him." The plight of J. W. D. Creath was now a dreary one. Margaret wrote, "How often I have thought his condition would be yours."[12]

By March, grief had become gloom for Margaret. Lonely and ill, she finally went to bed and confined herself to her room alone, contemplating her situation. Over her hung "that same dark cloud" that had haunted her for so long.[13] Frances Creath had been in her grave since January, "but here I am, still spared, a poor unworthy creature, while the good, the great, and the useful are taken."[14] Margaret wrote bitterly about her barren soul, attributing the tragedy of her spiritual insecurity to "the vanities of early youth" when she "wandered far away from the cross."[15] Margaret read her Bible diligently, a task perhaps more laborious with Frances Creath gone, for they had clung together in doubt. Days passed, and Margaret read: "Whosoever is born of God doth not commit sin, for his seed remaineth in him, and he can

[12] *Ibid.*

[13] Margaret Lea Houston to Sam Houston, Huntsville, March 11, 1856, University of Texas Archives.

[14] Margaret Lea Houston to Sam Houston, Huntsville, January 19, 1856, University of Texas Archives.

[15] Margaret Lea Houston to Sam Houston, Huntsville, March 11, 1856, University of Texas Archives.

not sin, because he is born of God." It was a favorite passage, and Margaret repeated it aloud.[16]

"All at once," she later wrote, "the true meaning of that passage flashed upon my mind. I had often heard it explained and had even explained it to others, but never until that moment, had my soul taken hold of it."[17] The seed referred to in the scripture was the soul. Sin was of the body, and salvation was freedom from that "poor perishing clay." A soul was eternal in spite of the evil tendencies of the flesh. The holy inner voice of the soul could not be silenced. Margaret wrote to General Houston: "I felt that I had never taken pleasure in sin, since the day of my conversion, and . . . there was ever a quiet admonition within me, that was grieved when I went astray. So then it was the poor frail body, that had so long weighed the spirit down with its infirmities." She concluded her letter: "Oh how my soul rejoiced. . . . This is the new birth. . . . Oh glorious hope!"[18]

Too late for Margaret already to have received the letter, General Houston had written, "Tomorrow is our communion day at E Street Baptist Church. If the Lord spares me, I expect to attend and partake of the sacrament of our Lord's supper."[19] Earlier he had written, "I am a poor dependent and sinful worm of the dust and constantly dependent upon an omnipotent and merciful God for my life. . . . Tomorrow, if spared, I will visit Bro. Sampson's church and invite him to spend as much leisure time with me as he can."[20] In her letter Margaret had said, "Present me affectionately to bro. Sampson. If I never see him in this

16 *Ibid.*

17 *Ibid.*

18 *Ibid.*

19 Sam Houston to Margaret Lea Houston, Washington, D.C., March 5, 1856, *Writings*, VI, 244–45.

20 Sam Houston to Margaret Lea Houston, Washington, D.C., January 6, 1855, Franklin Williams Collection.

world, I do believe I shall see him and know him in Heaven."[21]

By April 1, Margaret was in good health, filling vases with flowers that bloomed outside her window. Each day she sat with Maggie and Nannie at the piano and gave them music lessons. In the morning she and the children sang hymns together. The housekeeper, a disagreeable Indiana lady, was dismissed, and Margaret declined having another: "They require more management than a colored servant. And besides I take great pleasure in telling you that Nannie will soon be a fine manager. I believe she will make just such a woman as your mother."[22]

It is doubtful that Margaret believed Sam Houston would actually retire.[23] He was quickly bored and felt trapped by a domestic situation. The name Houston was a topic of discussion all over the country. His vote against the Kansas-Nebraska Bill had severed his relations with the radical Democrats, who were taking control of the party. Relatively new in Texas, the Democratic party, as an organized effort, used the Kansas-Nebraska Bill as its first major issue before the Texas public. The Democrats had used the bill as a specific means of fighting the long-established power of Sam Houston. They had fired their ammunition carefully. In the general's absence, insults were leveled at him, and Sam Houston's Texas public, having seen so little of Houston since annexation, listened intently. Rumors told of Houston's being challenged to duels. The possibility alarmed Margaret.[24] To calm her anxieties, Houston wrote, "A man who would dare . . . challenge me

[21] Margaret Lea Houston to Sam Houston, Huntsville, March 11, 1856, University of Texas Archives.

[22] Margaret Lea Houston to Sam Houston, Huntsville, February 5, 1856, University of Texas Archives.

[23] Margaret Lea Houston to Sam Houston, Huntsville, March 11, 1856, University of Texas Archives.

[24] Sam Houston to Mrs. Ana S. Stephens, Washington, D.C., March 22, 1856, *Writings*, VI, 299–300.

would be regarded as a *madman*, and . . . if I regarded it . . . I would be a fool."[25]

Parts of the North lauded Houston and spoke freely of him as a possible candidate for President of the United States. Houston's incessant speaking tours in the East prompted a neglect of his Senate post, to the disgust of General Rusk, who was overburdened with responsibility. The trips were expensive in hotel bills and railroad tickets, but Houston seems to have thought of it as an investment in the future. Audiences cheered Sam Houston as he remembered them cheering him in days past, though he sometimes overrated his ovations as representing a greater part of the nation than they actually did. The crowded Senate galleries applauded his oratory. He signed autographs, and he occasionally wrote flowery rhymes for pretty matrons or composed bizarre histories for the trivia he loved to present as rare artifacts to enchanted admirers.

From a political point of view, Sam Houston was on a bridge crumbling at both ends. He was allied with no political organization. The war he was waging was an outside attack against a highly developed version of the very system which, before he had left Tennessee, had made possible his first political achievements. If he had not left national politics back in Jackson's day but had remained and matured with the system, his position might better have favored presidential ambitions. The famous Texan who had returned to Washington had reached for too high a rung on the party ladder—as though it were his right—and had been rejected. He had begun to fight, and the fight had spread until he was a minor figure against a movement. While Sam Houston was a good fighter, initial success so encouraged him in his national pursuits that he continued optimistically in the course he had already

[25] Sam Houston to Margaret Lea Houston, Washington, D.C., January 6, 1855, Franklin Williams Collection.

begun. For the details of administration he had lost his taste. He moved continually from platform to platform, whipping with oratory the radical Democrats, who turned loathing eyes to him. He strutted on the national stage for thirteen years, and portions of his Texas foundation began, through neglect, to rot and nourish weeds.

That his eye was on the presidency was no secret at home. To Margaret he wrote:

> I often jest with my friends about having the doors of the "White House" widened and yesterday I was there and told the door-keeper that he must keep the house in good order as I might have to take it for the next four years. He is an Irishman, and was much delighted. He played it off quite handsomely. So you see my Dear, I am not very sensitive on the subject, worn out as it may [be]. I comment at times about the pretty play grounds for children! I never think of our humble home, but what emotions of deep and abiding affection swell in my heart.[26]

In Austin, the Democratic legislature contemptuously took a vote on whether to allow the turncoat into its chamber. Outside in the streets, the Know-Nothing party celebrated the senator's stand on Kansas and Nebraska. Houston actually toyed with the idea of associating himself with another party. He knew he would never be able to lead the Democrats, for even though he had supporters in the party, the pronounced tendency of the state party was more and more to adhere to the national radical machine. Between that machine and Sam Houston was mutual contempt, so the Know-Nothings caught Houston's cautious eye with their welcoming applause. Like Houston, but for different reasons, the Know-Nothings resented the Democrats' secrecy and complete sub-

[26] Sam Houston to Margaret Lea Houston, n.d., Sam Houston Hearne Collection.

ordination to party politics in spite of personal feeling. Although they were potentially guilty of similar conduct, the Know-Nothings were nativists reacting to forces of complex organization they suspected were undermining the American system. In many respects they clung to old Jacksonian principles as did Houston himself. While the Know-Nothings did make political gains, they lacked sufficient structure and strength to prevail. Houston abandoned them, and if he did not die with the Know-Nothings, his sojourn with them left him as politically alone as Margaret was alone at her fireside in Huntsville.

Houston turned to his wife for companionship. "I will send you a bundle of newspapers and in each one you will see something of me. They were selected by my two young friends Jno. Williams and Mr. Newman for you, so [you] will be indebted to them for the compliment, if it is even to make you read newspapers."[27] It was Saturday when he wrote, "Tomorrow, my Love, you know is the day to write as it is the Sabbath, but to you only. If I live to look around me, I may write you something of politics, though you take but little interest in such things."[28]

Early in September, 1856, General Houston was at home. The journey that once had taken six weeks now took eight days. He had gifts for each member of the family. Nannie received a locket, inside of which was a miniature of Margaret, entwined with a lock of Houston's hair. The general had worn it around his neck, "suspended by a blue and white ribbon" within his shirt. "I have a *fancy*," he told Margaret, "to have *you in my bosom*."[29] A similar present commissioned by the senator was a bracelet, upon which was painted a picture of Nancy Lea's tomb, framed under

[27] Sam Houston to Margaret Lea Houston, Washington, D.C., January 6, 1855, Franklin Williams Collection.

[28] *Ibid.*

[29] Sam Houston to Margaret Lea Houston, Washington, D.C., April 18, 1856, Texas State Archives.

glass by a rope braided from Margaret's, Varilla's, Antoinette's, and Nancy Lea's hair.[30]

A presidential campaign was in progress. Houston went on the road speaking for the American party's candidate Millard Fillmore, against James Buchanan, candidate for the Democrats. In November, he was home for two weeks, "quite lame" from old war wounds but "hardy as a bear and as young as ever."[31] Back in Washington his duties were heavier, for Rusk's wife had died, leaving his colleague disconsolate. Margaret had the sad duty to inform Houston that his old friend Henderson Yoakum had died at his country home. To make matters worse, Rusk committed suicide. Some thought that the excessive pressures of his office, brought on by Houston's flagrant abandonment of his own duties in favor of going on speaking tours, precipitated Rusk's suicide. Houston seems to have been cognizant of the appearance of Rusk's tragedy, for in Texas he missed no opportunity to blame the Democrats directly for Rusk's death.

During the last weeks of March, 1857, Houston made a slow trip home and honored many invitations to speak, telling of San Jacinto and his ardent desire to lay down the trophies of his long career and retire forever. That summer, however, he announced his candidacy as governor of Texas.

The Democratic State Convention at Waco had nominated Hardin R. Runnels, a radical, young, very avid admirer of the national party organization, to run on its ticket. It was politically necessary that the conservatives oppose him. Washington friends of Houston persuaded the general that there were enough "Jacksonian Democrats" in Texas to defeat Runnels and thereby weaken the radicals' growing hold on Texas. Houston discussed

[30] Item, collection of Mrs. Dan O'Madigan, Grosse Point, Michigan.

[31] Sam Houston to Thomas Jefferson Rusk, Huntsville, November 8, 1856, *Writings*, VI, 394–95.

with Margaret her wishes regarding his candidacy. Meanwhile provocative gossip drifted through the East Texas woods. A Runnels man was overheard saying Sam Houston "dared not run for office; that he would be met at every crossroads, and that he would be killed off."[32] Houston stood challenged. If the final decision was Margaret's, as he later claimed it was, she merely took the inevitable course, rather than to suffer the unpleasantness of being overlooked.[33]

The Democratic sentiments in Texas made the campaign hard to conduct. For example, stage lines refused passage to the hero of San Jacinto. Houston struck a bargain with a traveling salesman named Ed Sharp, who happened through Huntsville in a red buggy with "Warwick's Patent Plow" lettered in gilt on the side. The arrangement was advantageous to both Houston and Sharp, who traveled together through Texas that summer of 1857.

Margaret stayed at home, out of the heat. Through newspapers and occasional letters she was able to guess his progress over the state. She instructed the children in Texas geography by tracing their father's journey with her finger over the big, oiled map that hung in the loggia. The candidate maintained an unbelievable itinerary, but then one of Sam Houston's greatest talents had always been his mobility.

Houston, though not favored in the running, gave Texas a show. Stripped of his shirt, he spoke in a loose linen duster so as to be cooler in the intense heat. The speeches sometimes lasted several hours, depending upon the audience's attitude. In the manner of the old days, Houston paid scant attention to the issues, save in a word now and then, like "abolition." Personalities interested the people. With humor and audacity Houston described his opponents as possessed by greed and ignorance. He was not

[32] *Austin State Gazette*, July 25, 1857.
[33] *Ibid.*

restrained in his derogatory adjectives regarding other people nor in superfluous praise of himself. Sam Houston ignored the several violent incidents that accompanied his trip, and he returned home in August, quite pleased. Since his Senate term was not to end until March, 1859, he would have to resign if he won the gubernatorial race. He and Margaret would, in that case, be together in Texas on a permanent basis for the first time since annexation.

Margaret was sitting with him on the porch on the August afternoon that they received the election results. The messenger ran up the walk, and Houston heard him say that Runnels had won by a large majority. Sam Houston quietly walked to the bedroom door and closed it behind him.[34] In the election of 1857, Sam Houston met his only defeat. He gradually grew accustomed to the idea, and by late August was in good spirits. "The fuss is over, and the sun yet shines as ever," he wrote to Ashbel Smith. "In the result of the election I am cheered, and were it not for my friends, I assure you, I would rejoice at the result. If I am spared to take a seat in the Senate, I will, as the Frenchman said 'Have some fish to fry.' Had I been elected, I would have had 'other fish to fry.' " He made a deal with Ashbel Smith: "If you come to see me, I bind myself to make you laugh."[35]

Texas criticism of Houston was rampant that early November morning of 1857 when the senator waved goodbye to his family. The lonely Christmas to Margaret was prelude to a lonelier new year. April would bring Margaret's thirty-ninth birthday; after that, it would be a full year until the Senate term expired. She was pregnant again, but other than for the few ills that always accompanied her pregnancies, she was in good health, praying "that my mind will never again be clouded by the doubts and

[34] Lenoir Hunt (ed.), *My Master By Jeff Hamilton*, 34.

[35] Sam Houston to Ashbel Smith, Huntsville, August 22, 1857, *Writings*, VI, 447.

fears that have given me so many moments of mental anguish."[36]

Sam Houston missed her: "You will not wish me, I presume, to write any more love letters, but are willing that I should prattle about *love*, or the cherished regard which I entertain for you. . . . Now dearest our love letter days are over." He had dreamed that he ran home to her and found the new baby in her arms. "I would that I could realize the fact that I was with you."[37] Still the changing political times affected even his thoughts of her: "The latest news is from your state and points to *disunion*. I hope my dear that you have lived long enough from Alabama not to be infractured by such. . . . I am for UNION and OUR union as it is!!!!"[38] Elsewhere he apologized: "My Dear I have served you a dish of politics, merely for relish. Now I have only to tell you how much I love you and kiss my pen with which I write . . . Thy Devoted Houston."[39]

On May 25, the family was in Huntsville for the birth of the child. Sam was fifteen that day, and they celebrated the event. Late at night Nancy Lea held the seventh Houston child and the third son in her arms. He was named William Rogers Houston. Margaret saw the "pale little cripple," knowing that his birth had been the most difficult of all.[40] She was determined to build his strength and her own. As soon as she could rise and was able to travel, she and her family and her belongings would travel to Independence, for they had to vacate the Huntsville house, which

[36] Margaret Lea Houston to Sam Houston, Huntsville, March 11, 1856, University of Texas Archives.

[37] Sam Houston to Margaret Lea Houston, Washington, D.C., May 17, 1857, Texas State Archives.

[38] Sam Houston to Margaret Lea Houston, Washington, D.C., January 20, 1858, Franklin Williams Collection.

[39] Sam Houston to Margaret Lea Houston, Washington, D.C., April 22, 1858, *Writings*, VII, 99–100.

[40] Margaret Lea Houston to Sam Houston, Jr., Independence, July 1, 1864, Sam Houston Hearne Collection.

had been sold to pay campaign expenses. Sam Houston had not had a party to finance him in the expensive campaign. The house and surrounding farm were among the properties sacrificed to raise money.[41]

Mrs. Houston was ready to leave Huntsville. She anticipated the coming of great happiness. Twelve years thus far the general had served at the national capital, and Margaret had borne the separation bravely, believing that some day Houston would come home to stay. Now she knew better than merely to exist in expectation of a promised retirement which might never come. Margaret had learned long before that she must live in the meantime. Houston had been hurt by the loss of the race but not defeated. A family servant in later years remembered the day General and Mrs. Houston had heard the news of Houston's defeat. After the messenger had left, Margaret had returned to her chair on the porch, and in time the general had joined her. His first remark sounded the tone for the coming years: "Margaret, wait until 1859."[42]

Another campaign, perhaps, and another election might be in the future. But the Washington years were ending. That at least meant that Houston would return to Texas. He wrote to Margaret, "I have felt an exile in other lands, and from other homes, but then I was an exile that combined no wish or hope of return. . . . Our sunny home appears to me more bright and lovely than it has ever done in the realizations of the past. So many, so bright are the joys to my fancy . . . that I can scarcely contain myself."[43]

[41] In 1857, Houston sold the property to J. Carrol Smith, who, perhaps because the Houstons did not vacate the premises, neglected payment of the notes, but refinanced another purchase of the property from Houston November 19, 1858, at which time Margaret and her family left Huntsville. The purchase price was four thousand dollars.

[42] Hunt, *My Master*, 34.

In her Texas home, Margaret attended to her family and her church and awaited him.

[43] Sam Houston to Margaret Lea Houston, Washington, D.C., March 1, 1857, Sam Houston Memorial Museum.

8.

The Grand Finals

The yellow coach had never been impermeable, but in the laxity of old age it admitted more dust than usual. Margaret had learned that she could bear the discomfort by breathing through a handkerchief. Usually the smallest children slept against Eliza and their mother, rocked by the coach's climb and descent over the rolling land. Christmas, 1859, was three weeks away, and the Houstons would pass the holiday at home in Austin, a city neither Margaret nor her children had ever seen before. During the previous March, Houston had moved back to Independence from Washington. He had run for governor and had been elected. In his best tradition, Sam Houston had appeared at the right time. After his defeat in 1857, he had returned to Washington, leaving Texas to the Democrats, whose conduct in office had reflected the sectional hostility of the nation. The public had been wary of the Democrats' fanaticism. Houston entered the 1859 gubernatorial race with virtually no campaign, and the people of Texas welcomed him as a promise of the return of a serene past. He was known to all Texans, and he assumed an almost spiritual presence during the 1859 campaign in most parts of the state. The more wildly the Democrats had orated, the more sensible San Jacinto's hero had seemed.

While he was preparing to leave for Washington, Houston had expressed a wish to be a sheep farmer in Texas.[1] But not long afterward he had rented the Independence property, which was a good sheep farm, to bring immediate income to support his large family. The only house left was Cedar Point, and the increasing value of its four thousand surrounding acres probably accounts for its being retained more than the mere fact of Margaret's sentiment about it, because the Sam Houstons needed cash.

Margaret faithfully listened to Houston's plans for retirement. This time he was suggesting the Redlands again as a possible place of residence.[2] Margaret did not seem to care, for they were together, and that was what she had wanted for so long.[3] During the summer at Cedar Point she and the general had bathed Willie Rogers in the salt water and had walked him in their oak grove, and the boy's health was improved.

The Houston family climbed from the coach and saw the Texas Governor's Mansion in the second week of December, 1859. It was a tall brick house with Ionic columns and a wheat sheaf balustrade of wood enclosing a narrow second floor gallery. The bricks were yellow, like Baylor's building stones, with the contrast of white paint applied to the columns and other wooden trim. A small yard, bare and untended under the hot sun, was defined by a picket fence. Behind a stone stepping block the gate admitted one to the walkway that inclined up the hill to the porch.

[1] Sam Houston to Ashbel Smith, Huntsville, October 28, 1858, *Writings*, VII, 189.

[2] Sam Houston to Thomas Parnut, Huntsville, November 17, 1858, Texas State Archives.

[3] Sam Houston to Margaret Lea Houston, Washington, D.C., January 29, 1859, *Writings*, VII, 224–25; Sam Houston to Maggie Houston, Washington, D.C., January [?] 19, 1859, Sam Houston Hearne Collection.

Accustomed to the shade and clutter of little houses, Margaret was appalled by the big square chambers of the mansion. The windows were huge and the ceilings were high. Egyptian door frames and the circular stair were too pretentious for the Houstons' belongings. Former governor Runnels, a bachelor, had informed the legislature that the house needed furniture. Other affairs postponed a decision, and the topic came to the floor after the Houstons had moved in. A sarcastic Democrat rose and questioned the need of so much furniture, since the new governor was accustomed to having no better than a wigwam.

That was the attitude the heavily Democratic state government showed toward the unwelcomed governor. The Houstons' Austin reception was cold, and Margaret could but compare the contentment of Huntsville and Independence with her first days at the seat of state government. Although she had not lived in the public eye for fifteen years, her return confirmed the low opinion she had always entertained about politics. Austin was becoming an enemy camp. Recent occurrences in the United States had fortified the Democrats for bold action, and the Texas population was fickle.

On December 21, Margaret sat on the pillared piazza of the capitol for the inaugural ceremony. Sunshine lit the windy day, and a large crowd came to the terraced grounds of the capitol, where beyond them, in Margaret's line of vision, the sprawl of Austin was cut down the middle by Congress Avenue, which extended to the distant bank of the Colorado River. To her right, one block away, stood the mansion, its upper porch providing an unobstructed view of the capitol building. Houston stood in front of the obelisk that commemorated the Alamo's vanquished. He warned his listeners of the "wild ravings of fanatics." Secession was the tool of ambitious politicians, said Houston, encouraging his audience, and all of Texas, to think not as Southerners or

Northerners, but as Americans. He cast allusions southward, to Mexico: leave the lands beyond the Missouri free and extend slavery to the Isthmus of Tehuantepec. The balance would in that way be equalized, as Houston, the young congressman from Tennessee, had known it would. From the start the Anglo-Americans had been destined for those boundaries. There was support within Mexico for the protectorate, which was legalistic terminology for the conquest and supervision a considerable number of Mexicans wanted, in preference to the alternatives of an English or French take-over, or the consistently unstable governments that had cursed Mexico since her separation from Spain. As Houston spoke that day in Austin, a Mexican citizen named Juan Cortina occupied Brownsville, Texas, in a daring effort to provoke the Americans into pursuing him over the Río Grande. Certainly a lesser lure than Cortina would have drawn Houston to Mexico, had there been an army at his disposal. Governor Houston expounded promises that appealed to his audience. The years in the Senate had brought polish to his magical oratory. But he was only one man, speaking in a solitary place, against a historical movement which was far bigger than he.

In the new year 1860, the family settled to a quiet life in the Governor's Mansion. Margaret expected her eighth child in August, and she would be unable to appear in public after spring. Her seclusion was effective for the duration of her family's residence in Austin. Personal correspondence indicates that she was afraid for their lives. She took a protective attitude toward the children. It was an easy matter with the youngest ones, but difficult with sixteen-year-old Sam, who was a popular figure with the young people of Austin. The big house was not guarded. While Eliza and the nurses lived in rooms in the second floor of the mansion, Joshua and the others occupied quarters in the stable. There were twelve slaves with the Houstons in Austin, and none were hired out. The census lists half of them as mulattoes. Houston's stable included a team of mules, several saddle horses, and Sam's gray stallion, of which the boy was very fond.

Because of her withdrawal, few people saw Margaret in her career as governor's wife. Only written recollections, a single daguerreotype, and the stark lines of a steel engraving survive to describe her. A nephew of hers was prevailed upon to note that he had visited the mansion "many" times and that Margaret was "beyond the measurement that Grecian artists gave to their sculptured statues of the goddesses," and that her "gracefulness" had a "mysterious charm."[4] She still wore her hair parted in the middle, its gray streaks combed through festoons of finger curls that fell back from silver or tortoise tucking combs.[5] The vogue was to wear tight-sleeved, low-necked dresses on formal occasions, with mountainous skirts that spread to the floor over bell-shaped hoops. At home, women usually omitted the hoop, but their dresses remained very full. Pattern books provided the latest Parisian tastes, and Margaret and Eliza copied them, using the sewing machine Houston had bought. A fragment of one of Margaret's dresses survives. It is a shiny, greenish-gold-colored material in a florid lattice design, forming diamond shapes into which diminutive pink rosebuds are embroidered.

General Houston's features are simpler to trace, not only because he was famous and his pictures were in demand, but also because he liked to have his picture made. There is even a life mask of him, done while he was governor. In one picture he stands in a dark suit beside a Gothic Revival chair, his fingers cluttered with rings. Another picture shows him with a plaid scarf

[4] Essay on General and Mrs. Sam Houston by one of Margaret's nephews, possibly Mart Royston, Varilla's son and Sam's best friend, n.d., Barker Texas History Center, University of Texas Library.

[5] Sam H. Dixon, *Poets and Poetry of Texas*, 147.

swept around his neck, long mutton-chop whiskers, and a kind, paternal smile virtually concealing the reality of his difficult political days. His hair had become conspicuously white, thin in front, and thick and long at the back. The eyes were heavily overladen by a furrowed brow and the cheeks drooped in brushstrokes of wrinkles. He was sixty-seven. The poise so natural in his carriage seems to have intensified with age. The two were a handsome man and wife.

As governor and lady they continued their rural domestic life. Margaret's bedroom upstairs was the family living room, with the upper gallery easily accessible through tall windows. The bed in that room was of dark wood with thick octagon posts supporting a tester framed in heavy moulding. It was a comfortable room for its particular use. In apparent defense of the slow pace of their life, Houston had written four years before—"We were once young, but now we are old!!!"[6]

Margaret advertised in the *Mother's Journal of Philadelphia* for a governess to teach the girls and Andrew. When the "Young Lady" arrived, Sam Houston grumbled that she "would rather marry than teach other people's children."[7] With their schooling thus provided at home, there was no reason for the children to leave the safety of the mansion, except to play in the yard or walk with their mother down the street to the Baptist church.

For Sam's sociability General Houston found an immediate remedy. The boy was enrolled in Colonel R. T. P. Allen's military academy at Bastrop, located one day's coach trip east of Austin. Joshua drove the general and Sam to Bastrop in January. "Rearing, Tearing, Pitching Allen," as the cadets nicknamed the

[6] Sam Houston to Thomas Jefferson Rusk, Huntsville, November 8, 1856, *Writings*, VI, 394–95.

[7] Sam Houston to Sam Houston, Jr., Austin, April 3, 1860, Sam Houston Hearne Collection.

colonel, operated as near a facsimile of the Virginia and Tennessee academies as Houston knew in Texas. The original plan had been to send Sam east. When the time came, neither parent was willing to part with him.

Tall and good looking, Sam was the favorite of his parents, who indulged him and found him sometimes difficult to control. Drawing pictures and writing stories were his greatest pleasures. He liked to ride and hunt and had been reared with abundant leisure in which to partake of those interests as much as he wished. His education at Baylor had prepared him for any further schooling he might select, though his father believed that a boy should be taken out of school and put to clerking before he was twenty. Advanced studies in Latin and mathematics would make him a "graduated fool," the governor told a friend.[8]

Houston was not back in Austin a full week before he and Margaret were longing to see Sam. "I expected you to write to some ones of the family," the general wrote, "but to my surprise no letter has come from you. . . . You have time my son to write and I trust you will not fail to write at least once a week, to some member of the family."[9] In the same letter Houston described a "Shepperd Dog" given to him. "He is the finest large puppy that I have seen and quite intelligent." The children enjoyed all the dogs, which wandered at their own discretion through the house. Andrew, too, roamed the halls: "He [was] hugging the dogs the other day, and that night I had to get up, take off his flannels, turn them inside out and whip them in the Hall, as I think the fleas would have nearly eaten him up otherwise."[10]

[8] A. W. Terrell, "Recollections of General Sam Houston," *Southwestern Historical Quarterly*, Vol. XVI, 132.

[9] Sam Houston to Sam Houston, Jr., Austin, January 27, 1860, Sam Houston Hearne Collection.

[10] Sam Houston to Sam Houston, Jr., Austin, April 7, 1860, *Writings*, VIII, 457–58.

Margaret kept to her room and seldom sat with the family downstairs at meals. The long, hot seasons at Austin caused asthma flare-ups which contributed to the maladies related to her pregnancy.[11] Eliza and Nannie waited upon her, keeping the room dark in the heat of the day and silent when Margaret wanted to sleep.[12]

Visitors came to stay with the Houstons. Antoinette and Charles Power, with their son Tom and baby Lillie, arrived in March and left in April. Returning for a brief stay in the summer, the Powers were good therapy for a family uncomfortable in its situation. All the social news was brought by Antoinette. Power was upset over the secession talk, and he was certain that he and Antoinette and the children would go to England if hostilities broke out. Lean years had followed the hurricane. There was still a position available with the Liverpool company under whose auspices he had first come to Texas twenty years before.

Apparently Margaret's complaints alarmed Nancy Lea, prompting her to order Bingley to pack great quantities of vegetables and eggs into boxes at Independence and ship them to Austin aboard the regular stage. She was convinced that Austin was in a wilderness and that Margaret was not eating proper foods. Although they were perishables that she sent and none of them arrived in edible condition, she continued forwarding packages and incurring enormous freight bills in the process.[13]

Nancy Lea worried about Margaret until Varilla and Antoinette all but forced her to journey to Austin for peace of mind. The inconvenience of the stage trip exhausted her, then July northers came, laced with lightning and wind such as the widow had never

[11] See for example Sam Houston to Sam Houston, Jr., Austin, January 27, 1860, Sam Houston Hearne Collection.

[12] Author in conversation with Mrs. Jennie Morrow Decker, Houston, January 26, 1965.

[13] *Writings*, VII, 462–63, footnote.

seen. Doors and windows in the mansion rattled in their sockets. Nancy Lea was terrified of storms and ran about wailing, finally falling upon a featherbed and burying her face in it. The little children were never so amused as to see the fat, dignified old lady in animation. They piled on the bed with her and bounced in delight, laughing and screaming. When the storm stopped, Mrs. Lea scrambled for a switch with which she might correct her grandchildren's impudence. The children, particularly Andrew, who could easily goad her anger with a look, took the switching also as a game and hid under the bed. Nancy Lea bent down and switched under the bed indiscriminately.[14]

Other kinspeople called at the Governor's Mansion. One day a relative of Margaret's appeared on the front porch announcing himself as a cousin. He was Robert E. Lee of the United States Army and of that Virginia branch of the family that Nancy Lea idly pointed out on the family tree. Sent to take charge of the border patrol which supplemented the Texas Rangers in guarding the Río Grande against bandit invasions from Mexico, Lee had orders to pursue the troublesome Juan Cortina over the river if necessary. He was pleased to know Sam Houston, for he had met him many years before, when Houston was on a Congressional committee of inspection at West Point and Lee was a cadet.

Sam Houston took a particular interest in Lee's opportune position. Socially he warmed up to Robert E. Lee. Through other kin of Margaret he approached Lee about leading an army to Mexico and forcing the protectorate. Houston described himself as being a probable candidate for President of the United States, and in the event of his election he planned to make the protectorate an essential part of his program. Over stacks of maps Houston elaborated upon his scheme in the secrecy of his office

[14] Author in conversation with Mrs. Jennie Morrow Decker, Houston, April 12, 1965.

beneath the capitol piazza. Lee said that he was a United States soldier and responsible not only to his government but to its constitution. A genteel exchange of letters took place. And Houston discontinued his pressure.[15]

Houston's plan was realistic and seemed more so every day. For one thing, he was indeed a prospect for president, though there were many prospects. His desk was covered with letters from all over the country encouraging him to run. He knew the letters were by no means the expressions of the majority, but in his enthusiasm he exaggerated their significance. All day he kept to his thick-walled office. Margaret sent a servant with his lunch, then expected him after dark, unless from her windows she saw the glow of the Argand lamp in his office.

British support for an invasion of Mexico was mysteriously proposed in terms of partially financing an army of twelve thousand with General Houston at its head. The secret agents assured Houston that Margaret would have a guaranteed income for life if the general should fall in battle. Houston seriously considered the offer, for it took little foresight to realize that somebody was going to get Mexico. The French had made overtures, and other nations would be loath to permit Napoleon III so rich an asset. But even if the British were ready to move, Houston suspected that the Texans were not. He told the agents that to act "at this time" would not be wise.[16]

The low, rock buildings of Austin were within Margaret's vision from the second floor gallery of the mansion. In the rolling

[15] A. M. Lea to Sam Houston, Goliad, Texas, February 24, 1860, also Robert E. Lee to A. M. Lea, San Antonio, March 1, 1860, also A. M. Lea to Sam Houston, Austin, April 3, 1860, cited in Walter Prescott Webb, *The Texas Rangers: A Century of Frontier Defense*, 208–11; see also Edward R. Maher, Jr., "Sam Houston and Secession," *Southwestern Historical Quarterly*, Vol. LV, 451–53.

[16] Sam Houston to E. Greer, Austin, February 29, 1860, *Writings*, VII, 495.

terrain the capitol's walls gleamed in the sun, and the dust stirred by horses lingered in the air before it settled again into the dirt streets. A thief broke into the stable at the mansion and stole the general's horses. Margaret was left with nothing to pull her coach. Young Sam's gray stallion was not taken, and the parents expressed relief that it would be there for him to use when he came home on visits.[17]

A meeting of Unionists in Austin nominated Houston for President of the United States. Houston bided his time, waiting to see what his chances might be. At Baltimore the Texas delegation to the National Union Convention impatiently tried to push his name through for nomination. Houston listened closely. The Texas delegation failed, and Houston announced that he would run as an independent. Demonstrations in New York City's Union Square and in Texas suggested a strong following. Thus encouraged, Houston departed on a speaking tour in June, and he was not at home until early August.

On August 12, a maid was sent to the capitol to fetch the governor. Negro women rustled palmetto fans around Margaret's bed. Dr. Beriah Graham attended her, with Eliza close by, and in the evening Margaret gave birth to her eighth child, a boy. She named him for her father, Temple Lea Houston. Two weeks later the mother was able to receive visitors, having by that time risen from an illness during which Sam Houston kept a "constant vigil."[18]

Margaret must have been happy on August 18 when Houston withdrew his name from the presidential contest. He knew he had small hope of winning. Before the public his action savored of

[17] Sam Houston to Sam Houston, Jr., Austin, June 4, 1860, *Writings*, VIII, 127–28.

[18] Sam Houston to Charles L. Mann, Austin, August 27, 1860, *Writings*, VIII, 127–28.

sacrifice. All forces, he said, should be united against the abolitionist Republicans. Houston knew that Abraham Lincoln's election would be a triumph for the secessionists in the South and consequently another political blow to Sam Houston. Writing to Sam, he said, "My son I wish you to love and revere the Union. This is my injunction to all my boys!!! Mingle it in your heart with *filial* love."[19] The general saw danger in the public's temperament. In speeches he began to urge people not to react violently if Lincoln were elected and to keep peace so long as Lincoln followed the Constitution.

He spoke constantly on tour in Texas in September and October. The speeches echoed the old days: strong Union, individual freedom and Negro slavery, and a balm for the restless in Mexico's endless lands. Houston promised glory to the Texan who tilled a small farm but dreamed of more. But even in Texas, Sam Houston was no match for the Democrats, whose emotional philosophies were evangelical in tone and irresistible to that same man on the farm.

Governor Houston was with Margaret in November when Abraham Lincoln was elected President of the United States and the secessionist leaders in Texas moved to take political advantage of the public's dismay. A civilian army of several thousand, the Knights of the Golden Circle, offered itself to General Houston for Mexican filibustering. Perhaps the expedition would have buried the radical Democrats in dust, but Sam Houston stalled. The time must be right, the general said. Meanwhile Lone Star flags were raised over some Texas courthouses. Governor Houston had waited too long. The wild spirits that would have propelled an army to Mexico turned to more immediate outlets. Memorials began to arrive at the capitol requesting that the governor call a special session of the legislature.

[19] Sam Houston to Sam Houston, Jr., Austin, May 2, 1860, Sam Houston Hearne Collection.

An undecided Houston stalled in trivial legalities, attempting to slow the Democrats' enactment of events. He went on short speaking tours, trying, for the sake of his next political steps, to understand whether the people felt Texas patriotism or Southern patriotism. His tendency was to believe the former. Previously his appearance had softened tempers, but in Austin a woman drew a pistol on him, and similar incidents occurred elsewhere.

At the Governor's Mansion, Margaret lived in anxiety. She and the girls attended concerts. They sang in the choir of the big stone church Margaret had joined. To honor a dying churchwoman, Margaret journeyed with the congregation out two miles into the country to partake of the lady's final communion in the shade of the trees.[20] Margaret's self-imposed obscurity had made fear an easy emotion to waken in her. Her worry over Sam caused the governor finally to remove the boy from Colonel Allen's academy. When confining Sam to the mansion proved impossible, the state geologist, Nancy Lea's "one armed" friend, was dispatched on an expedition into Mexico, and Sam was sent with him.[21]

An impatient element of Texans began to drift into Austin. Noisy night meetings were followed by crowds of men climbing the hill to the mansion and watching its lighted windows from the darkness. Weary over Houston's procrastination in calling the legislature, Austin's visitors and the large secessionist group in town sent out a statewide request that delegates be sent to Austin in January for a convention. Houston had loathed these conventions since they had become the fashionable outlet of discontented people thirty years before. With no fanfare he summoned the legislature to meet January 21, one week before the convention.

[20] Terrell, "Recollections of General Sam Houston," 121.

[21] Margaret Lea Houston to Nancy Lea, Austin, January 21, 1861, University of Texas Archives.

Houston had shown his first sign of retreat.[22] The people reacted joyously. A throng marched down Congress Avenue then poured over the fence of the mansion, tramping Margaret's flowers and dumping potted plants off the porch. General Houston appeared and spoke to the mob, which cheered him and went home in tolerable humor.

One week later, news came to Austin that South Carolina had seceded from the Union. Newspaper editorials in fiery terms urged Texas to follow. Houston was less worried about the newspapers and the politicians than the strange silence of the public. He suspected that the Democrats were not as powerful with the people as they believed, and he continued making speeches.[23] Secession, he warned, would mean civil war; the coast would be blockaded. Europe, in spite of its need for cotton, would not interfere because of strong antislavery sentiment. Death and ruin would be the only fruits of a war at home. There was an alternative: Mexico.

Ashbel Smith came to Austin to try to persuade Houston to change his mind. The secessionists, among whom Smith was an important worker, were annoyed with Houston's conduct. Dr. Smith seems to have known Houston the politician well enough to suspect that Houston had his own political future close at heart. Few of the Democrats seem to have thought the people opposed secession. It was believed that East Texas and Southeast Texas by themselves could weigh the vote.[24] Houston was not convinced by the propaganda of his political enemies, and when Abraham Lincoln offered him an army with which to keep Texas in the Union, Houston refused. His only personal hope, and consequently what

[22] Maher, Jr., "Sam Houston and Secession," 452.

[23] Terrell, "Recollections of General Sam Houston," 452–53.

[24] Royall Tyler Wheeler to O. M. Roberts, January 6, 1861, cited in Maher, Jr., "Sam Houston and Secession," 454.

he believed best for Texas, was to prevent secession without bloodshed. He knew there was a large, but unorganized, antisecession element in the state. The problem was to call it up to support him, in spite of the Democratic workers, who were plentiful, often dangerous, and vigilant.

The beginning of January, 1861, brought blowing rain to wash the brick walls of the mansion, keeping the family inside and chilly. Houston was rarely with his family. Business was being conducted in his office during long hours, beginning in the early morning. To Nancy Lea, Margaret wrote late in the month, "General Houston seems cheerful and hopeful through the day, but in the still watches of the night I hear him agonizing in prayer for our distracted country."[25] Margaret wanted to leave Austin. She missed her mother, Varilla, and Antoinette, and the peaceful little church in Independence. "I cannot shut my eyes," she wrote, "to the dangers that threaten us. I know that it is even probable that we may soon be reduced to poverty, but oh I have such a sweet assurance in my heart that the presence of the Lord will go with us wherever we may go, and that even in the wilderness we may erect an altar of prayer!"[26]

Margaret wrote her letter, well aware of the importance of the day. It was the morning of January 21, 1861. "The legislature meets today and the town is filling up fast. Much depends upon their deliberations." Her windows at the mansion surveyed the spectacle of the capitol and the land beyond. Crowds of men ascended the slope to the portico; others tarried at the board fence where the horses were hitched. "God can incline their hearts to do right," Margaret wrote to her mother that morning. "See Bro. Ross as soon as possible and ask him to make it a subject of

[25] Margaret Lea Houston to Nancy Lea, Austin, January 21, 1861, University of Texas Archives.

[26] *Ibid.*

prayer that the executive and legislature may be guided by the hand of God in all they do."[27]

The legislature legalized the convention, but clipped its wings with the restriction that its decisions required a confirming vote of the people. Four days later the convention assembled. Houston was not welcome at its meetings, nor did he entertain any fantasies about what was going to be done. He was seated on the porch of the mansion when the secession vote was counted at the capitol. By the screaming and cheering that came from the capitol windows, he knew what had happened, but he seems not to have wanted to believe it. Later on, when a man ran down the street and yelled the news to the family seated on the porch, Houston sank back in his rocking chair and turned to Margaret. "Texas is lost," he said.[28]

But Sam Houston was still governor. He rambled about the immediate countryside making speeches, studying at close range the reactions of the people. The dangers of fanaticism were the themes of his oratory. His condemnation of the convention was even hesitant at times, and he told his audiences that their governor had the best interests of Texas at heart. On February 23, the general election on the question of secession was held. The people of Texas voted a majority in favor.

The secession convention then reassembled. Forming a committee of public safety, they ordered the surrender of General David E. Twiggs, commander of the large United States installation at San Antonio. Houston had anticipated the aims of the convention, and approached Twiggs with the request that the troops be surrendered to the governor personally.[29] The sympathy of General Twiggs was with the convention and, more specifically, with the Confederate States of America.

[27] *Ibid.*

[28] James, *The Raven*, p. 412.

[29] Terrell, "Recollections of General Sam Houston," 135.

Sam Houston's actions during the early spring of 1861 showed cautious experimentation. On March 4, he officially pronounced Texas' separation from the United States and considered that the status of the old Republic had returned. Houston's Mexican plan now seemed feasible. During his governorship, Houston had assembled all the weapons and ammunition the United States Army would send by magnifying the Mexican and Indian threat on paper, thereby increasing the flow of military supplies to Texas. His Mexican scheme did not need United States participation. Texas could effect it herself, with the aid of Indians and sympathetic Mexicans.

The convention united Texas with the Confederacy on March 5, after Houston's secession proclamation. Houston refused to recognize that union, on the grounds that legally the right to such a decision lay in the hands of the people. If necessary, Sam Houston was willing to pit himself against the convention or, more succinctly, the Democratic party, which, by its Confederate alliance, was merely reaffirming its national loyalties of the past decade. Houston had fought the Democrats in Washington; he would fight them and their Confederacy in Texas. The people had supported him in 1859, and he believed his Texas nationalism and his Mexican design would draw them to him again. The convention ignored the governor. Houston appealed to the people, which, as their elected leader, he had a right to do. In a letter he advised the secretary of war of the Confederacy that the convention's joining Texas to the Confederate States of America was illegal. The convention, hearing this, became hostile and took immediate steps toward silencing Sam Houston.

Dinner was being placed on the table at eight o'clock Friday evening, March 15, 1861, when a knock sounded at the door of the mansion. George W. Chilton, a member of the convention, was ushered into the house with an announcement. On the next day at noon all government officials, by order of the convention, were required to present themselves at the capitol and take an oath of loyalty to the Confederacy, or be removed from office. After Chilton went away, the family ate dinner, and when the dishes were cleared, Margaret ordered the two-volume Bible brought and placed before her husband. According to the usual custom the servants took seats along the walls. Having finished her prayers, Margaret took a lamp and went upstairs with the children. Fifteen-year-old Nannie asked her father not to be worried. Later Margaret told Nannie that General Houston's lamp burned until daybreak. When Margaret came downstairs the next morning, Houston met her saying, "Margaret, I will never do it."[30]

General Houston went to his office at the capitol, leaving Margaret alone with the children. One wonders whether she was watching the capitol or whether she drew her curtains. A noisy, jeering mass of people collected on the lawn, then completely covered it. Margaret must have heard the clock strike noon. During the afternoon Sam Houston crossed the capitol grounds. He had whittled while his dismissal took place on the piazza above his office. Monday morning he went before the legislature and demanded that the convention be dissolved. The legislature confirmed the convention's declaration that the office of governor was vacated.[31] The lieutenant governor had taken the oath and was now governor of Texas.

Margaret had begun packing. Late at night on Tuesday, March 19, she and the general and some friends sat by the light of a single candle among crates and barrels in the mansion. At the front door there came a quick, loud knock. They admitted several men who described an army of Houston supporters, sympathizers

[30] Temple Houston Morrow, Address to the Forty-Ninth Texas Legislature, Austin, February 27, 1945, *Senate Journal*, 282–83.

[31] Maher, Jr., "Sam Houston and Secession," 455.

with the Mexican plan, doubtless, and the revival of the Republic, waiting in the hills outside Austin to forcibly return Houston to the governorship. His word would set them moving. In the candlelight Margaret and her guests watched quietly as the general thought about the offer and spoke. Houston thanked the men but implored them to go to their army and say "for the sake of humanity and justice to disperse to go to their homes and to conceal from the world that they would have been guilty of such an act." To preserve "one poor old man in a position for a few days longer" was not worth the blood which would be shed.[32] The callers left him alone, muttering that were he twenty years younger, he would be with them.

In the last days of March, the Houston caravan moved out of Austin. From the window of the yellow coach, at the head of Congress Avenue, the lively throngs were visible milling in and out of the stores. Behind the coach stood the empty mansion. Over the capitol the flag of the Confederacy blew in the wind. Margaret and Sam Houston were bound for Independence. They had no money, but they were together, alive, and leaving Austin, and Margaret had more or less what she wanted. She was going home where her kin and her church waited for her. Had Houston led a filibustering army, he would have left her to worry in sleepless misery, believing that he was wounded or dead. He might have taken the oath of loyalty to the Confederacy and humbled himself before the Democrats he loathed, or he could have remained to contest the convention perhaps to a tragic ending before an assassin's bullet. The general had been wise to step down, even though in doing so he had voluntarily sacrificed his immediate political future to the forces he had fought since annexation. Undoubtedly

[32] An article by "A Friend Who Was Present," *Galveston Daily News*, April 3, 1892, *Writings*, VIII, 293; see also *Writings*, VIII, 312.

the thought of it hurt him. But his wife, who cared nothing for politics, felt differently. For twenty-one years she had yearned to have the assurance that she and Sam Houston would be together permanently. Her patience now seemed rewarded.

9.

Fierce Winds at Cedar Point

Independence usually seemed different from the rest of Texas, yet even Independence had not escaped the Confederate fever. The heat of public feeling prompted the preachers to stage a debate, in which the more vehement male students participated. Speakers for the Union won, and the United States flag was flown over the town. When news of secession came, the mayor went out with an axe and felled the pole, leaving it and the flag in the dirt. April cannons in South Carolina sent many Baylor boys to their hometowns to volunteer, lest the war be over before Independence got up a company. The Male Department became smaller, but the Female Department, four blocks away, remained the same, perched on its commanding hill.

The peaceful look of her house west of the square belied Nancy Lea's worry that everyone she loved was being swallowed up by the war. In Marion, Henry's sixteen-year-old daughter had married at Serena's house. Early the next morning she had cut up her wedding gown and had sewn it into a flag which she presented to the captain of the Marion volunteer company on the campus of

Judson College. The captain was her bridegroom, whom that day she bade goodbye at Judson's big oak tree that grew up on the edge of the street. One of Varilla's sons had already gone to the army. Charles and Antoinette had made plans to go with Charlie's brother Tom to Mexico for the purpose of seeking passage to England. Maybe Margaret had suffered more than anyone else. Her fifteen months in Austin had been frustrating ones. The obvious retreat was Independence, where Nancy Lea had welcomed the Houstons into her house. General Houston had gone to a bedroom, and he would not emerge. A preacher who came to call said Sam Houston was alternately praying, weeping, and sleeping.[1]

Nancy Lea was opposed to General Houston's plans to move to Cedar Point. She believed Independence was the right place for the Houstons. Houston, however, looked with dread upon retirement. Even now he could not refuse an offer to speak in public. At Brenham he had suffered the humiliation of seeing an onlooker brandish a Colt pistol so that the audience of noisy secessionists would allow him to continue. Back in Independence in May he spoke on the square beside the stub of the flagpole the mayor had chopped. He talked about the Confederacy to several hundreds assembled, reminding the people that he was a Southerner, too. "The time has come when a man's section is his country. I stand by mine." Texans had joined the Confederate States of America, and he stated, "I can but cast my lot with theirs."[2]

The state geological expedition ended when news of the events in Austin reached the party in Mexico. Sam was back, riding the fine gray stud, making quite an impression around Baylor. He was eighteen. Colonel Allen's drill instructions still rang in his ears,

[1] Burleson, *Life and Writings of Rufus Burleson*, 582.

[2] Sam Houston, A Speech At Independence, May 10, 1861, *Writings*, VIII, 301–305.

and he talked frequently of being a soldier. Margaret and the general became concerned that he would volunteer with one of the companies in the region. Houston wrote a long list of tasks needed at Cedar Point. Sam would be "overseer." Advising him to "be industrious," the Houstons waved him goodbye and when time had passed, Sam Houston wrote to his son:

> Keep the hoes in the corn. Keep them down. Have all *things* kept out of the field. See to the goats and stock. If it is too wet to do anything in the corn, put up a new cow pen; also one for the goats. . . . Do what you think best. . . . Keep the hands busy. I intend to be satisfied with whatever you may do.[3]

Nancy Lea was among the first to notice Houston's failing health. Her objections to his taking the family to Cedar Point were vocal. The first time they packed and made ready to go, she fell ill of the colic and ordered Bingley to bring out her coffin. For a long time the mother's moroseness had troubled Margaret: "It seems so strange that you should despond dear Mother, who has always been so hopeful and enduring, you who have enjoyed God's mercies for four and eighty years."[4] Margaret, back in Austin, had written to Mrs. Lea that she had asked God if "it might be my privilege to take care of you in your last days, and thus repay in some small degree the hours of anxiety you have endured on my account."[5]

Sam Houston had decided to go to Cedar Point, and there was no stopping him. Margaret obediently bundled up little Temple and, with Eliza, climbed into the coach. She had enrolled Nannie, Maggie, and Mary Willie in Baylor's Female Department and

[3] Sam Houston to Sam Houston, Jr., Independence, May 15, 1861, *Writings*, VIII, 305–306.

[4] Margaret Lea Houston to Nancy Lea, Austin, January 21, 1861, University of Texas Archives.

[5] *Ibid.*

had instructed them to respond to Nancy Lea's slightest wish. Shortly before June 1, the coach traversed the great oak grove where Ben Lomond stood, the log house a newlywed Margaret had decorated with seashells she and the general had gathered on the beach. The salt air at Cedar Point had strengthened Margaret in the past, and her children had profited from it more recently. Cedar Point had been many things to the Houstons, and now it was their sanctuary.

They were penniless, though Houston's credit was good because he owned huge tracts of land, valued on the tax rolls at $150,000. The Austin newspapers had made remarks about his being a rich man. He was in fact only on paper a man of means, for he loaned money unwisely and overinvested in land, a typical folly of the age. Little of the acreage was adequately surveyed. When asked to evaluate his real estate, he sometimes compiled extravagantly because he was proud and believed that anything he owned had endless potential and was worth more than it really was. His salary had not been paid in full by the Texas government, and, as always, expenses were high. After he had satisfied his Austin and Independence store debts, Sam Houston was without money. He needed to go to Cedar Point, hoping his family could exist on the fruits of its land.

Margaret established a household routine to please Houston. He was nervous, and his wounds pained him miserably. On warm afternoons Margaret walked with him or drove him along the edge of the water, down to the bay. He moved more slowly than he once did and now used a walking stick. If he mentioned a taste for oysters, oysters were before him the next time he sat down to eat. Some days he went to Houston City by land or by boat to Galveston, and mingled scarcely noticed among men in saloons and restaurants and listened to the talk. He called on old friends—and enemies—and came back to Cedar Point after a day or so, to an evening meal Margaret had delayed for him. During restless nights Margaret sat beside a sputtering candle and read to him from Harvey's *Meditations* or the Bible or, bitterly, from one of the newspapers that piled editorial assaults upon him. Summer's passage found him seldom mentioned any more.

Sam remained dutifully at Cedar Point during June and July. He was not happy and was uncomfortable listening to his father's reminiscences. Houston longed to be close to his son. For the first time he tried to speak to Sam as an adult. "I fear that within twenty days, or less, an assault will be made on some part of our coast, and how are we prepared to repel it? Have we men? Will we have means? Will . . . the gallant men made by the Convention, or the Committee of Vigilance, save us in our hour of peril?"[6] Houston knew Sam longed to be a hero in the army. He wrote as follows:

> When it is proper you shall go to war, if you really wish to do so. It is every man's duty to defend his Country; and I wish my offspring to do so at the proper time and in the proper way. We are not wanted or needed out of Texas, and we may soon be wanted and needed in Texas. Until then, my son, be content.[7]

It was not easy for General Houston to talk to Sam. In these eighteen years the General had given little of himself to his son, but had expected everything from the boy. Margaret had reared Sam to believe his father more a hero than a man, and Houston liked her adulation. It seems to have been difficult for Sam to reconcile the old man before him with his mother's hero. At Cedar Point they lived together under circumstances neither the father

[6] Sam Houston to Sam Houston, Jr., Cedar Point, July 23, 1861, *Writings*, VIII, 308–309.

[7] Sam Houston to Sam Houston, Jr., Independence, May 22, 1861, *Writings*, VIII, 306–307.

nor the son had known before. Houston had no clearly definable scheme for the future. Sam felt caged in the sudden closeness. In mid-July, when Mart Royston, Varilla's son and overseer of Ashbel Smith's Evergreen farm, wrote that Sam must visit him, the parents could only agree, thinking that it would ease the boy's boredom.

Not many days went by before Margaret received a letter from Sam, who confessed that he was drilling with Dr. Smith's volunteer company, the Bayland Guards, which Mart Royston had already joined. Margaret was upset. At his desk, which was kept in the open hallway, the general wrote to Sam. "If Texas did not require your services, and you wished to go elsewhere, why then all would be well, but as she will need your aid, your first allegiance is due to her and let nothing cause you in any moment of ardor to assume any obligation to any other power whatsoever, without my consent." Sam Houston was worried about more than loyalties. "Houston is not, nor will be a favorite name in the Confederacy! Thus, you had best keep your duty and your hopes together, and when the drill is over come home. Your Dear Ma and all of us send best love to you and Martin. . . . When will you be home, my son!"[8]

He was at home in August to tell them he had enlisted under Ashbel Smith in the Bayland Guards. Margaret's shock had not subsided by the day Sam left for Galveston Island, where his company was training. General Houston had done his best to rescue the household from chaos. He took Sam's side in the arguments, and Sam remembered it affectionately for the rest of his life. The last day Houston gave Sam a present from the family. Sam pulled from the box a Confederate uniform, and at once he put it on. Tearfully Margaret took a small Bible and tucked it in

[8] Sam Houston to Sam Houston, Jr., Cedar Point, July 23, 1861, *Writings*, VIII, 308–309.

his vest pocket. For days after he was gone, seven-year-old Andrew tormented Margaret's already unbearable grief demanding that he have a uniform and be allowed to follow Sam to war.[9]

General Houston was not content to cry. Sam, in his uniform, had looked very handsome, and Houston recalled the day in Maryville when he had bid his mother goodbye and had gone away with the army. The general had not known before how much the boy was like him. Throughout the autumn Sam Houston went to Galveston to watch the regiments in training. He visited in the camps, where he sat in his black buggy and watched Sam drill. The soldiers treated him with great respect, making him feel welcomed into their crowded camp, lessening the difficult imprisonment of Cedar Point and the seeming inevitability of obscurity.[10]

Margaret stayed at home, close to her Bible and the children. The strange circumstances of her realized dream of living at Cedar Point were melodramatic. Houston was away as much as he could be and was little comfort in her worries about Sam. A realistic Sam Houston, before leaving Independence, had written of Cedar Point, "We will be hard run to live, for the first year."[11] Had the Houstons, over the two past decades, endeavored to develop a paying farm at Cedar Point, they might have enjoyed abundant food and comforts in their retreat. But Cedar Point was as yet a wilderness much as it had been in the 1830's, with the exception of the grove of liveoaks that ran to the bayou.

Stranded that autumn of 1861, the Houstons looked for means of making money. When their need sharpened, Houston sent the Negroes out into the fringe of the grove to cut certain trees into cordwood, place them aboard barges, and ship them to Galveston

[9] Author in conversation with Mrs. Jennie Morrow Decker, Houston, January 10, 1965.

[10] James, *The Raven*, 418.

[11] Sam Houston to Sam Houston, Jr., Independence, May 22, 1861, *Writings*, VIII, 306–307.

to sell for firewood. The axe took more and more of the oaks, and by Christmas there were only a few trees left. In General Houston's desk were receipts for the Confederate taxes, which had been paid with some of the tree money.[12]

Christmas, the family was together at Cedar Point. Without its trees, the weathered cabin faced the elements. Maggie and Nannie and Mary Willie came from Independence by public stage, and General Houston made Sam put on his uniform for the girls to see. After New Year's Day, the girls returned to Independence to school, and the time came for Sam to go back to Galveston Island, where his company awaited orders to go to war. It was now more difficult for Margaret to surrender Sam than it had ever been. She wept when Sam and his father drove away in the buggy. Emotional pain affected her health, and Eliza put her to bed. A cold, blowing winter closed in on Cedar Point, whose residence was ill equipped to cope with such weather. The children suffered colds, but Margaret continued to tutor them in reading and the Bible. Her own condition of intermittent chills and fever did not improve. Houston told Nannie he had faith that she would revive "when the fierce winds cease."[13]

Sam's company left for Missouri on March 12. General Houston went to Galveston to see them off. Margaret wrote to her son, telling him to read the little Bible she had given him and not to forget his Christian upbringing. To Nancy Lea she recalled the scene of Sam's leaving her in January: "My weakness gave him the opportunity of displaying traits of character that made his father's heart swell with pride."[14] Over a packet of his letters, she

[12] Sam Houston to C. R. Johns, Houston City, July 11, 1861, *Writings*, VIII, 307; also author in conversation with Mrs. Jennie Morrow Decker, Houston, January 10, 1965.

[13] Sam Houston to "My Darling Daughter," Cedar Point, April 16, 1862, Sam Houston Hearne Collection.

[14] Margaret Lea Houston to Nancy Lea, Cedar Point, March 17, 1862, University of Texas Archives.

moaned that she would never see Sam again. Houston, returning from Galveston, left "nothing unsaid" in consoling her by boasting about Sam's manly farewell. She was not to be soothed by anybody. "I cannot forget that my boy, my darling, he that was to be the prop of my old age, is gone from me, probably never to return."[15]

Her grief increased to such proportions that her mind sought a familiar outlet. Sam had not been converted to the church, though he was "seeking religion most earnestly." Margaret, in remorse, turned to Nancy Lea. "My Darling Mother. . . . My heart seems almost broken, and yet I am astonished that I bear it all. Oh how I need your Spartan nerves and iron fortitude to sustain me." She had been able to bear Sam's joining the Bayland Guards, but when he left for Missouri, "I thought I would lie down and die. . . . It is strange how life will cling to such a poor emaciated frame as mine. . . . Oh Mother . . . reprove me as sharply as you please. It will do me good. I deserve it all."[16] In conclusion Margaret tried to analyze herself. "I find that I had really enshrined an idol in my heart. I did not love him more than the rest of my children, but he absorbed all my anxiety, all my hopes and fears. . . . Dear Mother, beg Brother Ross to . . . offer up a prayer of faith for my poor boy." If Margaret could be sure that Sam had accepted Christ, she wrote, "I would give him up, but this is my great source of distress. . . . Beg my Christian friends all to pray for Sam."[17]

The weeks passed into a warm April. Neither Margaret's poor health nor her sadness kept General Houston at home. He went frequently to Galveston and Houston City. Late at night he climbed down from the buggy to the porch, and they sat, listening to the peaceful sounds of the bay, and talked. Affectionate letters

[15] *Ibid.*

[16] *Ibid.*

[17] *Ibid.*

came from the girls at Independence. Margaret read them aloud, then heard the general speak on various subjects until late at night. Through newspapers they followed Sam's regiment. On April 6 and 7, it was involved in a surprise attack upon General U. S. Grant's forces at Shiloh, Tennessee. Grant was reinforced. The Confederates retreated to Corinth, Mississippi.

To draw themselves from worries about Sam and to amuse the children, Margaret and the general went on drives in the countryside. Sam Houston walked with difficulty. Since the horse theft at the mansion, he had bought Jenny Lind and Chester Lyons, the former being a good harness mare. After their excursions the Houstons returned, anticipating mail from the girls or a report from Sam. General Houston wrote to Maggie one afternoon, saying that he and Margaret had taken the children for a ride. In the course of the drive they passed under a China tree in bloom. "I stopped for your Ma to pull some [of] the flowers. She got a supply and Temple reached his hand, and your Ma gave him some. Coming on home, Andrew lit from behind the buggy & got some Primroses. Temple . . . held on to his flowers, and when he met Eliza he presented them to her as a present."[18] Margaret had been very proud and had pressed the flowers "as an evidence of his reflection, as well as affection for his nurse and friend."[19]

"We have heard," wrote Sam Houston, "of a great battle at Corinth, but we have not learned the result, nor have we heard from any of the Moroms Regiment, tho it was in the battle. Your Dear Ma of course is in a state of painful anxiety until she can hear from Bro. Sam. . . . We pray that God has shielded him from harm in battles hour."[20]

[18] Sam Houston to "My Darling Daughter," Cedar Point, April 16, 1862, Sam Houston Hearne Collection.

[19] *Ibid.*

[20] *Ibid.*

The girls' letters to their parents were detailed, giving long accounts of their exploits as Baylor students. They took Sam Houston into their confidence, telling him Nannie was reprimanded for talking during a lecture. Houston was a grateful accomplice: "PS I write this *since* your Ma's post script. . . . I have not . . . told . . . one word about your talking at the lecture."[21]

Early in May, a letter came from one of Sam's friends. The package was inscribed, "Battlefield of Corinth."[22]

> You have heard of [Shiloh]—I shook hands with Sam on the morning of the 7th. I was carried to camp 16 miles from the battlefield. . . . Sam and some 7 or 8 others were in no way accounted for . . . Some may have been wounded—and perhaps have fallen into the hands of the enemy. . . . I by no means despair of Sam's safety.

Margaret would believe nothing but that Sam was dead. Grief stricken in her belief, she took up her Bible and spent long hours alone beside her window.

General Houston passed much of the summer of 1862 in Galveston. The black buggy and his walking stick became the trademarks of a man who, for the first time in many years, could walk a public street in Texas and not be recognized. On a road at the outskirts of Houston City a Confederate soldier blocked the way, saying that nobody could pass without a permit from the provost marshal. Sam Houston snapped, "Go to San Jacinto and learn my right to travel in Texas," and drove on.[23]

That summer the girls came to Cedar Point to be with their mother. Had it not been for Sam's absence, summer would have

[21] *Ibid.*

[22] [Unknown] to General Sam Houston, Battlefield of Corinth, April 16, 1862, University of Texas Archives.

[23] "The Last Years of Sam Houston," *Harper's New Monthly Magazine*, New York, Harper Brothers, Vol. XXXII, 633.

seemed like old times in Huntsville or Independence. The little Cedar Point house brimmed with young people whose laughter cheered Margaret. Houston himself showed optimism about Sam: "The Bay Land Guards," he wrote, "are nearly naked and destitute, having lost all at the battle of Shiloh, where we lost our son, though we still hope to reclaim him some day."[24]

Margaret and the general followed every source of information about their son with a quick letter, then waited for a reply.[25] There was feeble promise of news until the last of August, when the letter came assuring them that Sam was alive. He had been captured, after being wounded in combat, and "kindly cured at the residence of a former friend of yours in Chicago."[26] The favor repaid Houston's defense of the preachers in the United States Senate ten years before.

Because of the close proximity of Cedar Point to Galveston, soldiers occasionally passed near the house on the way upcountry. They were a common enough sight, traveling alone. The Houstons gladly gave them food and a cool drink from the cistern.

One balmy afternoon late in September, Margaret was working among her flowers. General Houston was in Galveston, or she would have been sitting with him in the hall and would possibly have seen the thin, crippled soldier before she did. When at last she saw him and did not register surprise, he spoke: "Ma, I don't believe you know me!" It was Sam.[27]

[24] Sam Houston to S. M. Swenson, Cedar Point, August 14, 1862, *Writings*, III, 320–22.

[25] Margaret Lea Houston to Mrs. Anson Jones, May 6, 1862, and May 13, 1862, Jones manuscripts, University of Texas Archives.

[26] J. M. Worsham, C.S.A., to Sam Houston, Bay Come, July 20, 1862, University of Texas Archives.

[27] James, *The Raven*, 421, as related by Nettie Houston Bringhurst to Marquis James.

10.

Steamboat House

Margaret's coach and the wagons climbed the hill to Huntsville. It was chilly that December, and the odor of the pines was sweet. Margaret was glad not to have to spend another winter at Cedar Point. After the October capture of Galveston Island by Federal forces, the Houstons had gone to Independence, where the older children, including Sam, were enrolled in Baylor. General Houston silenced the boy's talk of returning to war and instructed him to remain with his sisters and Nancy Lea. Charles Power and Antoinette had been turned back by the blockade, so they were in Independence and could aid in managing matters for Nancy Lea.

The idea of moving back to Huntsville had not pleased Margaret. Everything favored remaining in Independence, for Nancy Lea's house was large and near the church, and there was ample space in which to make a vegetable garden to supply the family. Still, Sam Houston yearned to live in Huntsville again. His return from selling timber had been meager, a fact he covered very well with, among other purchases, a piano for Nannie.[1] He had become bored with Independence and decided to try to buy back the Huntsville house. Margaret, the youngest children, and several of the servants followed him to East Texas.

He registered at Captain Sims's hotel until he could permanently establish himself. Citizen Sam Houston found the Huntsville people as inhospitable toward his financial practices as they were toward his political views, and when he could not buy his old house on credit, he decided to rent a house. It was a peculiar two-story wooden house up the street from Oakwood Cemetery and across a meadow from the state penitentiary. Local people called it the Steamboat House. Tall and narrow, it had shallow porches which ran the full length of each side, upstairs and below, and were camouflaged in front by two crenelated towers set at each end of the façade. A steep and uncomfortable staircase led from the second floor parlor to the ground and was not sheltered from the weather. The side porches, the stair, and the shape of the building, taken collectively, did make a passable portrayal of a steamboat. Crude construction was compensated by genteel fittings, principally iron stoves, to replace the open fires Margaret disliked.[2]

The Houstons settled down in the Steamboat House and made a pleasant life for themselves, though they might have been happier in the old house across town. Houston was becoming feeble, and that troubled Margaret more than anything else. Time and the events of the last years had worn furrows. Houston's hair was very white, and he bent over the walking stick Joshua had carved for him out of hickory. When he was tired, he coughed

[1] Mrs. W. A. Wood, "The Houston Piano," The Baylor *Century*, November, 1940; item, Houston Collection, Baylor University.

[2] Lilla Kittrell to Mrs. I. B. McFarland, n.d., Wall Collection, Tennessee State Archives.

unceasingly. Margaret was perceptive. She must have seen how monotonous her life was for a man accustomed to being at the center of things. The children and the servants allowed little privacy. Houston selected the dark room behind the front stair downstairs for his bedroom. Unless he was in quest of a breeze, he remained on the ground level, for the climb upstairs was difficult for him. His wounds ached. There were seven of them on the front of his body, and the cut made by the Indian arrow a half-century before still abcessed and drained blood.[3]

"I would be most happy to see you," he had written to Ashbel Smith, who was at home recuperating from a battle wound. "If I were to do so, I would only say 'Another man ought not to leave Texas.' . . . Oh that our Governor would rise from his *lair* and shake the dew drops from his mane!!!" Texas, Houston insisted, should defend herself before she defended the Confederacy. "If Texas is ruined, what would the Confederacy be without her? She has been its *van* and *rear* guard." Galveston was lost. The future promised despair unless the Texans began to think more about their own homes than of the Confederate States of America, whose leaders, without one thought of Texas' welfare, were using Texans to protect the states nearer the front.[4]

On January 7, the news arrived upcountry that General John B. Magruder had recaptured Galveston Island in a bold morning attack on New Year's Day. Sam Houston wrote to the hero of Galveston: "You have breathed new life into everything." Texas, Houston hoped, "will yet show the world that she is capable of defending her own soil."[5] Houston's enthusiasm did not wane as the winter changed into spring and the wild azaleas and dogwood

[3] Ashbel Smith, undated notes on Sam Houston, University of Texas Archives.

[4] Sam Houston to Ashbel Smith, Independence, November 18, 1862, *Writings*, VIII, 323.

[5] Sam Houston to General J. B. Magruder, Huntsville, January 7, 1863, *Writings*, VIII, 314.

bloomed in the thickets beyond Steamboat House. Houston still considered himself governor of Texas. His departure from the capital had been a practical move more than a sacrifice. Perhaps the time was coming when he would return to the office of governor. He became occupied with improving his health, staying at home and taking medicines, claiming as his sole amusement an occasional walk over the side pasture to the penitentiary to visit the United States soldiers who were taken as prisoners of war at Galveston. Most of them were from the Union ship *Harriet Lane* sunk in Galveston Bay. Among those men Houston found congenial company. Most of Huntsville's inhabitants were old men and young boys, left behind with the women, and few of them sympathized with Sam Houston or interested him. In small ways Houston helped the prisoners by arranging conveniences, such as an honor system under which they could attend functions in town.

Houston suffered few of the family worries that increasingly bothered Margaret. When she could, she protected him from bad news. Maggie took scarlet fever. When she was able to travel, Charles Power brought her home to Huntsville. Once she recovered, Maggie was unable to re-enter Baylor, and she served her father as secretary, thus relieving Margaret of the tedious duty. Maggie was a strong, independent girl, and Sam Houston admired her spirit. A note informed the family that Sam had withdrawn from school. General Houston, enraged, dictated a letter of reprimand to Sam, who returned a disrespectful reply, saying that he was going back to the army and that he had a bill of credit at the store which must be paid. Whether the general saw the letter or not is questionable, for Margaret answered her son. "There seems to be every possibility that the Yankees will take Texas, but do not be uneasy. God rules over all. Some of the hottest Secessionists are becoming very mealy-mouthed." Sam, she wrote, must learn to act in a gentlemanly manner when corrected. In spite of his wound and his war record, he was still a boy not quite twenty years of age. "As to your store account, I do not know what to say. I do not think your father has the remotest idea that you have made any bills. Do not get any thing more, I beseech you."[6]

The room which housed the general's desk also contained a large number of books and an estimated eight trunks of papers, a veritable archive of Houston's life since he had left Tennessee.[7] It took a large wagon to transport these belongings, which Houston had always insisted on having with him at the family residence. His office was a nostalgic place. In a pensive moment his eyes could fall upon the Indian costume whose intricately beaded buckskin had clothed the exiled governor of Tennessee.[8] On another peg hung the inexpensive brass-handled sword he had carried at San Jacinto.[9] From a gilt oval, the face of an auburn-haired, blue-eyed young Houston looked back disbelievingly at an old man who remembered those days with Andrew Jackson at The Hermitage.[10] At his desk March 3, 1863, Houston wrote to his friend Eber W. Cave, who was also one of his most loyal supporters, "Yesterday, my friend, concluded my seventieth year; and now if I am not wise, I may at least claim to have experience, which is said to be nature's great teacher."[11]

[6] Margaret Lea Houston to Sam Houston, Jr., Huntsville, February 6, 1863, University of Texas Archives.

[7] The estimate of eight trunks is the nearest estimate the author could determine, going by various Houston family traditions. William Carey Crane is the only person ever allowed to see that material intact, and he left no indication of the size of the collection. Author in conversation with Mrs. Jennie Morrow Decker, Houston, January 10, 1965, and with Mrs. F. S. Baldwin, Houston, January 10, 1965.

[8] Item, Franklin Williams Collection.

[9] Item, Sam Houston Memorial Museum.

[10] Item, San Jacinto Museum of History.

[11] Sam Houston to Major Eber W. Cave, Huntsville, March 3, 1863, *Writings*, VIII, 326–27.

Memorabilia did not turn the general's head from the presence of opportunity. Provocative rumors came to the quiet of Steamboat House, and Sam Houston's name was returning to the major Texas newspapers through a ripple of anti-war feeling. There seemed to be present the flavor of Texas nationalism that Houston had known during the Republic. To satisfy his suspicions, he emerged from Steamboat House and took the stage to the coast.

In mid-March he spoke publicly at Houston City. "As you have gathered here to listen to the sentiments of my heart, knowing that the days draw nigh unto me . . . I know that you will bear with me, while I express those sentiments which seem natural to my mind."[12] He could still hold an audience, and he confirmed the fact at his Houston City appearance. "The gallant dead! How fell they? Heroes! Thousands of whom no monuments, save the memory of their everlasting valor. At the cannon's mouth . . . in the deadliest charge, with forlorn hope . . . at the first breach, there lay the Texan! The soldier of liberty died for her sake. . . . Such men cannot be conquered."[13] Of himself he said that in the ocean of time "I approach the narrow isthmus, which divides it from the sea of eternity beyond . . . the welfare and glory of Texas will be the uppermost thought, while the spark of life lingers in this breast. . . . Once I dreamed of an empire for a united people. . . . The dream is over."[14]

But not entirely over. One evening during his Houston City visit he called on Major Eber Cave, who had resigned as Texas' secretary of state rather than to take the Confederate oath. At Cave's residence were the major and A. W. Terrell, and Houston asked them what they thought of a plan to call the Texas soldiers

[12] Sam Houston, Speech at Houston City, March 18, 1863, *Writings*, VIII, 327–39.

[13] *Ibid.*

[14] *Ibid.*

home from the Confederate Army, then raise the Lone Star flag and tell the conflicting sections of the United States to leave Texas alone. Cave and Terrell said the "madness of the hour" would effect the ruin of any man who made such a proposal. They said that it would be called "treachery." Before Houston left them, he asked that the conversation not be repeated.[15]

He went home to Steamboat House a sick man. Margaret put him to bed in the room under the stair, but he could not rest because he was excited over the possibility of returning to public life. Friends irritated the situation by inquiring if stories they had heard were true. "My Dear General," wrote Charles Power, "I make no doubt but that the People will call you out yet for Governor. I never saw such a change in my life. If they elect you, well and good—but do not run except you are very sure."[16]

Power left on a trip to Mexico to try to arrange passage to England by way of Veracruz, and he invited Sam to go along as a guard. The boy gladly accepted the offer, which delighted the Houstons. The family had been afraid he would go back to the army as he had threatened to do. With Sam in Mexico, the only remaining family problems originating at Independence were minor ones, arising primarily from Antoinette's priggishness about the Houston girls' writing to soldiers. Houston wrote to Nannie, "I admit that the correspondence of Gentlemen who are friends of our family are well calculated to develop the minds of young ladies and greatly improve their style in composition." But at all costs Nannie must avoid the appearances of a "Love Scrape."[17]

Hardly had the general risen from his bed and resumed his visits to the soldiers than he suffered a relapse. Margaret became

[15] Terrell, "Recollections of General Sam Houston," 123.

[16] Charles Power to Sam Houston, Independence, April 4, 1863, Houston manuscripts, University of Texas Archives.

[17] Sam Houston to Nancy Elizabeth Houston, Huntsville, April 14, 1863, *Writings*, VIII, 344–45.

afraid that his symptoms were those of consumption. William Bledsoe and Vernal Lea had died of the sickness; Houston's thinness, his pale, weak look were fearfully familiar. She finally persuaded him to go to Sour Lake, near Grand Cane, for mud baths. Houston embarked on the journey by stagecoach. At home, Margaret considered the possibility of moving to a healthful town in the West if Sour Lake did not cure her husband. She wrote to Houston saying she prayed "that your life may be prolonged" by the waters and mud baths.[18]

Political enemies of Houston saw danger in the general's public appearances. In editorials they began to attack him, and he delighted at their notice of him and reacted as an offended patriot. Through a newspaper he said that he was not seeking the office of governor. "A man of three score and ten, as I am, ought, at least, be exempt from the charge of ambition, even if he should be charged with having loved his country but too well."[19]

They were afraid of him, even yet, and it gratified Sam Houston. He knew his old age had set its limitations on him, even though he tried to ignore his frail health. One of the slaves recalled in later years that Billie Blount, an Indian friend of the general, upon hearing Houston had been ill, sent eight Indian women and four braves to Huntsville to try to cheer him. According to their custom, they waited for the general in the meadow at the old house on the other side of town. On that particular day, Houston was unable to go there and meet them because his legs were in pain. So he sat on the little upper porch, tucked in a laprobe, and they took places at his feet, down the stair. They sang songs Houston had known among the Cherokees. At the last

[18] Margaret Lea Houston to Sam Houston, Huntsville, June 8, 1863, University of Texas Archives.

[19] Sam Houston to G. Robinson, Huntsville, May 27, 1863, *Writings*, VIII, 346–47.

song, a sad lament sung as they walked away, Houston wept and pressed Margaret's hand until they were gone.[20]

He had no intention of going directly to Sour Lake, for the curiosity in him could not resist a detour by way of Houston City and Galveston. It was invigorating to him to smell again the political breezes in important places, and a busy Sam Houston neglected to write to Margaret. She read about him in Houston City's *Tri-Weekly Telegraph.* "I was delighted to learn from the *Telegraph* that you had arrived in Houston and were looking so well. It is my daily prayer that you may be benefitted by the springs. . . . We have been very well since you left, but miss you very much."[21]

On Sundays, Margaret took the children to church, then returned home to let them play in the pine thicket beside the house. Her main intellectual interest was the sermons she heard. The preacher, she wrote to Houston, "preaches tonight on the Prophecies and the Confederate Government. I hope he will have better luck in predicting than he has had heretofore."[22] Seldom did she attend assemblies or large parties in town, though there were always such affairs held when some of the men were at home. On several occasions there had been unpleasantness. At Captain Sims's house some local youths, dismayed over the report that Vicksburg had fallen to the United States forces, tried to start a fight with several of the guests, who were prisoners of war from the penitentiary. Margaret knew there were people in Huntsville who called Sam Houston a Unionist and a traitor, and she avoided situations which might prove embarrassing.[23] Her household kept to itself. General Houston reached home again late in June, 1863,

20 Hunt, *My Master*, 114.

21 Margaret Lea Houston to Sam Houston, Huntsville, June 8, 1863, University of Texas Archives.

22 *Ibid.*

23 *Ibid.*

about the time Mary Willie and Nannie arrived to spend the summer. The family was together, except for Sam, who was still in Mexico.

The summer was hot and still. When the heat had waned in the afternoon, the children were allowed to leave the house and play in the yard. Margaret and General Houston sat under a great oak tree and watched them. In the shade of that tree, Houston spent most of his time, seated in a hide-bottom rocking chair, meditating. The wounds hurt him to the point of limiting his walking to sporadic, difficult crossings of the meadow to the penitentiary to call on the soldiers. Andrew or one of the servants sometimes accompanied him on his walks and gave him support when he needed it. On an afternoon in July, he returned home with chills and fever.

Margaret made him comfortable in the downstairs bedroom. A servant fanned him with a palmetto; the children made no noise. Hot, sunny days continued, but Sam Houston's chills were frequent. After three weeks, his condition was worse. He spoke aloud to himself about war and filibustering to Mexico. Margaret saw him sink and in desperation wrote to Ashbel Smith. The doctor appeared unannounced, dressed in his Confederate uniform. Houston submitted to a physical examination and was pleased to see Smith again. For about four days Smith remained at Steamboat House, but he was unable to do anything for Sam Houston.[24]

Pneumonia developed. The sultry pineland air became hard for Houston to breathe. To calm his anxieties as well as her own, Margaret stayed beside his bed and read to him. On Sunday afternoon, July 26, Margaret was reading from a volume of her Bible, which lay open across her lap. For the general, the day had been one that he knew only through semiconsciousness. The older girls and several of the servants were in the room, listening to

[24] Ashbel Smith, undated notes on Sam Houston, University of Texas Archives.

Margaret read the Twenty-Third Psalm. Dusk's dim light filtered through the painted glass doors. Houston stirred suddenly, and Margaret knelt at the bedside. He said, "Texas . . . Margaret—Margaret." Those were Sam Houston's last words.[25]

The window of Margaret's bedroom framed dark, thunderous skies Monday morning. Her children would always remember her composure. She had honored the request of the Masonic Temple that the general's corpse be dressed in ceremonial trappings. At the penitentiary the Union prisoners worked all night building the coffin, which was placed in the parlor upstairs. The Baptist preacher had gone to Galveston on business, so, ironically, a Presbyterian was called. His name was J. M. Cochran, and he was pastor of the Huntsville Presbyterian Church. Margaret's demands about the funeral were specific, and when the Reverend Mr. Cochran left her that morning, she pressed into his hand a small sheet of paper. It was a poem whose composition had consumed her sleepless night. She wanted it read at the funeral.[26]

At four o'clock in the afternoon, the rain began to fall hard upon Steamboat House. There were few people at the funeral, though the parlor in which it was held was so small that it must hardly have been noticeable. Black-bordered announcements had been circulated in the town. Maybe the people feared the rain, or maybe there were political resentments. Margaret seated herself with her children.[27] Mr. Cochran read Margaret's poem, whose last stanza said:

[25] Author in conversation with Mrs. Jennie Morrow Decker, whose account is from Nannie and Maggie, who, with Eliza, were present, Houston, Texas, January 10, 1965; see also James, *The Raven*, 433; see also *Tri-Weekly Telegraph*, July 29, 1863.

[26] Huntsville interviews, typescript, Sam Houston Memorial Museum.

[27] *Ibid.*; E. F. Estill to J. I. Cochran, Huntsville, January 20, 1937; see also Mrs. W. A. Leigh, notarized statement, Barker Texas History Center, University of Texas Library.

And now may peace, within thy breast,
From him descend, and there remain!
Each night oh mayst thou sweetly rest,
And feel thou hast not liv'd in vain.[28]

The minister then delivered a short eulogy. Through the rain the mourners followed the coffin and the pallbearers, who were the Masons, down the muddy street to the far end of Oakwood Cemetery. The Masons completed a ceremony over the grave, and the Reverend Mr. Cochran said a prayer. Nannie, Maggie, Mary Willie, and Nettie placed evergreen boughs over the raw dirt mound.

Eliza accompanied the children to their rooms. Alone, Margaret lighted a candle and opened her Bible. She dipped her pen and wrote on a blank page—"Died on the 26th of July 1863, Genl Sam Houston, the beloved and affectionate Husband, father, devoted patriot, the fearless soldier—the meek and lowly Christian."[29]

[28] Margaret Lea Houston, "To My Husband," Franklin Williams Collection.
[29] Margaret Lea Houston's two-volume Bible, Sam Houston Memorial Museum.

11.

The Receding Lantern

Margaret left Steamboat House for the last time in November, 1863. She was dressed in black, with a mourning veil over her face, and she must have noticed the contrast of herself against the whitewashed building. The high front stair presented a distant view of Oakwood Cemetery, where every day for the past four months Margaret and the children had marked Sam Houston's grave with flowers.[1] Each time they had gone to the grave Margaret had wept. It had been her own decision to return to Independence to live with her mother. Huntsville brought nothing but melancholy to Margaret, and such gloom was not healthful for the children to witness. In September, Margaret had sent the girls, except for Maggie, back to Baylor. By November, she and the executors of the estate had come to terms, and she left East Texas.

At a crossing near the old road to Raven Hill, Margaret's coach rattled away from the caravan southward, toward Cedar Point. The servants, with the household supplies and several of

[1] Author in conversation with Mrs. Edward A. Everitt and Mrs. Jennie Morrow Decker, Houston, January 15, 1966.

the little boys, proceeded to Independence. The long journey of the coach took Margaret to Grand Cane, where Vernal's widow, Catherine Davis Lea, still lived in the house Antoinette had built so long ago.[2]

Future prospects for Sam Houston's widow were not promising. The general's political campaigns and the speaking tours in the East had been costly. In challenging the Democrats, Houston had also challenged a monetary power greater than he could gather, and he had been driven to spending his own funds heavily. Margaret had lost two houses, one of them sold, the other leased apart from its farm to the Independence Baptist Church as a parsonage. The will had been probated in August. Thousands of acres of land were involved, and the taxes were due. With wartime land values low and money scarce, the executors of the estate agreed that it was unwise to sell. Margaret seems not to have felt that way at all. She saw no use in holding land when she needed the money. The Houstons' business had always been managed by an attorney, but after Henderson Yoakum's death, Houston had attempted to conduct business for himself. He was not successful. Money was put out at interest, and that money was not regainable. Margaret did not have the money to purchase a tombstone for the general's grave.

She found Cedar Point forlorn and cold, looking much the way they had left it after the fall of Galveston. Maggie developed chills but recovered under Eliza's attentions. Then they all climbed into the coach and were gone. Margaret had mixed emotions about Cedar Point. She loved it, but she knew that when the market was again high, she should sell it, for Cedar Point was one of the two most valuable properties in the Houston inventory, and it produced no income. On the way to Independence, Margaret

[2] Public Deed Records, Liberty County. Catherine Lea married the Reverend J. W. D. Creath a few years after this.

stopped in Houston City so that Maggie could rest and see a doctor. In her lodgings she again read a depressing letter postmarked Galveston. Sam had gone back to the army.

Margaret had done everything to keep him from going. When he and Charles Power had returned from Mexico, Sam had enrolled in Baylor. Margaret encouraged his interest in a local girl, hoping that he would marry and stay in school.[3] She remembered the Bible she had put in his vest before he left for Missouri and how its thickness had diverted a Shiloh bullet from Sam's heart.[4] Next time Sam might not be so lucky. At Houston City, Margaret wrote to him, "My Darling Boy, In a few days, I suppose, from all accounts, you are to meet the enemy."[5] Her fears for him were the same as always: "If you should fall in battle what will be the condition of your soul? You may laugh with your gay companions, and put these sad things out of your sight, but in the evil day there will be no mirth or laughter. . . . I am told there is still a great revival going on at Galveston. Oh my son, will you not tear yourself away . . . and go where God is pouring out his Spirit, and try to have your sins forgiven? Time is short, oh, so short."[6]

When Maggie was stronger, the coach again progressed toward Independence. In December, they ferried over the Brazos at Washington and passed down the vacant Ferry Street of other times. The ashes and rubble of Independence Hall nourished weeds; lightning had struck the building the year before, and it had burned down to its dirt floor. There was little left of the forgotten capital of Texas. Out on the road to the west, Major Hatfield, the old saloonkeeper, had built a fine brick house with

[3] Margaret Lea Houston to Sam Houston, Jr., Independence, February 18, 1864, Sam Houston Hearne Collection.

[4] Item, Sam Houston Memorial Museum.

[5] Margaret Lea Houston to Sam Houston, Jr., Houston City, November 24, 1863, University of Texas Archives.

[6] *Ibid.*

exotic frescoes inside. Rocking in a chair on his portico, he might have been mistaken for a retired preacher or a planter instead of "grocer" to the Republic of Texas, as history would remember him. Margaret knew the country well. As a bride she had slept in a tent under its stars when she and Sam Houston had traveled as newlyweds. Just that autumn she had pulled the tent out of storage at Cedar Point and sent it to the army to shelter "those who might otherwise suffer from . . . the wet and cold."[7]

She hastened to be with her mother at Independence. Her asthma was aggravated by her regret over Sam's flight to the army. He was the one she had wanted to depend upon. Her little boys were fatherless and in need of a man's guidance. Margaret resented Sam's abandoning her. "I am but dust and ashes!" she scolded him. "A few more days and this feeble frame shall cease to suffer."[8]

Nancy Lea put Margaret and Maggie to bed in one of the low attic rooms of her house. Promptly the old lady took charge of the other six children and the servants. For the past few years Mrs. Lea had indulged herself in comforts because she was fully expectant of death. The coming of Margaret's lively children into the calm household proved too much. Andrew was the real problem, for, at not quite ten years of age, his ability to waken the worst in his elders was prodigious. Nancy Lea's custom of inspecting her tomb was well known. A more recent custom, but one kept secret, was the widow's interest in reassuring herself that the metallic coffin was the correct size, for she had become very fat since she bought the coffin. War's scarcity of supplies had compelled her to take special precautions against the servants' stealing

[7] Margaret Lea Houston to the Commander of the Second Texas Infantry, Huntsville, October 26, 1863, University of Texas Archives.

[8] Margaret Lea Houston to Sam Houston, Jr., Houston City, November 24, 1863, University of Texas Archives.

the sugar, salt, coffee, and flour. In so doing she pushed the coffin under her bed for the storage of goods, and superstition became her watchman. During naptime one day, Andrew peered through the closed blinds of Nancy Lea's first floor bedroom. He saw her tug the coffin from under the bed, empty it of its tin containers, and lower herself into the upholstered rectangle. She stretched out, crossing her hands over her stomach. At about that time Andrew sprang into the room and danced about, mocking her. In boundless wrath, Mrs. Lea vaulted up in the direction of the switch she kept in the corner. But she was stuck at the hips and was reduced to the humiliation of negotiating with Andrew to help her out.[9]

Similar incidents convinced Margaret of the urgency of moving her family under a private roof. After New Year's, 1864, she bought the Root house, an old place in sight of her mother's, facing the main avenue leading to Baylor. The tall house had been empty for a while, and its owners were anxious to sell, so Major Cave was able to trade some of Margaret's land for it.

The house was crowded, though no more so than Cedar Point or the Huntsville house had been. Upstairs was the boys' room and across the hall, the girls' room. Below was Margaret's room and a parlor, which contained the two pianos, Margaret's and Nannie's, and a high-post bed. Rock chimneys warmed the four principal rooms, and there was a double chimney connected to the kitchen and dining room, which were housed in a separate building in the yard. Trunks of papers were hauled up to the low attic. The pictures of Sam Houston were hung on the bare plank walls, with wreaths the girls had woven from pigeon feathers and hair of deceased family members.

Eber Cave came up from Houston City whenever Margaret needed business advice; and when he happened to be in the area,

[9] Author in conversation with Mrs. Jennie Morrow Decker, Houston, January 15, 1966.

which was often, he stopped in Independence to visit her. Of all Sam Houston's friends, Eber Cave remained the most loyal and considerate toward the widow Houston. Cave was married to Adolphus Sterne's daughter. A newspaperman by profession, he was also a good businessman, and though he was not an executor in Houston's will, he became Margaret's main adviser in matters of economics.

A few weeks after Margaret settled in the new house, Nancy Lea fell sick from an "affection of the stomach." To her three daughters she spoke affectionately of the past, of Marion and Pleasant Valley. Her sons were all dead, and six of her grandsons were away at war. One of the grandsons—Varilla's boy—had been slain in the war, and Nancy Lea reasoned that maybe more would die. Nancy Lea sank into deep sleeps. From one of these, on the morning of February 7, 1864, she did not waken. Her bell tolled at the Independence Baptist church, and its clanging reverberated in Margaret's brain a week after, when she wrote to Sam, "I delivered your last message to her, not many hours before her death. She expressed much pleasure and always spoke of you with the greatest affection. Her remains were put in her metallic coffin and deposited in her vault. The attendance was very large." Margaret had expected her mother's death, but she was unable to quiet her sorrow. From her house she saw the people walking to the funeral. "I am sure you will not be surprised to know," she wrote to Sam, "that I had not the strength to be present. Oh my son do write to me."[10]

Widowhood brought with it responsibilities Margaret had never accepted, even in the general's long absences. She knew little about money matters. They had always lived on credit, and while the general was at home and was able, he had paid her debts.

[10] Margaret Lea Houston to Sam Houston, Jr., Independence, February 16, 1864, Sam Houston Hearne Collection.

Soon Margaret would be forty-five. In some respects she had remained a child. She had not had to provide so much as a needle and thread to contribute to her existence. Long evenings she squinted through her spectacles over the pages of her Bible. She became uncertain, not only because of the future, but because of the present. "A great sorrow," she wrote to Sam, "fell upon me and crushed my spirit." She wondered, "in my loneliness and desolation . . . how I could ever guide my little flock through the dreary wilderness."

Again Margaret sought peace in religion. Through the spring and into the summer, she read her Bible and meditated in the privacy of her home. The war continued, though she scarcely noticed it, except to worry about Sam. Panic stricken, Antoinette and Charles Power once more packed their belongings and went to Galveston to try to run the blockade and reach England by way of the West Indies. Power's brother Tom, with his wife Sallie, had effected an escape. Antoinette and Charles felt that they must flee before the enemy armies began the rapine of Texas.[11] In midsummer the Powers returned to Independence, disappointed. The widowed Varilla moved into Tom Power's house in town, thereby living a short walk from Margaret. Charles Power traded his Independence farm for a cattle ranch, where he, Antoinette, and the two children moved.[12]

Almost oblivious to the constant activity, Margaret studied the scriptures. Her attitude slowly improved and lifted her spirit from the depression that for "a few months" had stayed with her.[13] She opened her eyes to the fact that her lot was better than some. A friend in Huntsville had lost five sons in the war. Star-

[11] Margaret Lea Houston to Sam Houston, Jr., Independence, May 13, 1864, Sam Houston Hearne Collection.

[12] *Ibid.*; clipping (1869?) in the collection of Mrs. John L. Little, Sr.

[13] Margaret Lea Houston to Sam Houston, Jr., Independence, July 1, 1864, Sam Houston Hearne Collection.

vation crippled Alabama. "I can truly say," she wrote, " 'Yes thereto hath the Lord helped me.' Not one of his precious promises has failed."[14] She had children who needed her, and she wanted their lives to be "wholly consecrated" to God.[15] Her usefulness, she reasoned, was far greater than it had ever been.

Thus Margaret saw another pinnacle toward which to climb. To her own satisfaction she defined her path and placed her feet upon it. The eight children must grow into men and women who would make their father proud. They would be an eternal testimony to her and to Sam Houston. She and Eliza opened the curtains and spread white tablecloths. At mealtime the monogrammed silver ornamented a table sometimes spare of meat but abundant in vegetables from Bingley's garden and fruits from the parsonage orchard. The girls walked up the street to Baylor every day. Margaret stayed at home and played with Willie Rogers and Temple in the shady front yard. When soldiers came through, there were parties for them at Baylor. Margaret opened her jewelry boxes and drew forth earrings and pins and necklaces, gifts to her in the past as Sam Houston's wife. She allowed Nannie and Maggie to wear what they wanted, except the cameo of their father. That was only for Margaret.[16]

Sam's letters were a great joy to the family. One of the girls usually read them at the dinner table, for everyone to hear. "We left Camp Pilham yesterday," he wrote to Margaret. "I went up to tell my . . . acquaintances 'goodbye.' . . . The prettiest one threw her arms around my neck and said, 'Houston, I guess I had better kiss you for I know you are not coming back to see me'—of course I

[14] *Ibid.*

[15] *Ibid.*

[16] Author in conversation with Mrs. Jennie Morrow Decker, Houston, January 15, 1965; also with Mrs. John L. Little, Sr., Beaumont, March 1, 1965; see also appropriate items in the Sam Houston Memorial Museum and in the Franklin Williams Collection.

had not the slightest objections."[17] War had not entirely changed Sam. He sent poems home with exact instructions about who was to receive them. His Aunt Antoinette received his pen-and-ink sketches of army camps in the Louisiana lowlands. All her life, his little sister Nettie would treasure his drawings of the Battle of Shiloh.[18]

The romance Margaret had encouraged Sam to pursue had brought difficulties to Lieutenant Houston. Margaret had to call on the girl's parents and apologize because there had been a misunderstanding—Sam had offered no proposal of marriage. "I blame myself a good deal," she wrote to Sam about the involvement. Margaret had plotted the marriage to keep her son home from the war.[19] The alienation his leaving had created between himself and his mother lasted through the winter and spring. And she still failed to understand how he could abandon her. "Ma I was reckless and ambitious, and I was restless when out of hearing of the boom of the cannon—it almost seems now that the death groan and bursting shells had a music for me—I was proud that I could ride fearlessly through it all, and show to friend and foe that I was not afraid to die." He could always win Margaret. "Ma it was not for myself alone—I was proud of my name and I wanted to show to the world that the blood of a Houston ran untainted."[20]

While Margaret kept her spirits high in the presence of her

[17] Sam Houston, Jr., to Margaret Lea Houston, Camp Magruder, Louisiana, August 15, 1864, University of Texas Archives.

[18] Shuffler, *The Houstons at Independence*, 55; see also sketches by Sam Houston, Jr., in the collection of Mrs. John L. Little, Sr., who inherited them from Antoinette Lea Power.

[19] Margaret Lea Houston to Sam Houston, Jr., Independence, February 18, 1864, Sam Houston Hearne Collection.

[20] Sam Houston, Jr., to Margaret Lea Houston, Wills Plantation, Louisiana, July 5, 1864, University of Texas Archives.

children, there were times when loneliness drove her from the house out into the empty land, to walk undisturbed and think. The children's merriment seemed somehow irreverent to her. She had not been so unfeeling when Temple Lea had died; she remembered very well how she had taken her grief to secret places to ponder and try to understand. Now the widow sought refuge in the sweeping hills around Independence. At her desk she found still further escape in poems.

Stranger behold you silent mound
Where waves the rank grass tall,
There, beneath that hallowed ground,
Is deposited my all.[21]

The older children realized her loneliness when time had passed. One autumn afternoon, Nettie came home early from school to find Margaret seated in the parlor as though she awaited someone. Nettie moved unnoticed into the room and studied the look of "deep longing" on Margaret's face, as the mother studied the flames in the fireplace. Quietly Nettie watched, before she said to Margaret, "No wonder my father loved you so."[22]

The spring of 1866 brought excitement to the Houston household. Nannie was to be married. She was nineteen, and the announcement of her engagement surprised people because she had said many times that she would never marry a man who could not pay the preacher fifty dollars in gold and take her to Niagara Falls on her wedding trip. Since the war, a declaration such as that, even from a girl as pretty as Nannie, seemed certain promise of spinsterhood.[23]

[21] Dixon, *Poets and Poetry of Texas*, 147.

[22] *Ibid.*, 153.

[23] Author in conversation with Mrs. Jennie Morrow Decker, Houston, May 10, 1965.

She had no notion of marriage before Joseph Clay Stiles Morrow appeared in Independence. He owned a mercantile house in Georgetown, two days west, and had made money. Young, handsome, and single, the Kentuckian rode the stage to Independence to attend parties at Baylor, where he met Nannie. He returned bringing presents and stayed to relate his war experiences. Nobody was more delighted than Margaret when they became engaged. The wedding was scheduled for August.

That spring was a happy season for Margaret. Sam was home, confused about his future to be sure, but home nonetheless and recuperating rapidly from excessive exposure during the Louisiana campaign. Margaret and her eight children were together. There was money to spend. The Texas legislature had voted to present her with the balance of General Houston's unpaid salary, a little under two thousand dollars.[24] Some of the people whose notes Margaret held had paid her small percentages, which she took as eagerly as though they were the full debt. Even Joshua, who had become a successful blacksmith in Huntsville, brought his savings to her and insisted that she take the whole amount, which was something over two thousand dollars in cash. But Margaret refused to accept the gift and urged Joshua to return to Huntsville and spend the money to provide "Christian educations" for his children.[25]

Stories of Mrs. Houston's poverty had spread, and indeed her need seems to have been acute until the coming of the unexpected money. Most of her servants remained with her in freedom. Bingley, her mother's former slave, attached himself to Margaret's household. The children in the immediate family needed

[24] William Alexander to Margaret Lea Houston, Austin, April 20, 1866, University of Texas Archives.

[25] Undated newspaper clippings, *Dallas Morning News*; see also notes of the author, various conversations with Mrs. Jennie Morrow Decker; see also James, *The Raven*, 457.

shoes, shirts, and dresses. Tuition at Baylor was demanded, in spite of General Houston's generosity to the Baptists in better times. Sam tried to build profitable herds with the farm animals his grandmother Lea had left and the ones which had survived the family's wartime famine.[26] His walk over the rocky ground was stumbling and uncertain, but Andrew, Willie Rogers, and Temple followed him admiringly.

With frugality, Margaret's household stayed intact. Even the tombstone she erected in Huntsville was simple and inexpensive. Eliza's vegetables and Sam's beef fought hunger very well. Whitewash and unpruned crepe myrtles covered the disrepair of the house. Clothing was patched, as were shoes. Thrift applied in all instances except one: Sam Houston's eldest daughter was to be married, and Margaret's pride demanded opulence. Her new and close friends, the Reverend and Mrs. William Carey Crane, who were going to New Orleans, were asked to buy materials for Nannie's wedding dress. When the Cranes returned, Mrs. Crane, partially from excitement and partially to apologize for spending so much money, offered to do the sewing. The offer made Margaret very happy. Through the spring and summer Catherine Jane Crane walked from the parsonage and sat at Margaret's sewing machine all the day at her task.

On occasions, the Reverend Crane accompanied his wife. He was an educator of wide national experience. Texas Baptists had called him to take over the presidency of Baylor. Passionately fond of history, he had been a cofounder of the state historical association in Mississippi. Margaret approached him about writing a biography of Sam Houston.[27] The attic was filled with trunks of

[26] Sam inherited Nancy Lea's stock, and Margaret got the house and its contents. See Margaret Lea Houston to Sam Houston, Jr., Independence, February 18, 1864, University of Texas Archives.

[27] Crane, *Life and Select Literary Remains*, 3.

letters, drafts of speeches, and mementos. People had not forgotten the general. Margaret had selected a portrait of him at the request of some politicians, who hung it in the capitol in Austin. In the month of April, *Harper's New Monthly Magazine* would run a highly sympathetic article called "The Last Years of Sam Houston" and would say of Houston's life that a novelist could "truthfully make facts appear stronger than fiction," but "we will not print a romance, lest some scribbler should fail properly to mould the useful and ready material into shape."[28]

Margaret wanted a proper history written, with some reservations. Crane divulged only one of these reservations, the one that called for a chapter "setting forth Gen. Houston's religious character."[29] It is possible that Crane himself elected to omit certain personal details, if he ever knew them. The Indian woman Diana Rogers was deleted, though Crane was quite frank about Houston's liquor problem.[30] At first, Crane did not feel "competent" to write the biography because he had "only seen the General twice in my life, once in the President's house in 1846, and again on the floor of the U.S. Senate in 1852."[31]

The historian in Crane won out. Margaret ordered the trunks brought down from the attic. In the parlor she read papers and then passed them to Crane, while Mrs. Crane sat by sewing the white dress for the bride. When Margaret wearied of reading, Crane had free access to the trunks, and sometimes he labored until dawn, at which time he laid the papers aside and walked to his office at Baylor.

In March, Crane enthusiastically wrote an inquiry to a Philadelphia publisher. Margaret's excitement seems to have matched

[28] "The Last Years of Sam Houston," *Harper's New Monthly Magazine*, April, 1866, 635.

[29] Crane, *Life and Select Literary Remains*, 3.

[30] *Ibid.*, 253.

[31] *Ibid.*, 3.

that of the scholarly preacher. They awaited the promise of a contract in advance of the manuscript. The answer arrived:

> It does not seem to me that there is any pressing urgency to present the Life and Labors of Gen. Houston to the world. It is true that they will possess a paramount interest so long as the Republic, or State, or Country of Texas, whichever it may be, shall possess an interest for men; yet even in this view there is an advantage in bringing out a book in an opportune time. At the present time every mind that thinks is powerfully, often painfully preoccupied with the strange anomalous, grave condition of our affairs, with the uncertainty of our future and that of the gigantic Government of the United States.[32]

Deep disappointment filled the parlor that had been so animated with ambition for literary success. All the misery a publisher's kindly discouragement can bring sank over Margaret and the Reverend Mr. Crane.

Margaret broke the silence. If the world was not interested in the true Sam Houston now, then it had missed the chance forever. The public had always been Margaret's enemy. She had heard its lies and its laughter. Perhaps now she contemplated revenge, for it was the first time in her life that the opportunity presented itself. With random approval from the older children Margaret began casting handfuls of the letters into the fireplace and watching the flames consume them.[33] William Carey Crane gathered up his

[32] *Ibid.*

[33] Author in conversation with Mrs. Jennie Morrow Decker. The Reverend Mr. Crane kept his notes. When his manuscript was completed some years later, the Houston children each gave a rather reluctant consent to its publication. Of course a controversy arose at once over Crane's qualifications to publish the book. An unsigned letter appeared in the *Galveston Civilian and Gazette* in August, 1869, saying "No two men ever lived more unlike than Gen. Houston and Dr. Crane. Dr. C. is an Old Line Whig. Gen. Houston was an old Jackson Democrat.

extensive notes and unfinished text and departed. Margaret sat beside the fireplace with her iron poker, filling the small rock mouth, stopping now and then to read a familiar line of sweeping penmarks. Summer's hot light burned outside. The fire was neglected. Margaret took refuge from the heat by pulling her parlor chairs into the hall, where the breeze blew unobstructed when the doors were opened.

Kate Crane's needles moved fast. In the hot though rainy July, preparations for the wedding were begun. There would be many guests. The house was too crowded with furniture. Margaret dispatched the unnecessary and the embarrassingly threadbare articles to the barn loft. Away went the trunks of letters, the bulk of their contents intact, to hide for years among the hay bales, broken furniture, and discarded things.[34]

Dr. Crane is a fine Virginia gentleman of the kid glove school. Gen Houston was a plain, rugged frontiersman, of intense earnestness." Thereafter the letter attempts delicately to insult Crane. It was suggested that Eber Cave or the distinguished newspaperman Hamilton Stuart, who had written a moving essay on visiting the Houstons at Cedar Point during the Civil War, take on the task. A cuttingly genteel exchange erupted, and many people wrote to the newspapers claiming closer friendship with Sam Houston than they had ever enjoyed in fact. The authorities were myriad. Reverend J. W. D. Creath even put in a word: "Mrs. Houston was a woman of no ordinary intellect," he wrote, "at different times [she] discussed the merits of each [possible biographer], gave her opinion freely, but in a kind and lady-like manner." Mr. Crane's work was published in Philadelphia after all. It appeared in the 1880's and with some exceptions endures as one of the best, most clearly drawn portraits of Sam Houston.

[34] While one cannot help wondering how much Mrs. Houston burned, no figures exist to indicate the exact amount, for very obviously no figures were kept. I have been told by descendants that over the years "hundreds" of letters were burned as "uninteresting" or, in the true legacy of Margaret's reasoning, "too intimate." Great numbers of letters, stored in trunks, stayed in the barn and in the attic of the Independence house until well into the twentieth century. Some of those were subsequently destroyed or fell victim to mildew or silverfish. Others passed to Houston descendants through Maggie, who lived in the Independence house for most of the rest of her life and was in possession of the great majority of the Houston artifacts.

By midsummer, engraved cards had circulated among some three hundred people.

Mrs. M.M. Houston
AT HOME
Wednesday evening, August 1st 1866

A smaller card was inscribed "Nannie E. Houston" and enclosed with the large one. August 1 dawned as Catherine Jane Crane knotted her last thread.

Flowers from the gardens of Independence garlanded the stairs and mantels of the house. People crowded into the rooms and out into the yard, and both pianos played. The wedding guests had not seen such a dress since the outbreak of the war. It was cream brocade, very full over hoops, with a lace veil. A wide sash, tied at the back, fell to the train with such grace that a country lady gasped, and a townswoman, bursting with Kate Crane's whispered news, remarked officiously, "It cost twelve dollars a yard!"[35] On the white tablecloth the Houston silver and Margaret's china were as civilized as anything in Texas.[36] Joe Morrow paid the Reverend Mr. Crane fifty dollars in gold, which caused considerably more of a sensation than Nannie's song, a farewell lament she sang to her mother. They took the stage to Galveston, where they set sail to New York.

The Morrows were hardly gone when Margaret made another announcement. Maggie would marry Weston Lafayette Williams of Independence. West Williams, in his twenties, had roomed at

[35] Author in conversation with Mrs. Jennie Morrow Decker, Houston, January 12, 1965; see also various newspaper clippings from the 1930's showing photographs of the actual dress, in the collection of Mrs. Jennie Morrow Decker. In 1940 the dress was placed in a glass case in the Sam Houston Memorial Museum, where, left in the direct sunlight, it rotted and disappeared.

[36] Items, Sam Houston Memorial Museum and the Franklin Williams Collection.

Nancy Lea's while a student at Baylor, and in that way he had first known the Houstons. War's disillusionment left him unprepared for the hard times he found at home. So he had left Independence and leased a farm at Labadie Prairie, in a remote part of Washington County.

Maggie's wedding took place October 17 before the family and close friends. Probably at the bride's insistence the celebration was simple, for she had worried about her mother's extravagances. Margaret was fond of West Williams, but she and Eliza cried when Maggie went away with him to Labadie. In spite of her stability, Maggie's health was poor, and she was sometimes unable to care for herself. Margaret offered to deed Nancy Lea's house to Maggie and West Williams if they would stay in Independence. Their refusal of the offer irritated Margaret, who was not accustomed to being refused.[37]

The months passed peacefully into Christmas and the new year of 1867. Margaret listened happily to Sam's schemes for his future. He had settled on the idea of going to medical school, with the intention of returning to Independence and building a practice there. Farming would always be a problem because of his physical limitations. When he was only ten years old, Sam Houston had bought him some farm animals, so that he might learn to love husbandry. Many events had taken place since those days, and the world had changed. Sam was a good student. His best future would be as a professional man.

In April, 1867, Margaret was forty-eight. Illness had taken a measure of her good looks away. Heavy responsibility showed in her face and in the austere back-swept hair, combed and tucked for practicality rather than appearance. There had been leisure in her life before. Now Eliza's mornings were occupied with little

[37] Margaret Lea Houston to Margaret Houston Williams, Independence, n.d., Sam Houston Hearne Collection.

else than combing Margaret's hair, which, when undone, fell in long tresses to her waist. Margaret's figure had thickened since Houston's death. Her face had gained a gaunt, sunken look, and the eyes which had been so lively and young were serious and humorless.

Antoinette and Charles Power wrote regularly. They were settled on their ranch, and the adaptable Antoinette was happy. Power said that the future was in cattle. Joe Morrow agreed and purchased land for himself near Round Rock. That year Varilla was sixty-six. Aged over her loss in the war, she fluttered like a mother hen around Margaret and the Houston children. She lived alone. In the afternoons, while the children napped, Margaret walked down to Varilla's and sat with her sister on the porch. They read Nettie's poems, or they worked on a dress for Mary Willie, who was becoming the most beautiful of the Houston girls.

Early in the spring, Nannie and Joe Morrow were in Independence. They had traveled from Niagara Falls to Kentucky to visit the Morrow relations. Nannie was pregnant. Margaret insisted that she remain in Independence until the baby was born. Captain Morrow agreed. He rode the stage to Georgetown, taking thirteen-year-old Andrew with him. Margaret was completely unable to control the boy, who was constantly into mischief, which more often than not was provoked by irrational discipline at Baylor. Morrow was not as easily dominated as Margaret and proved to be the only one able to deal with Andrew.

Nannie's baby was born in June. She was named Margaret. The grandmother was content to have Nannie turn the baby over to her and Eliza. Nannie's being at home gave Margaret a strange feeling of safety, for both Nannie and Maggie were more capable managers than their mother. Where Margaret liked to smother Maggie with affection, Nannie was Margaret's strength and released Margaret from domestic duties which she loathed. But

Nannie wanted to join her husband, and though Margaret protested tearfully and tried to make Nannie feel guilty for leaving, Nannie was on the westbound coach late in June. Eliza was with her, wearing a yellow hat with ostrich feathers. Only on the condition that Eliza go to nurse the baby would Margaret allow Nannie to leave. Nannie had never seen Georgetown, nor had Margaret or Eliza. It was two days westward in good weather, about thirty miles north of Austin. As Nannie departed, Margaret pressed a small package into her hands. From the moving coach Nannie looked back to see her mother weeping in the doorway. The youthful Mrs. Morrow opened the package and held up the cameo of Sam Houston.[38]

That summer, Sam left for Philadelphia to attend the medical school of the University of Pennsylvania. He and his mother had burned many candles over the account books to find money to make his further education possible. Unable to mortgage the house, Margaret finally rented Cedar Point for $300, with $110 paid in advance. A family friend, probably Major Cave, signed her note for $200 more, asking "a mere verbal promise" that she would repay the debt.[39]

Margaret had presented her situation to Sam as better than it was. He was proud, and she did not want him to worry. In September, she wrote to Joe Morrow, "I am in sad need of money. My house is ruining for want of repairs. What shall I do?" Brother Baines had paid her $100 on his note. The preacher was now teaching in Salado, north of Georgetown, after having had trouble with the Baptists. Margaret calculated that perhaps if Joe and Nannie "would represent my situation to him as I have described

[38] Mrs. Edward A. Everitt to William Seale, Houston, July 29, 1965, author's collection.

[39] Margaret Lea Houston to Joe Morrow, Independence, September 3, 1867, University of Texas Archives.

it, he would let you have something for me." Morrow's wagons passed through Independence on the way to Georgetown with stock for the store. "I took the liberty of appropriating two of your bacon sides," Margaret wrote. "I did not pay for them, for the simple reason that I had not the money."[40]

In her financial distress, Margaret developed a passionate concern that her children be provided for. She told Sam goodbye, probably glad he was leaving the dismal problems of home. Philadelphia would present the new life Sam needed, and though Margaret had never seen Philadelphia, she had faith that Sam would find fulfillment there. Maggie and West Williams worked hard on their Labadie farm; Margaret believed they worked too diligently for their own good. The Morrows' prosperity pleased Margaret more than anything else. Captain Morrow had built Nannie a new house with new furniture, curtains, oil chandeliers, and coal stoves. Nannie ordered dress materials from New Orleans. She pleaded with her mother to come to Georgetown so that they could make dresses together and devise something for Margaret other than the drab mourning costumes. Andrew and Eliza had not come home from Georgetown. The boy was improved, and he wrote his mother a "dear letter" about his adventures exploring Bat Cave.[41]

Margaret's immediate responsibilities were her younger children. Mary Willie was seventeen and Nettie was fifteen; Willie Rogers was eleven and Temple was seven. Margaret knew that it would not be many years before the girls married, so it was the little boys who were her specific charge. Sam Houston had been specific in his wishes for the boys. "My will is that my sons should receive solid and useful education. . . . I wish my sons to be early

[40] *Ibid.*

[41] Andrew Jackson Houston to Margaret Lea Houston, Georgetown, July 15, 1867, University of Texas Archives.

taught an utter contempt for novels and light reading. . . . I wish particular regard to be paid to their Morals, as well as the character and morals of those with whom they may be associated or by whom instructed."[42]

With her duty mapped before her, Margaret rose stubbornly to comply. Her errand seemed to her strangely sublime and appealed to her more than the mundane occupations of the housewife. When Nannie and Joe Morrow asked her to move to Georgetown to live with them, she declined, saying that Independence was home. Independence was between Georgetown and Labadie, and far enough away from both. The general had never liked living with other people, and she remembered what it was like to live as a guest. If times were hard, Margaret, in her characteristic way of dismissing things, believed they would improve. One day Sam would return to Independence as he had promised. Margaret wanted to be able to open her doors to him and to the rest of the children. She wanted to preserve the domestic entity that had entwined Sam Houston and herself in its pleasures over all the years.[43]

The epidemic began in early September, 1867. According to the doctors it was "a congestion of some sort," and Margaret wrote to Joe Morrow that "sickness and death have been busy among us."[44] When the plague reached Independence, Baylor closed down. White sheets labeled the houses of the afflicted. By October, the town was silent, except for the public dead-wagon which, now and then, rattled to the cemetery. Margaret imprisoned herself and the children in the house until she received a letter from

[42] Will of Sam Houston, Huntsville, April 2, 1863, Sam Houston Memorial Museum.

[43] Author in conversation with Mrs. Jennie Morrow Decker, Houston, December 29, 1964.

[44] Margaret Lea Houston to Joe Morrow, Independence, September 3, 1867, University of Texas Archives.

Maggie, who said that within several weeks she planned to visit Independence.

Terrified that Maggie might take the sickness, Margaret ordered her coach to the back door, quickly loaded the children and a few belongings, and was gone to Labadie Prairie. Her decision was beneficial. Labadie was away from the disease, a "pleasant quiet place" in which to stay.[45] West and Maggie's house was small but adequate in the cool autumn season. Letters and newspapers were Labadie's sole connection with the outside world, whose tidings were sad.

Fever burned over Texas. Even Huntsville in its highlands had not escaped tragedy. Old friends had been laid to rest among the cedars of Oakwood Cemetery. Dr. Evans' wife and Edaline Yoakum and scores of children were dead. Doctors did not know what to do, for, as Margaret wrote, "They know so little about it." Margaret clasped her hands and thanked God. "While the pestilence is sweeping around us the Lord seems to shield me and my dear ones from its breath."[46] In desperate fright Margaret cried, "Why am I so blessed while so many households are made desolate?" Her mind lingered on doleful possibilities. "Oh do not neglect your religious duties," she implored her children. "You will be safe as long as they are kept up. Form a habit of singing hymns while you are working."[47]

Cold November weather slowed the disease. One thousand people had died in Galveston; tentacles of the fever had trailed up into Arkansas. Newspapers anticipated the new year with hope, believing the fever was under control. The refugees at Labadie Prairie heard the news with great joy. Margaret had in her hands

[45] Margaret Lea Houston to Nannie Houston Morrow, Labadie, October 25, 1867, University of Texas Archives.

[46] *Ibid.*

[47] *Ibid.*

a letter from Nannie. The whole family was invited to spend Christmas in Georgetown in Nannie's big house. There, before warm coal fires, Margaret would have nothing to do but play with her grandchild.[48]

She waved Maggie and West goodbye from the yellow coach. Out on the road, Margaret told the driver to stop in Independence, where she had forgotten some needed belongings in her hurry to leave. She believed she might decide to stay in Georgetown longer, maybe until spring, or even until summer. Strong wind rattled the windows of the house and whistled through the broken panes. Margaret endured unanticipated delays in packing —the weather, and the callers who had seen the coach and knew that she had returned from Labadie. The epidemic had killed many people in town. Margaret made the necessary calls and left her card, but her main effort was spent at home, gathering the items she would want to have on her visit with Nannie. Georgetown, the "pure air of Georgetown," was a sanctuary to her.[49] The central Texas town already seemed a home, not only because of Nannie and baby Margaret, but because Andrew and Eliza were there too.

Yellow fever begins with a gripping sensation in the pit of the stomach and graduates, depending upon the victim's resistance, to throbs in the head and vomitous burning in the throat and chest. Margaret's resistance was small.[50] She was stricken before people realized that the fever had come back in a second wave. White sheets reappeared along the streets of Independence. Mary Willie

48 Author in conversation with Mrs. Jennie Morrow Decker, Houston, May 25, 1965.

49 Margaret Lea Houston to Nannie Houston Morrow, Labadie, October 25, 1867, University of Texas Archives.

50 William Carey Crane's diary, Barker Texas History Center, University of Texas Library.

and Nettie came running home from Varilla's crying that the family must flee. Already Margaret had gone to bed. She begged her daughters to take the little boys and proceed to Georgetown without her, but they refused to leave. Nettie in later years remembered going to close the curtains and seeing the wagons and horsemen racing west from the town crying "*Yellow Fever! Yellow Fever!*"[51] Nettie was the poet of the Houston children. Perhaps the emotion of the hour lingered to distort her memory.

For two days the girls listened to the religious threads of their mother's delirium. Not until the last moments were they able to enlist a doctor. Major Cave had chanced through town and saw the sheet jerking from the upper porch in the wind. When he was told that there was no doctor in Independence any more, he rode to Brenham and returned with a physician, who arrived in time to pronounce Margaret dead. It was the afternoon of December 3, 1867.

At about eleven o'clock that night four people lifted the homemade coffin onto the cart. The doctor had advised them of the regulation that yellow fever victims must be buried at once in the ground, and Major Cave and Bingley assisted the girls in performing the duty. Three of them pushed the cart behind Nettie, who led with a lantern. The procession moved down the dark avenue. Behind it was the house, in whose upper bedroom William Rogers and Temple were sleeping. Ahead was the old Houston place where lived the Baptist preacher William Carey Crane, presumably asleep at that late hour. He would not conduct a funeral for fear of contamination.[52] The party turned into the street that ran beside the church and stopped before the tomb of Nancy Lea.

[51] Author in conversation with Mrs. James A. Darby, Mr. Sam Houston Hearne, and Mrs. Jennie Morrow Decker, Independence, May 15, 1965; also Mrs. John L. Little, Sr., Beaumont, May 16, 1965; see also Shuffler, *The Houstons At Independence.*

[52] Crane was pastor of the Independence Baptist church and occupied the

Bingley had dug a grave at the tomb's side. It was deep in the ground, in accordance with the regulation. The coffin was lowered into the earth, and Bingley and the major shoveled the dirt over it. When that was done, Nettie and Mary Willie spread a quilt of evergreens over the mound.[53] Back up the street the four figures walked with the cart. The December wind was cold, and in the dark, Nettie's lantern blinked smaller and smaller until it had vanished into the doorway of the house.

"Hines Place" as the Houstons' former house was called. Margaret received no rent for the minister's use of the property, and at the time of her death, only a small amount of property remained around the house, most of the original farm having been sold in small plots for income; see also undated clipping in the collection of Mrs. F. S. Baldwin.

[53] Author in conversation with Mr. Sam Houston Hearne, Mrs. James A. Darby, Mrs. Edward A. Everitt, and Mrs. Jennie Morrow Decker, Independence, May 15, 1965, and various times in the spring of 1966; see also Shuffler, *The Houstons at Independence*, 52; see also undated clippings in the collection of Mrs. F. S. Baldwin.

On the Sources

An explanation of my use of interviews, sites, and artifacts will, in preface to my listing of the major sources, serve as an epilogue to Margaret Houston's life.

Of course there is nobody living who remembers either Sam Houston or Margaret Lea Houston. Most of the Houston children enjoyed long lives. Their grandchildren, and in some instances their children, who knew them intimately, are alive. These are the people I sought out for some of the domestic details that I present in my work. I questioned and requestioned and challenged the answers of one person against those of other people, and, whenever possible, against material in the manuscripts from which I had gleaned my original questions and the bulk of the information in this book. To demonstrate the closeness of the present Houston descendants to the children of Margaret Houston, it will be useful and interesting to know, with dates, what happened to each of the eight.

Sam Houston, Jr., M.D., practiced medicine briefly, then unfortunately abandoned medicine for creative writing. Upon the death of his wife, he closed his medical practice and moved to

Independence to live with Maggie, who occupied Margaret's last home. He died in 1894 in Independence.

At Christmas, 1867, Temple was taken to Georgetown with Willie Rogers, Nettie, and Mary William. Nannie and Captain Morrow reared him and the other younger children to adulthood, and like his fellow younger members of the family, he always thought of Nannie's house as his home. As a young lawyer, the dashing Temple Lea Houston went to Oklahoma to practice. There and in the Texas Panhandle he led a colorful, if brief, life. He died in 1905.

Maggie and West Williams lived in Independence and in the summers entertained many family members in the tall white house on the avenue. From the shady porch they watched Independence die. Nancy Lea's house rotted to the ground, and Baylor moved away to Waco. Maggie, a friend of many artistic people, did not like to talk of the past but consented to write a memoir shortly before her death in 1906. She left the house virtually unchanged after Margaret's death, and most of the artifacts have come through her heirs.

Nannie lived in Georgetown in a big, sunny house for the rest of her life. She and Captain Morrow were prominent in cultural affairs in Central Texas. When Southwestern University was brought to Georgetown, Nannie became one of its ardent supporters. She died in 1920. In that same year, Willie Rogers was found fallen from his horse, dead of an apparent heart attack, in Hugo, Oklahoma. He was an Indian agent and the only one of the eight Houstons to leave no children.

Mary Willie, a postmistress in Abilene for much of her life, was left a beautiful young widow soon after having married Joe Morrow's cousin. She died in 1931.

Nettie inherited Margaret's love of literary romance and wrote poems under the name Mignonette. She was a pillar of the

Daughters of the Republic of Texas. Most of her life was spent in San Antonio, where in 1932 she died in an automobile accident.

The last child to die was the indomitable Andrew. He wrote books about Texas history and saw the past in a glowingly heroic light. A military man, a sportsman, and a dapper figure in social circles from Washington, D.C., to Texas, Andrew was a visionary and a dreamer, with an intense love of his family background. Colonel Houston once filed suit against a Hollywood motion picture company whose film *The Raven*, starring Richard Dix, offended him on two counts: in the first place it showed Houston eating raw meat with his bare hands, and in the second place it represented him as living with an Indian woman, the forgotten Diana Rogers Gentry of the Cherokees. Andrew Jackson Houston died in 1941 and is buried in the San Jacinto Battleground State Park, Texas.

Family interviews can be viewed askance sometimes, when dealing with Sam Houston. And yet too often they are completely overlooked. Recollections have survived; indeed, even one of the slaves later wrote a book. There has been a historical mania on the subject of Sam Houston, and it has produced over fifty biographies and many more articles since the general's death. Some of the family recollections have come down among the descendants clearly and consistent in every detail. "My father," wrote Maggie in her memoir, "was with us so little of the time, that his visits stand out as 'pictures on memory's wall.' " Traditions about Margaret seem more candid. She was always with her children, and within their families the children talked more about her than about General Houston. On the subject of Mrs. Houston, the descendants had not been seriously approached before. No pressure was exerted for them to remember when there might be nothing to recall. What they patiently gave me was valuable both in the sense of its being useful descriptive detail and in its providing small lamps with which I might search in the often confusing dark of the voluminous manuscripts.

The Houstons' several residences or their sites were helpful in rounding out the life presented in this book. In each case I have examined the written record in effecting my restorations of the houses and towns, as well as extensive studies of the physical remains of the buildings.

Out "Green" Street, Henry Lea's residence stands changed, though the windows of its library still present through ripply glass views of the town of Marion. Galveston Bay flows over the site of Cedar Point, but the imagination needs little encouragement to build upon ample, known facts in recreating Margaret's beloved retreat. Raven Hill was torn down many years before a hurricane washed Cedar Point away, and the Bledsoe house near Grand Cane burned down. At the sites, the visitor's eyes sense life in what was lifeless in the archives. Tucked away in a woodland park in Huntsville, the Houstons' log house and the Steamboat House stand together in an idyllic pasture. They are strange companions—the one a scene of joy, the other a house of sorrow. White paint and clipped lawns there draw the historian from his vision of the raw Texas frontier. On through the woodland is a Jeffersonian pavilion housing the personal effects of the Jacksonian Houston and his wife and children. Through glass shields one may see dresses, shoes, spectacles, books, and pens that the Houston household used every day. Across town, Houston's grave is under an ambitious marble pile that replaces the original marker, extravagant in its simplicity, which he doubtless would have preferred. One can follow the iron fence of Oakwood Cemetery up the hill to the former site of Steamboat House. Margaret's crepe myrtles still bloom there in the summer.

At Austin, the mansion is yet the home of the Texas governors.

It is one of the most historic houses in the Southwest and of course has suffered, in that particular light, because it has had to serve as a home all these years and has had to shelter people who loved it and those who did not. Margaret did not love it and was glad to leave in that spring of 1861. The rubble and ruins of old Independence are scattered in weedy pastures. All that remains of the first Baylor College is a file of rock pillars; before the pillars extends an avenue of shells and foundations. A tumbling corncrib and a clear spring are what is left of the Houstons' house, though on down the street the wooden house in which Margaret died is probably about the same as it was. The Baptist church still rings Nancy Lea's bell. The wooden church is gone, replaced by a pleasant stone building. Across the road Mrs. Lea's tomb has suffered the indignity of having a tree grow up from its floor through the roof. Nancy Lea was removed from the vault in the 1880's, and she and her metal coffin were buried nearby. Margaret lies beside her. A third grave bears more inscription than the others: "Aunt Eliza. Died March 9, 1898. Aged 75 years. FAITHFUL UNTO DEATH."

There is left some savor of the Houstons' world, faint though it may be. A biographer must endeavor to see as his men and women saw. Toward this goal the investigator can sometimes move very far. His most consequential source is his collection of manuscripts, the actual words of the characters and the people who knew them. Elsewhere he follows with caution and honesty any clue which might lead him through the concealing fog of the years that have intervened.

Selected Bibliography

Primary Sources

Original Letters and Papers and Museum Materials

Duke University Library:
David Christy Manuscript Collection
Library of Congress:
Andrew Jackson Manuscripts
James K. Polk Manuscripts
New York Public Library:
Sam Houston Manuscripts
Margaret Lea Houston Manuscripts
Rosenberg Library, Galveston:
Personal belongings of Sam Houston
Sam Houston Memorial Museum, Huntsville:
Personal belongings and letters of Sam and Margaret Houston
San Jacinto Museum of History:
Personal belongings of Sam and Margaret Houston
Stephen F. Austin State College, Nacogdoches:
David Rusk Manuscripts
East Texas Collection

Tennessee State Archives:
Bernhart Wall Notes
Texas State Library (Archives Division), Austin:
Frank Brown Manuscript, "Annals of Travis County and of the City of Austin"
Governors' Letters
Houston Unpublished Correspondence
Thomas Jefferson Rusk Manuscripts
University of North Carolina Archives, Chapel Hill:
Green Collection
Polk Collection
University of Texas Archives, Austin:
Ashbel Smith Manuscripts
Henderson Yoakum Diary
Houston Unpublished Correspondence
Personal Collections:
Andrew Jackson Collection, The Hermitage, Nashville
Franklin Williams Collection, Houston:
Manuscripts and personal belongings of Sam Houston
Sam Houston Hearne Collection, Houston:
Manuscripts, letters, and personal belongings of Sam Houston

Books and Articles

Boney, F. N. (ed.). "The Raven Tamed," *Southwestern Historical Quarterly*, Vol. LXVIII (1964), 90–92.

Burleson, Georgia Jenkins (ed.). *Life and Writings of Rufus C. Burleson.* Privately printed, 1901.

Burleson, Rufus C. *Address of Dr. Rufus C. Burleson on the One-Hundredth Anniversary of the Birth of Gen. Sam Houston.* Austin, Jones Co., 1893.

Butler, Ruth L. and W. Eugene Hollon (eds.). *William Bollaert's Texas.* Norman, University of Oklahoma Press, 1956.

Coleman, Robert M. *Houston Displayed, or Who Won the Battle of San Jacinto.* Velasco, 1837.

Ellis, J. H. H. *Sam Houston and Related Spiritual Forces.* Privately printed, Concord Press, 1945.

Fisher, Orceneth. *Sketches of Texas in 1840.* Springfield, Walters and Weber, 1841.

Gulick, C. A., et al. *The Papers of Mirabeau B. Lamar.* Austin, Von Boeckman Jones, 1922–26.

Hunt, Lenoir (ed.). *My Master by Jeff Hamilton.* Dallas, Manford Van Nort and Company, 1940.

Jones, Anson. *Memoranda and Official Correspondence Relating to the Republic of Texas, Its History and Annexation: Including a Brief Autobiography by the Author.* New York, Appleton and Company, 1859.

Linn, J. J. *Reminiscences of Fifty Years in Texas.* New York, Sodlier and Company, 1883.

Lockhart, John. *Sixty Years on the Brazos.* Privately printed, 1930.

McCalla, William L. *Adventures in Texas, Chiefly in the Spring and Summer of 1840.* Privately printed, Philadelphia, 1841.

Nevins, Allan (ed.). *Polk: The Diary of a President, 1845–1849.* New York, Longmans, Green and Company, 1929.

North, Alfred T. *Five Years in Texas, or What You Did Not Hear During the War from January 1861 to January 1866.* Cincinnati, Elm Street Printing Company, 1871.

Olmsted, Frederick Law. *A Journey Through Texas; or, A Saddle-Trip on the Southwestern Frontier.* New York, Dix, Edwards, and Company, 1857.

Peareson, P. E. "Reminiscences of Judge Edwin Waller," *Southwestern Historical Quarterly*, Vol. IV (1900), 33–53.

Richardson, Willard, et al. *Galveston Directory, 1859–1860, with a Brief History of the Island, Prior to the Founding of the City.* Galveston, Galveston News, 1859.

Smith, Ashbel. *An Account of the Yellow Fever Which Appeared in the City of Galveston, Republic of Texas, in the Autumn of 1839, with Cases and Dissections.* Galveston, Hamilton Stuart, 1839.

Smither, Harriet (ed.). "The Diary of Adolphus Sterne," *South-*

western Historical Quarterly, Vols. XXX through XXXVIII (1926–35).

Terrell, A. W. "Recollections of General Sam Houston," *Southwestern Historical Quarterly*, Vol. XVI (1912), 113–36.

Terrell, A. W. "The City of Austin From 1839–1865," *Southwestern Historical Quarterly*, Vol. XIV (1910), 113–28.

Williams, Amelia W., and Eugene C. Barker (eds.). *The Writings of Sam Houston*, 8 vols. Austin, University of Texas Press, 1938–43.

Interviews

Baldwin, Mrs. F. S., great-granddaughter of General and Mrs. Houston. Interviewed April, 1964.

Darby, Mrs. James, great-granddaughter of the Houstons. Interviewed at various times in May, June, and July, 1964, and in May, 1965.

Decker, Mrs. Jennie Belle Morrow, granddaughter of the Houstons and daughter of Nancy Elizabeth Houston Morrow. Interviewed in April, May, June, September, and November, 1964, and in January and May, 1965, and variously in 1966.

Everitt, Mrs. Colonel Edward Allan, great-granddaughter of the Houstons, and intimately associated with the Houston children. Interviewed with Mrs. Decker, and privately April, 1965, April, 1966, January, 1967, and April, 1968.

Hearne, Sam Houston, great-grandson of the Houstons. Interviewed May, 1964, and April and May, 1965.

Herrin, Mrs. T. S., of Marion, Alabama, and a student at Judson College in the late nineteenth century. Interviewed in Houston, Texas, May 15, 1964.

Johns, Mrs. Ruth Sanders, a great-granddaughter. Interviewed in 1963, died in Cuernavaca, Mexico, 1965.

Jones, Mrs. Roland. Interviewed at various times in 1967. Used collection of artifacts and manuscripts from Huntsville and San Augustine, Texas.

Little, Mrs. John L., Sr., granddaughter and intimate acquaintance of Antoinette, Margaret Houston's sister. Interviewed variously in 1963, 1964, and 1965.

O'Madigan, Mrs. Dan, Antoinette's great-granddaughter. Used collection of jewelry and similar items which belonged to Antoinette as Mrs. Power. Interviewed January, 1965.

Secondary Sources

Books and Articles

Alexander, Drury Blakely. *Texas Homes of the Nineteenth Century.* Austin, University of Texas Press, 1966.

Barr, Alwin, "Texas Coastal Defense, 1861–1865," *Southwestern Historical Quarterly*, Vol. LXXV (1961), 1–31.

Brewster, Willis. *Alabama: Her History, Resources, War Record, and Public Men.* Montgomery, Barret and Brown, 1872.

Brooks, Elizabeth. *Prominent Women of Texas.* Akron, The Werner Company, 1896.

Bruce, Henry. *The Life of General Houston.* New York, Dodd, Mead, and Company, 1891.

Carroll, James M. *A History of Texas Baptists.* Dallas, The Baptist Standard Printing Company, 1923.

Connally, Ernest A., "Architecture At the End of the South: Central Texas," *Journal of the Society of Architectural Historians*, Vol. XI (1952), 9–20.

Crane, William Carey. *Life and Select Literary Remains of Sam Houston of Texas.* Philadelphia, Lippincott and Company, 1884.

Creel, George. *Sam Houston: Colossus in Buckskin.* New York, Cosmopolitan Book Corporation, 1928.

Culberson, Charles. "General Sam Houston and Secession," *Scribner's Magazine*, Vol. XXXIX (1906), 26–40.

Daughters of the Republic of Texas. *Fifty Years of Achievement.* Dallas, Banks, Upshaw, and Company, 1942.

Davis, J. Frank. *The Road to San Jacinto.* New York, Bobbs-Merrill and Company, 1936.

Dixon, Sam Houston. *The Poets and Poetry of Texas.* Austin, Dixon and Company, 1885.

Featherstonhaugh, G. W. *Excursion Through the Slave States from Washington on the Patomic to the Frontier of Mexico,* 2 vols. London, Murray and Company, 1844.

First Baptist Church of Galveston, Texas. *Historical Sketch.* Galveston, News Steam Job Press, 1871.

Flanagan, Sue. *Sam Houston's Texas.* Austin, University of Texas Press, 1965.

Ford, Hoyt. "The Life and Works of William Carey Crane." MA thesis, University of Texas, 1926.

Fornell, Earl W. *The Galveston Era.* Austin, University of Texas Press, 1961.

Friend, Llerena Beaufort. *Sam Houston: The Great Designer.* Austin, University of Texas Press, 1956.

———. "The Great Designer, Sam Houston in the American Political Scene." PhD thesis, University of Texas, 1951.

———. "The Texan of 1860," *Southwestern Historical Quarterly,* Vol. LXII (1958), 1–17.

Gage, Larry Jay, "The City of Austin on the Eve of Annexation," *Southwestern Historical Quarterly,* Vol. LXIII (1960), 428–36.

Gambrell, Herbert. *Anson Jones.* Garden City, Doubleday and Company, 1948.

Graham, S. B. (ed.). *Galveston Community Book, a Historical and Biographical Record of Galveston and Galveston County.* Galveston, Cawston and Company, 1945.

Guild, Josephus Conn. *Old Times in Tennessee, with Historical, Personal, and Political Scraps and Sketches.* Nashville, Tavel, Eastman, and Howell, 1878.

Hartwell, Joan M. "Margaret Lea of Alabama: Mrs. Sam Houston," *The Alabama Review,* Vol. XVII (1964), 271–84.

"Historical Sketch of Washington County," *The American Sketchbook*, Vol. IV (1878), 15–21.

Hogan, William R. *The Texas Republic: A Social and Economic History*. Norman, University of Oklahoma Press, 1946.

Hoovestall, Paeder Joel. "Galveston In the Civil War." MA thesis, University of Houston, 1950.

Houston, Samuel R. *Brief Biographical Accounts of Many Members of the Houston Family*. Cincinnati, Elm Street Printing Company, 1882.

James, Marquis. *The Raven: A Biography of Sam Houston*. Indianapolis, Bobbs-Merrill Company, 1929.

James, Marquis. *Andrew Jackson: The Border Captain* and *Portrait of a President*, 2 vols. New York: Bobbs-Merrill Company, 1937.

Jennings, Vivian. "History of Sam Houston's Governorship of Texas." MA thesis, University of Texas, 1934.

Kelley, Dayton, "BU Hourglass," *The Baylor Line*, Vol. XXX (1968), 13.

Lester, E. Charles. *Life of Sam Houston, Hunter, Patriot and Statesman of Texas*. Philadelphia, G. G. Evans, 1860.

Lovelace, Julia Murfee. *A History of Siloam Baptist Church, Marion, Alabama*. Birmingham, Siloam Baptist Church, 1943.

Maher, Edward R. "Sam Houston and Secession," *Southwestern Historical Quarterly*, Vol. LV (1951), 448–58.

Martineau, Harriet. *Retrospect of Western Travel*. London, Saunders and Otley, 1838.

Miles, Susan. "A Famous Romance," *West Texas Historical Yearbook*, Vol. XXXVIII (1961), 135–53.

Morrow, Bobbie M. "A Rhetorical Analysis of Two Speeches Delivered in 1854 and 1856 by Samuel Houston in Congress." MA thesis, University of Texas, 1963.

Nichols, Annie Lee, "Early Days in Marion," unpublished lecture delivered at Judson College in 1962. Collection of Miss Annie Lee Nichols, Marion, Alabama.

Pickett, Albert James. *History of Alabama.* Birmingham, Roberts and Son, 1851.

Pinkney, Pauline. *Painting in Texas: The Nineteenth Century.* Austin, University of Texas Press, 1967.

Power, Tyrone. *Impressions of America in the Years 1833, 1834, and 1835.* Philadelphia, Carey, Lea, and Blanchard, 1836.

Rankin, Melinda. *Texas in 1850.* Boston, Damrell and Moore, 1850.

Schlesinger, Arthur M., Jr. *The Age of Jackson.* Boston, Little, Brown, and Company, 1949.

Shearer, Ernest C. "The Mercurial Sam Houston," *The East Tennessee Historical Society's Publication*, Vol. XXXV (1962), 8–27.

Shuffler, R. Henderson. *The Houstons at Independence.* Waco, The Texian Press, 1965.

Sibley, Marilyn. *Travelers in Texas 1761–1860.* Austin, University of Texas Press, 1967.

Siegel, Stanley. *A Political History of the Texas Republic, 1836–1845.* Austin, University of Texas Press, 1956.

Smith, J. H. *The Annexation of Texas.* New York, Barnes and Noble, 1941.

Smith, Culver H. "The Funeral of Andrew Jackson," *Tennessee Historical Quarterly*, Vol. IV (1947), 195–214.

Stenberg, Richard R. "Jackson's Neches Claim, 1829–1836," *Southwestern Historical Quarterly*, Vol. XXXIX (1936), 1–18.

Strickland, Rennard and Jack Gregory. *Sam Houston with the Cherokees.* Austin, University of Texas Press, 1967.

Turner, Martha Anne. *Sam Houston and His Twelve Women.* Austin, Pemberton Press, 1966.

Webb, Walter Prescott. *The Texas Rangers: A Century of Frontier Defense.* Boston, Houghton Mifflin Company, 1935.

Wheeler, Kenneth W. *To Wear a City's Crown: The Beginnings of Urban Growth in Texas, 1836–1865.* Cambridge, Harvard University Press, 1968.

White, Olive Branch, "Margaret Lea Houston: Wife of General

Sam Houston," *Naylor's Epic-Century Magazine*, Vol. III (1936), 30–42.

Williams, Alfred M. *Sam Houston and the War of Independence In Texas*. Boston, Houghton Mifflin Company, 1893.

Wisehart, M. K. *Sam Houston: American Giant*. Washington, Luce Company, 1962.

Yoakum, Henderson. *History of Texas from Its First Settlement in 1685 to Its Annexation to the United States in 1846*. New York, Redfield and Company, 1855.

Youngblood, Frances, et al. *Historic Homes of Alabama and Their Traditions*. Birmingham, Birmingham Publishing Company, 1935.

Newspapers

Alabama State Review, Montgomery, Alabama.
Austin State Gazette, Austin, Texas.
The Bee, New Orleans, Louisiana.
Civilian and Galveston Gazette, Galveston, Texas.
Commercial Bulletin, New Orleans, Louisiana.
The Daily Bulletin, Austin, Texas.
Dallas Morning News, Dallas, Texas.
Flake's Bulletin, Galveston, Texas.
Galveston Daily News, Galveston, Texas.
The Herald, New York, New York.
The Houston Post, Houston, Texas.
Marion Herald, Marion, Alabama.
The Morning Star, Houston City, Texas.
Nashville Union, Nashville, Tennessee.
Nile's Weekly Register, Baltimore, Maryland.
The Red-Lander, San Augustine, Texas.
Telegraph and Texas Register, Houston, Texas.
Texas Sentinel, Austin, Texas.
The Texas State Gazette, Austin, Texas.

Selected Bibliography

Public Records

United States Census Returns for the years 1850 and 1860.

County Records

Texas counties of Chambers, Galveston, Hardin, Harris, Liberty, Nacogdoches, Polk, San Augustine, Travis, Walker, Washington, and Williamson.

Alabama counties of Perry and Mobile.

Davidson County, Tennessee.

Index

Abolition: 91, 185, 201
Adams, President John Quincy: 21
Alabama: 10, 15, 17, 48, 67, 88, 107, 145, 154, 187; in War Between the States, 241
Alamo, fall of: 26, 192
Allen, Eliza (Mrs. Sam Houston): 21–22, 29, 56
Allen, Mrs. Eliza (editor of *Mother's Journal of Philadelphia*): 111 & n., 112
Allen, John: 21
Allen, Colonel R. T. P.: 195–96, 211
American party: 184
Anderson, Texas: 159, 164
Anglo-Americans in Texas: 25, 61, 90–91, 101, 193
Anna (housekeeper): 112–13
Annexation (of Texas) to United States: 90, 109, 186, 208; Houston's views on, 91–93, 98; annexation proposal made by United States, 96; convention to consider, 99; Texas sentiment on, 99–101, 104
Arkansas, yellow fever in: 255
Austin, Texas: 16, 38, 45, 65, 85, 129, 161, 170, 182, 203, 213, 252, 262; character of, 48; archives trouble, 69–70, 72–73, 77; abandoned by officials, 70; Texas government returned to, 108; the Houstons move to, 190; Houstons in, 190–208; Unionists' meeting in, 200; secessionist convention call in, 202; Houston's portrait in capitol, 246
Austin College, Huntsville, Texas: 135, 151, 161 & n.

Bagby, Tom: 93, 146
Baines, Rev. George W.: 144, 159, 164, 168–70, 252
Baines, Melicia: 141, 144, 152–53, 159, 164
Baptist church, Independence, Texas: 162–63; house leased to, 235; bell for, 173–74, 239
Baptists: 8, 166, 168, 171, 245, 252; at Grand Cane, 94; in Huntsville, 135–37; in Independence, 149, 163; in Austin, 195
Barbecues: at Washington-on-the-Brazos, 60; in Tennessee, 103
Bastrop, Texas: 195
Bayland Guards: 215, 218, 221
Baylor, Judge R. E. B.: 168, 170
Baylor University, Independence, Texas: 161, 163, 173, 196, 210–11, 234, 238, 241, 245, 250; Sam Houston, Jr., at, 161, 222, 236; Houston daughters enrolled at, 212, 220; closed by yellow fever epidemic, 254; moved to Waco, 260
Ben Lomond (cabin at Cedar Point): 39, 44, 50–51, 54–57, 133, 213
Bingley (servant): 174, 197, 212, 241; with Margaret Lea Houston,

244; and burial of Margaret Lea Houston, 257–58
Blackburn, Dr.: 169
Bledsoe, Antoinette Lea: 5, 6, 10–11, 15–16, 37, 42, 47, 52–53, 65, 68, 76, 78, 93–94; and founding of Concord Baptist Church, 100; Galveston-bound, 105; married to Captain Power, 111; *see also* Antoinette Bledsoe Power
Bledsoe, William: 5, 10–12, 16, 37; illness of, 14–15, 37, 42, 52–53, 78; death of, 104–105, 107, 229
Bledsoes, the William: 35, 41, 43ff., 47, 68, 78, 99; sugar plantation of, 37–38, 41, 93
Blockade: 203, 222, 240
Blount, Billie: 229
Blount Springs, Ala.: 14; Houstons at, 104
Blue, Ben (slave): 38
Brazos River: 35, 72, 74–75, 85, 89, 236; Indian treaty talks on, 95
Brenham, Texas: 166, 169–70, 211, 257
Brownsville, Texas: 193
Buchanan, President James: 184
Burleson, Georgia Jenkins (Mrs. Rufus Burleson): 164
Burleson, Rufus (president of Baylor College): 163–64, 166, 170–71
Burnet, David G.: 53, 56, 58–59

Cameo portrait of Sam Houston: presented to Margaret Lea, 14, 241; presented to Nancy Elizabeth Houston Morrow, 252
Cass, Lewis: 139
Catholic church, Roman: 25, 62–63
Cave, Major Eber W.: 226–28, 238–39; at death and burial of Margaret Lea Houston, 257–58
Cedar Point (Houston's farm): 35, 38–40, 44–45, 47, 73–74, 96–97, 132 & n., 133, 158, 211, 221–22, 235, 237–38, 262; plans for permanent house at, 50; the Houstons at, 54–59, 172, 213–21; rented, 252
Charlotte (slave): 17, 40, 44–45, 122; sold to planter, 128
Cherokees, the: 19, 22–23; and Sam Houston, 22–24, 114, 145–46; at Huntsville, 229–30
Chevalier, Charles: 63
Chicago, Ill.: 221
Chilton, George W.: 206–207
Christy, William: 76, 100, 145
Cincinnati, Texas: 135, 149
Civil War: *see* War Between the States
Clay, Henry: 140
Cluis, F. V.: 12
Cochran, Rev. J. L.: 232–33
Coffin, Nancy Lea's: 163, 237–38
Comanche Indians: 24
Committee of Vigilance: 214
Concord Baptist Church, Grand Cane: 100, 105–106
Confederate Army: 215, 219, 228
Confederate States of America: 205, 208, 210–11, 224, 230; Texas united with, 206, 211; Texas officials' oath of loyalty required by, 207, 227
Constitution, United States: 199, 201
Corinth, Miss.: battle at, 219–20
Cortina, Juan: 193, 198
Cramayel (French agent): 92
Crane, Catherine Jane (Mrs. William Carey Crane): 245, 247–49
Crane, Rev. William Carey (president of Baylor University): 9 & n., 245, 249, 257 & n.; author of Houston's biography, 245–48

Crawford, Rev. Peter: 7, 18, 31, 45–46
Creath, Frances (Mrs. J. W. D. Creath): 110, 135, 141, 144, 152, 159, 173–74; illness and death of, 177–78
Creath, Rev. J. W. D.: 135–36, 144, 174, 177–78
Creath, Luther: 174
Creek Indians: 19, 21

Democratic National Convention, 1852: 157
Democratic party: 96, 139, 156, 157, 206, 208; radical branch of, 161, 180–82, 185; in Texas, 180, 190–91, 201
Democratic State Convention, Waco, Texas, 1857: 184
Democrats: 115, 184–85, 202–204, 206, 235; view Sam Houston as presidential candidate, 155–56; Kansas-Nebraska bill of, 165; James Buchanan as candidate of, 184; in Austin, 191–92
Donelson, Andrew Jackson: 96; at Raven Hill, 98; Houstons visit, 102
Douglas, Stephen A.: 168

Eliza (servant): 17–18, 32, 40–41, 43–45, 51, 53–55, 65, 70, 77–78, 89, 93, 109–10, 122, 127–28, 131, 138, 163, 167, 190, 193–94, 197, 200, 212, 217, 219, 233, 235, 241, 250–52; with Nancy Elizabeth Houston Morrow, 252–53, 256; death and burial of, 263
Elliot, Charles (British agent): 92, 98
Ellis, Joseph: 94
England: Republic of Texas recognized by, 78; diplomats from, 92; Houston's denial of collusion with, 100–101; possible Mexico takeover by, 193; sanctuary sought in, 197
Esaw (slave): 38, 44
E Street Baptist Church, Washington, D.C.: 141, 179
Etheridge (Houston's courier): 94
Evans, Dr.: 141, 159
Evans, Mrs.: 141, 152, 159, 255

Fanin Artillery: 64
Filibustering: 77, 86, 201, 231
Fillmore, President Millard: 184
Fort Jesup, La.: 26
Fosgate, Dr.: 59–60
France: 66, 68; Republic of Texas recognized by, 78; diplomats from, 92; Houston's denial of collusion with, 100–101; possible Mexico takeover by, 193, 199
Frankey (field hand): 40, 59

Gadknew, H.: 152
Gaines, General Edmund Pendleton: 26
Galveston, Texas: 13, 29, 42, 53–54, 67–68, 70, 73, 80, 89, 96, 99, 104, 109, 111, 120, 127, 213, 216, 218, 221, 224, 230, 232, 235–36, 240, 262; Nancy Moffette Lea in, 16, 35–38, 45, 52; Antoinette Lea Bledsoe in, 105; prisoners of war taken at, 225; fellow fever epidemic in, 255
Galveston Bay: 13, 26, 35, 111, 132; ship *Harriet Lane* sunk in, 205
Galveston Island: 10, 26, 34, 43, 215, 219; captured by Federal forces, 222; recaptured, 224
Gentry, Diana Rogers (Mrs. Sam Houston): 23, 56, 261; *see also* Diana Rogers

Georgetown, Texas: 244, 251–54, 256–57, 260
Georgia, University of: 5, 47
Gibbs, Tom: 145, 174
Gillespy, Aunt: 108
Goree, Mrs. L. J.: 18, 104, 161; move to Madisonville, 172
Goree, Professor L. J.: 45, 104, 161; move to Madisonville, 172
Gott, Thomas: 133, 136, 150; and Virginia Thorne, 140–41, 147–49; Mrs. Houston sued by, 151–53; *see also* Virginia Thorne
Governor's Mansion, Austin, Texas: 191–98, 207–208, 262–63
Graham, Dr. Beriah: 200
Grand Cane, Texas: 37, 41–43, 53, 73, 76, 78, 81, 85, 89, 94, 96, 99, 122, 124, 127, 133, 140, 158, 229, 235, 262; Concord Baptist Church at, 100, 104–106
Grant, General Ulysses S.: 219
Greensboro, Ala.: 104

Harding, William G.: 13
Harper's New Monthly Magazine: 246
Harriet Lane (Union ship): 225
Hatch, Captain Frank: 121, 127, 132, 147–49
Hatfield, Major: 74, 77, 236–37
Hermitage, The, Nashville, Tenn.: 13, 20, 24, 92, 100, 103, 226; Houstons at, 101–102
Hines, Mr.: 161
Hockley, George Washington: 39–40, 56–57; resigns government post, 74; at peace conference, 90
Holland: Republic of Texas recognized by, 78
Houston, Andrew Jackson: 167, 195–96, 198, 216, 219, 231, 245; at age two, 175; and coffin-inspection incident, 237–38; in Georgetown, 251, 253, 256; adult life of, 261; death of, 261
Houston, Antoinette Power (Nettie): 157–58, 242–43; at age four, 175; poems of, 251, 260; at age fifteen, 253; and yellow fever epidemic, 256–57; at death and burial of Margaret Lea Houston, 257–58; death of, 261
Houston, Elizabeth Paxton: 19, 21, 30, 120
Houston, Margaret (Maggie—Mrs. Weston Lafayette Williams): 131, 142, 147, 180, 217, 219, 234–37, 241, 253–56, 260; at age eight, 175; enrolled at Baylor University, 212; illness of, 225; quits Baylor, 225; secretary to Houston, 225; at father's burial, 233; engagement of, 249; wedding of, 250; Independence visit planned by, 255; death of, 260
Houston, Margaret Lea (Mrs. Sam Houston): 32–35, 37, 40, 43, 46–48, 66–67, 74–77, 91, 100, 109, 142–43, 155–60, 176–79, 183–84, 186–89, 208–209, 211–12, 214–18, 228–29, 252, 259; in Galveston, 36–39, 45, 52, 54; trips to Cedar Point, 38–39, 47, 132–33, 158, 191, 235; illnesses of, 42, 51, 57, 59, 70, 93, 95, 113–14, 122–27, 158, 163, 218, 237; fears about Houston's drinking, 43, 70, 72, 82–83, 116; in Houston City, 45, 64–66; gossip spurned by, 48–53, 89; poetry of, 52–55, 57–58, 67, 95, 111–12, 173, 232–33, 243; at Grand Cane, 53–54, 78–81, 89, 93–96, 104–106, 122–27, 132–33, 158–59, 235; in

Marion, Ala., 70–71, 104–106; and yellow coach, 89–90, 97, 99, 122, 158, 190, 208; birthday party for, 93; and Virginia Thorne, 93, 127, 140–41, 147–49, 151–53; at Raven Hill, 97, 110–22, 127–28; and founding of Concord Baptist Church, 99–100; reform of Houston, 106–108, 115–16, 120, 136, 144, 151, 153–54, 160, 167; surgery, 125, 127; at Huntsville farm, 127, 128 & n., 129, 133–37, 144–47, 154–57, 159, 172–75; and Indians at Huntsville, 146; sued, 151–53; brooding on death, 160, 166; in Independence, 161–63, 166, 187–90, 211, 234–58; return to Huntsville, 172–73, 183; letters of, 175; and death of Frances Creath, 177–78; in Austin, 191–208, 211–12; move to Cedar Point, 213–21; at Steamboat House, 223–33, 234; move to Independence, 234–37; finances of, 235, 239–40; sale of Cedar Point considered by, 235; efforts to keep Sam Houston, Jr., out of army, 236, 242; in Nancy Lea's home, 237–38; new house in Independence, 238, 239–59; loneliness of, 242–43; Houston's salary received by, 244; note payments made to, 244; poverty of, 244–45, 252–53; and Houston biography, 245–46, 247; disposal of documents, 247 & n., 248 & n.; and Nancy Elizabeth Houston's wedding, 248–49; engagement of Margaret (Maggie) Houston announced by, 249; and wedding of Margaret Houston, 250; at age forty-eight, 250–51; and first granddaughter, 251, 256; cameo portrait of, 252; Cedar Point rented by, 252; rejects move to Georgetown, 254; at Labadie Prairie, 255–56; stopover in Independence, 256; stricken with yellow fever, 256–57; death and burial of, 257–58; *see also* Margaret Lea

Houston, Mary (sister of Sam Houston): 151

Houston, Mary William (Mary Willie): 150, 217, 231, 251; at age five, 175; enrolled at Baylor, 212; at father's burial, 233; at age seventeen, 253; and yellow fever epidemic, 256–57; at death and burial of mother, 257–58; death of, 260

Houston, Nancy Elizabeth (Nannie—Mrs. Joseph Clay Stiles Morrow): 120–22, 124, 126–27, 142, 147–48, 159–60, 164–65, 167, 180, 183, 197, 207, 217, 222, 228, 231, 241, 254, 256; in Independence, 162; at age nine, 175; enrolled at Baylor, 212, 220; at father's burial, 233; wedding of, 243–45, 248–49; on visit to Independence, 251; in Georgetown, 252–53; prosperity of, 253; death of, 260

Houston, Sam: 5, 8, 13, 36, 38, 40, 45–47, 79, 89, 93, 111, 123–24, 131, 135, 137, 150–51, 155, 172, 174–76, 208–209, 214–17, 222, 235, 237, 241, 244–45, 252, 254, 259; meeting with Margaret Lea, 10–11; courtship of, 12–17; marriage of, 5, 17–18, 30–33; as president of Texas Republic, 10, 28, 60, 65–66, 68–93; drinking of, 12, 23, 28–29, 31 & n., 34 & n., 43, 58, 62, 70, 80–81, 115–16, 246; as governor of Tennessee, 12, 21, 22, 40, 226; hero of San Jacinto, 14, 19,

26–28, 62, 109, 118, 137, 145, 171, 184–85, 191; in Texas Congress, 16, 40, 42, 44, 45–53; early life, 19–20; aided by Jackson, 20; Jacksonian views of, 20–21, 183; marriage to Eliza Allen, 21–22, 29, 56; citizen of Cherokee Nation, 22–23, 229; marriage to Diana Rogers Gentry, 23; ambassador for the Cherokees, 23, 114; on Texas mission for Jackson, 24; ambition for Texas empire, 24–25, 28, 90–91, 121, 227; land speculation, 24–25; and Anna Raguet, 28–29; on religion, 46, 90, 106, 114, 120–21, 130, 136, 157, 160, 163–64, 179; (Texas) presidential campaign of, 52–59; finances of, 55, 57, 85, 113, 121, 223; token conversion to Catholicism, 62–63; in Washington-on-the-Brazos, 72–93; clothes of, 77, 138 & n., 166; Mexican territory coveted by, 91–92, 199, 206; and annexation, 91–93, 98, 100–101, 139; campaigning for Anson Jones, 94–95; at Huntsville, 94, 96, 97, 144–47, 153, 157, 183; visit to Grand Cane, 99, 105–106, 126–27; denounced as traitor, 99; elected to U.S. Senate, 107–108; reform of, 106–108, 115–16, 129–30, 144, 151, 153–54; war with Mexico envisioned by, 109; in Washington, D.C., 109, 113–16, 121–26, 131, 137, 139–41, 143–44, 147–53, 156–57, 161, 164–67, 172, 179, 181, 184, 188, 190–91; military commission sought by, 117–19, 121, 126; U.S. protectorate over Mexico endorsed by, 121, 193, 198; re-elected to Senate, 129, 161; decline of popularity in Texas, 139–40; political philosophy of, 139; church attendance of, 141, 159; in U.S. presidential race, 155–56, 157, 200; in Independence, 161–63, 166; on Texas speaking tour, 162; Kansas-Nebraska bill opposed by, 165, 167–68, 180; presidential ambition of, 165, 181, 198; popularity in New England, 166, 180; baptism of, 170–71, 173; and Democratic party, 180–82, 202–206; and Know-Nothing party, 182–83; campaigning for Fillmore, 184; as governor of Texas, 184–86, 190–208; pictures of, 194–95, 226, 238, 246; and Robert E. Lee, 198–99; speeches of, 201, 203, 205; secession opposed by, 201, 203–204; Lincoln's offer refused, 203; relationship to Confederacy, 206, 207, 217; governor's office vacated by, 207, 225; move to Cedar Point, 211–12, 213–21; failing health, 212, 223–24, 228, 231; in Steamboat House, 223–32; on Texas defense, 224; prisoners of war aided by, 225, 228, 231; archives of, 226 & n., 238, 245–48; at age seventy, 226; speech in Houston City, 227; at Sour Lake, 229–30; called Unionist and traitor, 230; illness and death of, 231, 232–33; will of, 235, 239, 253–54; grave of, 262

Houston, Sam, Jr.: 100–101, 112–14, 117–18, 121–22, 124, 126–28, 132–33, 142–43, 147–48, 150–51, 155, 157–58, 164–65, 167, 187, 193–94, 200–201, 239–41, 254; birth of, 86; at Washington-on-the-Brazos, 86–89; at Grand Cane, 93, 95–96, 99, 104–106; at Huntsville, 97–98; in Alabama, 104; enrolled at Baylor University, 161, 222, 236; in Independence, 162, 244–50; at age twelve, 175; enrolled in military academy, 195–96; withdrawn from academy, 202; trip to Mexico, 202; return from Mexico, 211; at Cedar Point, 212, 214; in Confederate Army, 215–19; at battle of Shiloh, 220–21; capture of, 221; return home, 221; return to army, 225, 236–37; in Mexico with Charles Power, 228, 231, 236; poetry of, 242; drawings of battle of Shiloh, 242; farming, 245 & n.; medical school plans of, 250, 252–53; medical practice of, 259–60; death of, 260

Houston, General and Mrs. Sam: 36, 78, 121, 127–29, 159, 188, 208–209; on trip to Redlands, 40–42; in Houston City, 44–45, 67–69; at Ben Lomond, Cedar Point, 54–57, 172; finances of, 55, 57, 85, 113, 187–88, 213, 223; Redlands tour of, 59–65, 70; in Washington-on-the-Brazos, 72–75, 77, 81–93; visit at Grand Cane, 99, 105–106; in Nashville, Tenn., 101–104; at Blount Springs, Ala., 104; on Marion, Ala., visit, 104; at Huntsville house, 144–47; move to Independence, 161–63, 187–90, 211; move to Austin, 190; at Cedar Point, 191, 213–21; in Austin, 191–208; in Steamboat House, 223–32

Houston, Major Samuel: 19

Houston, Temple Lea: 200, 212, 219, 241, 245, 257; at age seven, 253; law practice of, 260; death of, 260

Houston, William Rogers (Willie Rogers): 187, 191, 241, 245, 257; at age eleven, 253, 260; death of, 260

Houston City (Houston), Texas: 28–29, 38, 47, 53, 58–60, 64–65, 68–70, 72–73, 79, 84, 93, 96, 99, 213, 218, 221, 227, 230, 236; Sam Houstons move to, 44–45; Texas archives ordered moved to, 69; Sam Houstons' house rented, 74; house sold, 146

Houston Dragoons: 64

Huntsville, Texas: 94, 110–11, 116–17, 119, 121, 135, 148, 151, 154–55, 158–59, 174, 192, 221–23, 225, 231, 238, 240; Houston house at, 94, 96–98; Houstons in, 97; Raven Hill, 97; plantation exchanged, 127–29, 131; Huntsville farm improvements, 133 & n., 134, 146; Baptists in, 135–37, 163; Indians at, 145–46, 229–30; house rented to L. J. Goree, 161; Houstons move from, 161–62; return to, 172–74, 183; house sold, 187–88 & n., 262; Steamboat House in, 223, 226–28, 234, 262; prisoners of war at, 225, 228, 231–32; yellow fever epidemic in, 255

Huntsville Male Academy: 135

Hurricane on Gulf Coast: 160, 197

Independence, Texas: 149, 154, 158–61, 168, 170–73, 187, 192, 195, 197, 204, 208, 210–11, 213, 216–17, 219, 221–22, 228, 249; Houstons in, 161–71, 190–91, 210, 249; Margaret Lea Houston in, 234–58; yellow fever epidemic, 254–58; decay of, 260

Indians: 43, 48, 57, 77, 88, 206; in treaty talks, 95; at Huntsville, 145–47

Irion, Anna Raguet (Mrs. Robert Irion): 29, 63–64, 76, 86
Irion, Dr. Robert: 29, 63–64, 86
Irion, Sam Houston: 64
Isabella (housekeeper): 155, 158, 162

Jackson (coachman): 17, 40, 54
Jackson, President Andrew: 13, 20, 24, 27, 96, 109, 114–15, 118, 226; defeat of, 21; election of, 21; Sam Houston's annexation views sought by, 92–93; illness, 98; death and funeral, 101–103
Jackson, Rachel Donelson (Mrs. Andrew Jackson): 20–21, 102
Jacksonian Democrats: 22, 184
Johnson, Daniel: 150
Johnson, Joe: 150
Jones, Anson: 92, 94, 105, 139; president of Republic of Texas, 95
Jones, Mrs. Anson: 91
Joshua (slave): 41, 60, 74, 96, 109–10, 132–33, 159, 167, 193, 223; carpentry of, 94, 97, 122; blacksmith in Huntsville, 244
Judson Female Institute (Judson College), Marion, Ala.: 4, 7, 9–10, 18, 104, 161, 210–11

Kansas-Nebraska Act: 167–68, 182
Kansas-Nebraska bill: 165
Kellum, Major Nathaniel E.: 146
Kennedy, William: 79
Kentucky: 251
Knights of the Golden Circle: 201
Know-Nothing party: 182–83
Kountz Creek: 170–71

Labadie Prairie (Labadie), Texas: 250, 253–56
Lafayette Hotel, Marion, Ala.: 4, 17, 32
Lamar, Mirabeau B. (president of the Republic of Texas): 40, 53, 56, 58–59, 66, 72, 86, 95
Laredo, Texas: 90
Lea, Antoinette: *see* Antoinette Bledsoe *and* Antoinette Bledsoe Power
Lea, Catherine Davis: 147, 158–59, 235 & n.
Lea, Senator Henry: 4–6, 13, 15, 18, 47, 56, 71, 104, 129; death of, 160
Lea, Lucy Ann: 136
Lea, Margaret: 5–9, 12–18; marriage of, 5, 17–18, 30–33; conversion of, 7, 18, 45–46; at Judson Female Institute, 7, 9; poetry of, 8, 14; meeting with Sam Houston, 10–11; engagement, 13–17; *see also* Margaret Lea Houston (Mrs. Sam Houston)
Lea, Martin: 6, 11, 16–18, 32; government post filled by, 70; financial problems of, 74; mystery surrounding death of, 85
Lea, Mary (wife of Vernal Lea): 5, 127; in Galveston, 47; at William Bledsoe home, 47, 79–80; visit to Washington-on-the-Brazos, 88; semi-invalid, 93; death of, 105, 107
Lea, Nancy Moffette: 5, 6, 8–10, 12–16, 38, 40, 42, 44, 47, 51, 53–54, 76, 78, 93, 110–12, 120, 132–33, 143, 145–46, 158, 160, 163, 167, 174, 184, 187, 197–98, 204, 213, 217–18, 245, 250; business interests, 10–13; in Galveston, 16, 35–38, 45, 52; at William Bledsoe home, 52, 94, 105; sued, 73; and Virginia Thorne, 80; in Washington-on-the-Brazos, 84–90; and Concord Baptist Church founding, 100; at Grand Cane, 122–23, 147; at Independence, 148; return to

Huntsville, 149–50, 154; preparations for death, 150, 154, 163, 212, 237; in Independence, 154, 158–59, 161–62, 210–11, 222; tomb built by, 163, 166, 183, 257, 263; church bell bought by, 173–74, 239, 262; coffin inspection of, 237–38; illness and death of, 239; grave, 263
Lea, Serena (wife of Henry Lea): 4, 5, 15, 72, 89, 104, 210
Lea, Temple: 6, 7, 17, 33, 154, 243
Lea, Vernal: 5, 6, 37, 111, 123, 133, 140, 235; in Galveston, 47; at William Bledsoe home, 47, 79–80; guardian of Virginia Thorne, 80; on visit to Washington-on-the-Brazos, 88; sugar plantation cultivated by, 93; postmaster at Grand Cane, 105; remarriage of, 147; move to Bledsoe place, 147; illness, 151, 158–59; death, 160, 229
Lebanon Pike (Nashville, Tenn.): 101
Lee, General Robert E.: 198–99
Letcher, William H.: 108
Liberty, Texas: 37, 76, 79, 125, 127
Lincoln, President Abraham: 201, 203
"Lines To a Withered Pink" (poem): 8
Lockhart, Mr. and Mrs. John: 75, 81
Lone Star flag: 228
Louisiana: 41, 67, 69; army camps in, 242
Louisiana military campaign: 244

McLean, Mr.: 45
Madisonville, Texas: 172
Magruder, General John B.: 224
Marion, Ala.: 3, 4, 9, 12–17, 30, 33, 35, 50, 63, 70–71, 79, 89, 110, 129, 160, 168, 210, 239; Margaret Lea Houston's visit to, 104–107
Maryville, Tenn.: 19–20, 216
Masonic Temple (Huntsville): 232
Matagorda Bay: 123, 150, 159
Memphis, Tenn.: 101
Merritt, Mrs.: 110, 117
Mexican Army: 69, 72, 117
Mexicans: 57, 66, 118, 193, 206; raiding parties of, 77
Mexico: 24–25, 44, 66, 69, 84, 86, 109, 121, 193, 201, 203, 211, 228, 231; instability of government, 25; in revolution of 1835–36, 26–28; territory coveted by Sam Houston, 91–92, 206; invaded by United States, 117–21; U.S. protectorate advocated for, 121, 193, 198; bandit invasions from, 198; British support for invasion of, 199
Mexico City, D. F.: 118
Milam Guards: 64
Military Academy, Colonel R. T. P. Allen's: 195–96
Miller, Washington: 72, 87, 98; on mission to The Hermitage, 92
Missouri Compromise, the: 165
Mobile, Ala.: 10, 13, 16, 32, 34, 78, 104, 144; land speculators at, 86
Montgomery County, Texas: 99
Montsabert, Baron de: 68
Moore, Elizabeth Houston: 116, 120; death of, 151
Moore, Houston: 116
Morocco, Sultan of: 145
Moroms Regiment at Corinth, Miss.: 219
Morrow, Joseph Clay Stiles (Joe Morrow): 244, 249, 252, 254, 260; land purchased near Round Rock, Texas, 251; on visit to Independence, 251; prosperity of, 253
Morrow, Mrs. Joe: 251
Morrow, Margaret: 251, 256

Mother's Journal of Philadelphia: 111, 195

Nacogdoches, Texas: 28, 41, 60, 62–64
Napoleon III: 199
Narbonne, Count de: 68
Nashville, Tenn.: 13–14, 21–22, 25, 92; Sam Houstons in, 101–104
National Union Convention, Baltimore, Md.: 200
Neches River: 27
Neuces River: 48, 77
Newman, Mr.: 183
New Mexico: 109
New Orleans, La.: 10–11, 17, 20, 27, 34, 76, 83, 89, 100, 104, 118, 122–23, 163, 245, 253; Houston's annexation speech in, 100–101
New York: 86, 174, 249
New York (steamer): 34–35, 70, 100
Niagara Falls, N.Y.: 243, 251

Oakwood Cemetery (Huntsville): 223, 234, 255, 262; burial of Sam Houston in, 233
Oriole (steamboat): 99

Pennsylvania, University of: 252
Perry County, Ala.: 3, 39
Philadelphia, Pa.: 252–53
Philabeauscourt, M. and Mme de: 68
Pleasant Valley Academy (Alabama): 7, 18
Polk, President James K.: 102, 115, 117–18, 121
Polk County, Texas: 147
Power, Antoinette Bledsoe (Mrs. Charles Power): 111, 123–25, 151, 159, 166, 184, 197, 204, 211, 228, 235, 240, 242, 251; political power sought for husband, 123; visit to Huntsville, 150; daughter born to, 160; in Independence, 160–63, 222, 240; turned back by blockade, 222; renewed effort to flee, 240; *see also* Antoinette Lea Bledsoe
Power, Captain Charles: 111, 124–25, 197, 211, 225, 228, 236, 251; affluence of, 123; political favor sought by, 123; plantation destroyed by hurricane, 160, 197; in Independence, 160, 162, 167, 222, 240; turned back by blockade, 222; passage to England sought by, 228, 240; cattle ranch of, 240
Power, Lillie: 197
Power, Margaret Houston: birth of, 160; death of, 166
Power, Sallie (wife of Tom Power): 240
Power, Tom: 197
Power, Tom (brother of Charles Power): 211, 240
Presidential campaign of 1856: 184

Raguet, Anna: 28–29, 64; *see also* Anna Raguet Irion
Raven, The: 261
Raven Hill (Huntsville plantation): 97–100, 104, 108–11, 116–17, 121, 123, 126–29, 234, 262; exchanged, 127, 128 & n., 129; part retained by the Houstons, 132; *see also* Huntsville, Texas
Redlands, the: 29, 40, 43, 52–53, 57–59, 109, 191; land speculation in, 54, 61, 94; Houstons' tour of, 59–65, 70
Red-Lander (San Augustine newspaper): 61–62
Republicans: 201
Republic of Texas: 10–11, 28, 34, 53–60, 66, 68, 82, 96, 109, 206,

208, 227, 237; emergency precautions for, 69; government factions in, 70; Washington-on-the-Brazos as capital of, 72–75; archives conflict, 77; recognition of, 78; finances of, 86; greater security of, 90; congress of, 91; Mexican territory viewed by, 91
Rhodes, Mary: 93
Río Grande: 48, 66, 69, 77, 165, 193, 198; envisioned as border, 109; General Zachary Taylor south of, 117
Rise, Progress, and Prospects of the Republic of Texas, The: 79
Rocky Creek: 171
Rogers, Diana: 246, 261; *see also* Diana Rogers Gentry
Ross, Brother: 204, 218
Royston, Martin: 111
Royston, Robert: 15, 88
Royston, Varilla Lea: 6, 14–15, 88, 111, 148, 184, 197, 204, 211, 251, 257; in Independence, 154, 159, 162–63; son killed, 239; move into Tom Power's house, 240
Runnels, Hardin R.: 184–85, 192; election of, 186
Rusk, Senator Thomas Jefferson: 109, 126, 181; death of, 184

Sabine Pass, Texas: 10
Sabine River: 26, 29, 67, 81, 99, 101, 109
Salado, Texas: 252
Saligny, Count: 92, 98
Samson, George Whitfield (Baptist minister): 141; Washington, D.C., church of, 159, 179
San Antonio, Texas: 48; taken by Mexican Army, 69; Mexican withdrawal from, 72; surrender ordered for military installation at, 205
San Augustine, Texas: 29, 40–41, 44, 60–63, 65
San Jacinto, battle of: 14, 19, 26–28, 40, 56, 67, 77, 91, 109, 118, 137, 145, 171, 184–85, 191, 220, 226; Sam Houston wounded in, 27, 76
San Jacinto Battlefield State Park: 261
San Jacinto River: 26
Santa Anna, General Antonio López de: in revolution of 1835–36, 26–27, 145; captured, 27; dictatorial rule of, 91; return to Mexico from exile, 117; march against United States, 117–18
Secession: 192–93, 197, 201; Houston opposed to, 201, 203–204; of South Carolina, 203, 210; of Texas, 205
Secesssionists: in Texas, 201, 225; Austin convention called by, 202, 205
Sharp, Ed: 185
Shiloh, Tenn., battle of: 219, 221, 242
Siloam Baptist Church, Marion, Ala.: 3, 7, 18, 32
Simmons, Anne: 63
Sims, Captain: 230
Slavery: 165, 193, 201
Slaves, Negro: 4, 19, 80–81; in Cherokee Nation, 23; at William Bledsoe farm, 38, 79; Sam Houston's, 38, 44, 89, 97, 121, 193
Smith, Dr. Ashbel: 18, 28, 36–39, 42, 57–59, 79, 133, 151, 186, 224; on yellow fever, 56 & n.; minister to France, 66, 68, 78, 87; at Galveston luncheon, 68; summoned to Grand Cane, 124–25; illness, 126; on visit to Houstons, 146, 203; at Steamboat House, 231

Sons of Temperance: 146
Sour Lake, Texas: 129, 229–30
South Carolina, secession of: 203, 210
Speculation, land: 24–25; in Redlands, 54, 61, 94; speculators from New York and Mobile, 86
Steamboat House (Huntsville): 223, 226–28, 234, 262
Sterne, Adolphus: 62–64; daughter of, 239
Sterne, Eugenia: 64
Sterne, Eva: 62–63
Subletts, the Philip: 61–62

Taylor, General Zachary: 117–18
Tecumseh campaign: 76
Tehuantepec, Isthmus of: 90, 121
Tennessee: 12, 19, 21–22, 100, 107, 120, 151, 170, 181, 193, 226
Terrell, A. W.: 227–28
Texans: filibustering of, 77, 86, 201, 231; origin of, 89; on annexation, 91; Jacksonian principles of, 140; and winter of 1856, 172; reluctance to move against Mexico, 199; Sam Houston's promise to, 201
Texas: 10–11, 15–16, 24, 26, 29, 32, 35, 59, 63, 76, 78, 86, 89, 97, 103–104, 107, 109, 114–15, 121, 131, 137–39, 155, 165, 167–68, 186, 189, 192, 201, 203, 240; land titles, 25; violence in, 61, 67, 94; army urged for, 66, 77, 84; Mexican invasion threat to, 66–67; Mexican Army in, 69; annexation, 91–93, 96, 99–101, 104, 139; new political views in, 140, 156, 161; Houston viewed for presidency, 155–56; new party organization in, 162; Houston's popularity decline in, 168, 180–82; Radical Democrats in, 184–85, 190; Houston elected governor of, 190; secession of, 192–93, 201, 203–204, 205–206; delegation at Unionists convention, 200; united to Confederacy, 206; Houston on defense of, 224; Yankee takeover feared in, 225; anti-war feeling in, 227; yellow fever epidemic of 1867, 254–55
Texas Rangers: 198
Thomas, Iredell D.: 61
Thomas, Penelope: 61
Thorne, Virginia: 80, 93, 127; baptism of, 136; and Thomas Gott, 140–41, 147–49; suit against Mrs. Houston, 151–53
"To My Husband's Picture" (poem): 52–53
Towns, Major: 32–33
Trinity River: 35, 41, 47, 54, 78, 85, 93, 99, 104–105, 109, 122, 125, 159
Tri-Weekly Telegraph (Houston City): 230
Truth (campaign articles): 55, 58–59
Twiggs, General David E.: 205

Union, the: 201–203, 210
Unionists: 200
United States: 66, 69–70, 86, 98–99, 109, 206; Republic of Texas recognized by, 78; Texas annexation question in, 91–93; annexation proposal made by, 96; invasion of Mexico, 117–21; boundaries extended, 137
United States Army: 198

Veracruz, Mexico: 228
Viannah (Negro woman): 17
Vicksburg, fall of: 231

War Between the States: 210, 239–41, 250
Washington, D.C.: 21, 23, 109, 113–16, 121–26, 131, 137, 151–52, 156–57, 159, 165, 167, 172, 181, 184
Washington-on-the-Brazos, Texas: 60, 79, 85–89, 94–96, 154, 162, 170; capital of Republic of Texas, 72–75, 77, 81, 236; Houston's house in, 83–84; Texas declaration of independence signed at, 88; decay of, 236
Washington County, Texas: 250
Webster, Daniel: 140
West Point, New York: 198
Wiley, A. P.: 152
Williams, John: 183
Williams, Weston Lafayette (West Williams): 249–50, 253, 255–56, 260; farm leased at Labadie Prairie, 250
Woods, Colonel: 117

Yellow fever, epidemics of: 35, 54, 56, 80; Baylor University closed by, 254; in Independence, 255–58; in Huntsville, 255; in Galveston, 255; yellow fever symptoms, 256
Yoakum, Edaline: 255
Yoakum, Henderson: 138, 145, 151–53, 174; diary of, 153; death of, 184, 238

The paper on which this book is printed bears the watermark of the University of Oklahoma Press and has an effective life of at least three hundred years.

University of Oklahoma Press

Norman